This Is Paradise

An Irish mother's grief, an African village's plight,
and the medical clinic that brought fresh hope to both

Suzanne Strempek Shea

*This Is Paradise: An Irish mother's grief, an African village's plight,
and the medical clinic that brought fresh hope to both*

PFP, INC
publisher@pfppublishing.com
144 Tenney Street - Georgetown, MA 01833

Printed in the United States of America
© April 2014 Suzanne Strempek Shea

First PFP edition © 2014
(also available in eBook format)

*A portion of book sales to benefit
The Billy Riordan Memorial Trust*

Some ages and surnames were withheld at the subjects' requests.
All names of the family in Chapter 7 have been changed.

Publisher's Cataloging-In-Publication Data
(Prepared by The Donohue Group, Inc.)

Shea, Suzanne Strempek.
This is paradise : an Irish mother's grief, an African village's plight,
and the medical clinic that brought fresh hope to both / Suzanne
Strempek Shea. -- First PFP edition.

pages ; cm

Issued also as an ebook.
ISBN-13: 978-0-9892372-9-1
ISBN-10: 0-9892372-9-X

1. Riordan, Mags. 2. Mothers--Ireland--Biography. 3. Parental
grief--Ireland. 4. Children--Death--Psychological aspects. 5. Clinics-
-Malawi. I. Title.

DA990.U452 R56 2014
941.6082/092/4 B

Also by Suzanne Strempek Shea

Fiction

Selling the Lite of Heaven

Hoopi Shoopi Donna

Lily of the Valley

Around Again

Becoming Finola

Nonfiction

Songs from a Lead-Lined Room: Notes — High and Low — from My Journey through Breast Cancer and Radiation

Shelf Life: Romance, Mystery, Drama and Other Page-Turning Adventures from a Year in a Bookstore

Sundays in America: A Yearlong Road Trip in Search of Christian Faith

Praise for Suzanne Strempek Shea's Work

Fiction

Selling the Lite of Heaven

"I barreled through this bighearted and precisely drawn story, marveling at the author's gifts and accompanying myself with the laugh track of my own involuntary guffaws. And the second time I read *Selling the Lite of Heaven*, I loved it even more. Suzanne Strempek Shea has created a multifaceted, unflawed gem." — Wally Lamb, author of *She's Come Undone*

"Shea's witty yet warm rendering of a community where strong mothers rule and meek daughters find creative ways to rebel is satisfying on many levels." — *Glamour*

Hoopi Shoopi Donna

"She's what Amy Tan is to Chinese-Americans, Isaac Bashevis Singer to the Jews, Jimmy Breslin to the Irish, Mario Puzo to the Italians, Terry McMillan to African-Americans — She's Suzanne Strempek Shea." — *Rocky Mountain News*

"Shea has a distinctive voice — comic, bittersweet, a bit old-fashioned — and a distinctive sense of place. In her novels, the author has quietly created a quirky American version of English village fiction, wry and closely observed." — Amanda Heller, *Boston Globe*

Lily of the Valley

"It is a gift to take the ordinary and make it extraordinary, to reveal the lives we see unfolding every day, and add a charm and warmth to them that those of us who move around them sometimes forget to notice. But this is the way Suzanne Strempek Shea does it for her readers." — Ann Hood, author of *Comfort: A Journey Through Grief*

Around Again

"Shea brings uncommon depth and richness to her narrative, which powerfully conveys both the adolescent push for independence and the adult need for connection." — *Booklist*

Becoming Finola

"An engaging tale, deftly crafted and plotted, with plenty of Irish whimsy, charm, and blarney." — *Kirkus Reviews*

"Shea returns to fiction in another delightfully enchanting tale about the unorthodox ways dreams can come true . . . Sophie is a beguiling heroine, a plucky, lucky American minx who becomes the sort of Irish lass that would have made Maureen O'Hara proud." — *Booklist*

Nonfiction

Songs from a Lead-Lined Room: Notes — High and Low — from My Journey through Breast Cancer and Radiation

"This is one of those books that changes our life forever. I am deeply grateful that I got a chance to read it, and will recommend it to everyone I know." — Anita Shreve, author of *Fortune's Rocks*

"When bad things happen to a talented, insightful, witty reporter and virtuoso novelist, her notes delivered a brilliant silver lining. I'm not the same person I was before reading *Songs from a Lead-Lined Room*, Suzanne Strempek Shea's brave, honest, enthralling, darkly funny story. I couldn't put it down, and I'll never forget its lessons about friendship and good intentions gone awry. I loved many books, but never before have I come away with the conviction that I've just read the one that's been missing from the world." — Elinor Lipman, author of *I Can't Complain: (All Too) Personal Essays*

Shelf Life: Romance, Mystery, Drama and Other Page-Turning Adventures from a Year in a Bookstore

"With her sparkling humor, reporter's eye for detail, raconteur's love of anecdote, literary passion, and affection for humankind, Shea fashions a fresh and rousing tribute to the grand and quirky tradition of bringing books and readers together, with insight, finesse, and enthusiasm."   — *Booklist*

"Book enthusiasts who pine for a friendly, like-minded community will love this light, funny memoir."

— *Publishers Weekly*

Sundays in America: A Yearlong Road Trip in Search of Christian Faith

"Do you believe in miracles? You will after you read *Sundays in America*. This book will lift you up. If you've stopped going to church on Sundays, it will lasso your lost faith. If you never left, it will remind you why you gather, why you pray, why you are part of the flock. Suzanne Strempek Shea writes with soul, straight from her heart; this book was just what I needed to read."   — Luanne Rice, author of *The Lemon Orchard*

"*Sundays in America* is unlike any other book you'll ever read. While born and raised Roman Catholic, Suzanne Shea invites us to accompany her on a year-long pilgrimage to weekly services in non-Catholic Christian churches . . . Like all pilgrimages, this one will enlighten you and change your life too; and I might add, you will not find a pilgrim guide more fun to be with than Suzanne Shea."   — Karol Jackowski,
author of *Ten Fun Things to Do Before You Die*

For Susan Tilton Pecora, who holds down the fort and lifts up the heart. And, in memory of Mary Jean Baker, who changed her own personal village.

Acknowledgments

I am indebted to Mags Riordan for allowing me to follow and write about her life and work. I thank all who agreed to be interviewed for this book, and am especially grateful to Steve Free and the volunteers and staff of the Billy Riordan Memorial Trust for their kindnesses while I was in Cape Maclear.

I also send much gratitude to Tommy Shea, Julie Strempek, Elinor Lipman, John Talbot, Peter Sarno, Elizabeth Searle, Roland Merullo, Mary Shea, Maureen Shea, The Grimanis Family, Jeff Kern, Michele Barker, Ted and Annie Deppe, Carol Leary, Melissa Morris-Olson, Caron Hobin, Michael Konig, Briana Sitler, Annie Finch, Robin Talbot, Avery Rome, Brendan Buzzard, Ann Hood, Ollie Jennings, Elisabeth Wilkins Lombardo, Rachael Raffel, Brenda Edmands, Morgan Callan Rogers, Barry Schatz, The DuComb Family, Tanya Barrientos, Mary Ellen Lowney, Fran Ryan, Stephani and Dana Sawyer, Allan Hunter, Cat Bennett, Aine Greaney, Dori Ostermiller, Lauren DuComb, Barbara Greenbaum, Barbara Hurd, Deb Marquart, Jaed Coffin, Cait Johnson, Bunny Goodjohn, Kate Whouley, Kelli Hadfield Faherty, Kerri Kerber Dieffenwierth, Chuck Smithson, Beth Slattery, Connie McKee, Patricia Reis, Ian Romboletti, Yvonne Milewski, Cece Hewinson, Janet Edwards, Flora Edwards, Christina Rose Giliberti, Mary McLaughlin, Ray Kelly, Anne-Gerard Flynn, Gerry Donnelly, Sister Kathleen Popko, Sister Mary Caritas Geary, Paul Donoghue, Elsie Ostrowski, Elsie Osterman, Alice Piechota, and Lorraine and Andrew Milewski.

ONE

The sound of their footsteps — a muted crunch beneath sneakers and sandals — is that of any walk to the shore. The temperature of 98 degrees Fahrenheit also is that of a day at the beach, and the brash early morning light makes sunglasses and wide-brimmed hats more than fashion choices. But this group is walking away from the water, Lake Malawi — turquoise and inviting — at their backs as the two doctors, two nurses and three medical students open the reed gate of their lodge and step into the sandy lane to begin their commute to work.

The one-mile route is flat except for its start, a fifty-yard gradual incline that leads to the edge of Chembe Village, which is at the edge of Cape Maclear, which is at the edge of the Nankumba Peninsula, which is at the eastern edge of the country of Malawi, which is at the western edge of Lake Malawi, which is at the western edge of Mozambique, which is at the southeastern edge of the continent of Africa. In electric blue or teal scrubs — except for the lone male, who wears forest green dress trousers and long-sleeved blue shirt and carries a pristine white doctor's coat — the seven break into clusters of two and three, chatting quietly about a patient's prognosis, or about plans for a day off, but are mostly silent as they trudge up this alley of sorts edged by tall reed fences bordering small mud-brick or straw homes, the thatched roofs of which poke heavenward above the enclosures. A child dashes in front of the group, chasing a goat. The air is thick with the briny smell of tens of thousands of finger-long silvery fish drying on chest-high tarps strung from poles set into the sand next to many of the dwellings. The lodge's pair of resident dogs passes the group, then circles back to lead it over the crest of the hill, where the landscape opens to a wide, nearly barren plain ending in rocky hills half a mile ahead. Spaced around the trunk of a nearby baobab tree like numerals on a clock face, eight goats lie neatly, their legs folded in card table fashion. To the left of the trail, their herdmates scavenge the hill that marks the rear of the village, and amble through the rectangular pits from which earth has been excavated in the first of many steps involved in creating mud bricks.

After clearing the crest, the doctors and the nurses turn left, onto a hardpacked dirt thoroughfare that is the route from one end of Chembe Village to the other. Younger children in white shirts and blue skirts or trousers also head to the left, in the direction of the primary school. Groups of teens in larger versions of the same uniforms move in the opposite direction, en route to the secondary school. The traffic also includes a man on a bicycle; another on foot and carrying a machete; a woman bearing a stack of six eight-foot-long logs atop her head; and a trio of young women, each with an infant bound to her back by a colorful length of fabric. Past the football pitch that at the tail end of the dry season looks simply like just another arid rectangle of earth, in the direction of the lonely line of poles that delivers electricity to less than 5 percent of the community — most of that percentage the handful of bars, eateries and lodges catering to tourists — the doctors and the nurses and the medical students and the dogs turn right, follow a path along shallow dry gulleys etched during the last rainy season and head up a trail edged with low vegetation and the stumps of trees long ago leveled for firewood. After passing a lone and unassailed mango tree, fully leafed and glistening a deep emerald, the group snakes left, toward the neat brick-and-concrete building that is its destination, the Billy Riordan Memorial Clinic.

It's ten minutes to eight and patients have been queuing on the clinic porch for fifty minutes. With no regular hours at the clinic since Friday, and only emergency cases — including an unresponsive forty-year-old woman pronounced dead shortly after being brought in during the night — seen since, the day promises to be busy. A line has formed at the pair of louvered windows marking reception, just to the right of the archway over which the word "clinic" has been painted in bright blue capital letters. The word and the building face the one and only road leading to the nearest town, and the rest of the world beyond. The positioning wasn't intentional for more than the fact that it makes sense to have the entry facing the village's gateway. But the mere presence of those six letters, and the building they're painted on, shouts to the world another word, and there's no exaggeration in saying that word is hope.

Prior to the opening of the Billy Riordan Memorial Clinic in 2004, that dirt road equaled death for many locals in need of medical care. The nearest hospital is in the village of Monkey Bay, eleven miles — down an often twisting and completely corrugated road that can partially disappear beneath torrents during the November-to-April rainy season. While a thirty-five minute trip might be relatively easy to make in parts of the world where public transportation awaits on most corners, or where few homes are without at least one vehicle waiting in the driveway, this sprawling village of 15,000 people includes only five automobiles and has no public transport affordable for villagers. With home remedies or a witch doctor session being the limits of health care in a region having only one doctor for a catchment of eight hundred thousand people, infection from a simple cut easily could turn fatal and further underline the country's median age of seventeen and a life expectancy the World Health Organization estimates is fifty-seven or fifty-eight years.

"Before, when there was no clinic, most of the people died because of lack of transport," says Sofina Katumala, a forty-four-year-old woman who's lived at the Cape all her life and who's worked as registrar Monday through Friday since the day the clinic opened, August 24, 2004. "I knew them," she adds. "But I can't count them, because it is too many."

For those with the finances, transportation choices for any trip from the village are limited to two. The first and cheaper, at 500 Malawi *kwacha* still would consume your weekly salary — that is, if you are among the country's employed 10 percent. Wait for the 5:30 a.m. arrival of the *matola* — a flatbed truck heaped often taller than its cab with boxes and luggage and passengers and flying along a road so jarring it is easy to lose one's grip and tumble off. The pricier and swifter choice, at a whopping 5,000 kwacha: pay for a lift in one of those private cars. Whatever the vehicle, the trip often is too long for someone on the brink of — or far into — a crisis. It ends in the ramshackle yet relatively modern community of Monkey Bay, at 11,600 inhabitants smaller than Cape Maclear but including a main road lined with such luxuries as a few tiny grocery stores, a gas station and rows of busy vendor stalls. However, taking the left at the God is Able Phone Accessories stand and reaching the gate of the handsome one-story brick Monkey Bay Community Hospital doesn't mean you've arrived at anything close to a state-of-the-art facility.

Don't blame the village. Even if a patient survived the 148-mile, three and a half hour trip west to the capital, Lilongwe, or to Malawi's largest city, Blantyre, (163 miles south and four hours away), subpar would be the norm at hospitals and clinics throughout this densely populated country that *Global Finance* magazine ranks as the eighth poorest country in the world. More than half its 15.4 million citizens — 84 percent of them in rural areas — live below the poverty line, nearly half that group scrapes by in extremely dire conditions, and not a single resident receives social services, because Malawi offers none.

Expect a health facility to suffer from unsanitary conditions, poorly equipped facilities and sparse staffing. In 1998, Malawi had only one orthopedic surgeon. The 2002 opening of an orthopedic hospital in Blantyre raised the figure, with one surgeon now available for every three million citizens, but compare that to American stats of one for every 12,000 people. However, if you're in your thirtieth hour of labor, or your child has cerebral malaria, you don't stop to first check reports from the WHO. You just try to get to a hospital. For residents of Chembe Village, help is now just a trip up the hill, or across the plain, past the soccer pitch and the mango tree, up the slope and through the archway beneath the word "CLINIC," where, at 8 a.m. on this early October Monday in 2010, thirty-six people await a doctor or nurse to emerge from the hallway and invite the person at the head of the line into a consultation room. Bigger than the word painted on the archway is the reality that now, here, as has been the case since the clinic's opening, lives daily are saved. So many men, women and children getting the chance to live. All because one mother's son did not.

Eight thousand one hundred thirty-seven miles north, that mother is walking purposefully toward an airline desk in London's Heathrow Airport, pushing a trolley containing a large hard-shelled lilac suitcase and a rectangular black fabric tote, and dressed for long-haul comfort in white T-shirt, blue sweater and faded Levi's, her feet sockless in metallic silver flats. The bangs of her blonde updo cascade as she looks down to fish through the bag until she spots the maroon cover of her passport, *An tAontas Eorpach*/European Union printed in gold above the words *EIRE* and IRELAND, and the image of a harp. She also locates the printout of the reservation for her two-leg fifteen-hour flight on South African Airlines. Past security, she gives nothing more than a sideways glance toward Harrods and Prada and the gauntlet of other high-end shops delaying most of Terminal One's passengers in their progress toward the gates, then treats herself to a coffee-shop chocolate croissant, her last such indulgence for the couple of months until her return. In the first row of the plane's main cabin, a seat she continually claims due to her silver level of frequent-flierness, before a tray holding a cup reading, "Traveling opens a window to the world," she will pick at her rectangular dish of chicken (never beef — she's eaten none since a scare regarding Irish beef decades ago) and green beans, avail herself of two glasses of free merlot, down the Xanax that will usher her to onboard sleep, and curl against the window. The next time she sleeps will be, as she likes to say, not just in another country, but in another world.

She will need rest for what lies ahead. In her first seven days back in that other world — Chembe Village, Cape Maclear, Malawi — she will, in this order, grill airline officials about a piece of missing luggage containing vital medical supplies; argue for the best rate from a money changer who visits her porch in cargo pants packed with the paper currency of several countries; ensure personal hydration by constantly refilling a series of bottles with water pumped from the local bore hole and boiled in her kitchen's electric tea kettle; and lecture night watchmen who are allowing anyone who wishes to draw water from the limited supply in the well at the Billy

Riordan Memorial Clinic.

She will meet with a friend to kindly ask that the friend's daughter stop being one of those helping themselves at that well. She will counsel a volunteer doctor from Ireland who, after two years of fundraising for his trip to Cape Maclear, and after less than a week there, must make a sixteen-hour flight home to a father who is gravely ill. She will review job applicants and seriously consider hiring a man once arrested and beaten by authorities for robbing her of CDs from a window-sill and her clothing from a line, belongings he left stacked at her door after being released from custody.

She will hand wash a week's worth of underthings. She will field in a single afternoon four lengthy, elaborate and passionate requests from friends and strangers in need of money. She will weather three regional power outages, including one that lasts ten and a half hours. She will review the case of a nervous sixteen-year-old village boy who wants to relinquish the sponsor-funded slot she helped him receive at a private high school that will be his first chance at a real education. She will drive two staffers along eleven miles of mostly unpaved roads for a pointless meeting with health officials.

She will be shadowed for two days by an Irish newspaper reporter writing a feature about the clinic and its founder, including as she gets stood up by the chief's sister — the highest authority in the village — and a host of other vital participants meeting to respond to a villager's ongoing allegations that the land on which the clinic stands, land granted by the chief's late father for the clinic's use, belongs to him. She will arrive at the chief's sister's home at the other end of the village only to be told by the chief's sister's husband, after he sweeps the porch and lays out a reed mat for her, that the chief's sister is out of town, and only to be asked by him, "What are you doing here?"

The chief's sister's husband is not the first one to wonder this. Not about Mags Riordan's mid-afternoon presence on his porch, but about her curious presence in Chembe Village in general. Why this thin, white, middle-aged Irish secondary-school teacher and mother of two would materialize in the village ten years earlier as a source of rare possibility for this community. Why three years later she would lift a shovel and heft a wheelbarrow full of concrete to help build the twelve-room clinic staffed by a revolving team of a dozen international volunteer doctors and nurses who, as of the end of 2013, has seen 275,000 patients and who tend to those in an extension holding two inpatient wards, a laboratory, and services including a porridge program, family planning, HIV/AIDS counseling and drug distribution.

The goals of whites normally are far less altruistic here at the headland of the western-slanting Nankumba Peninsula on the rough-sand shores of what is the fourth-largest lake in Africa and the ninth largest in the world. Working on a tan, going for a snorkel, taking a lounge in a hammock and settling into the latest gap year campsite are more the aims for out-of-towners who head toward the throbbing reggae of the several neatly tended tourist bars and lodges oddly punctuating the closely placed rows of unadorned brick-and-straw homes in a community not only 90 percent unemployed but 90 percent illiterate, 50 percent malnourished and 100 percent beyond the American middle class mind's concept of poverty.

For those with the kind of kwacha that allows ensconcement beyond the metal gates of the guest lodges and foreigners-only bars, Cape Maclear is "the sort of place where you sit on the beach, have a few beers, and the next thing you know your visa's run out," says *The Lonely Planet Guide to Mala-*

wi, Mozambique and Zambia. And *Coast to Coast – The Backpackers Guide to Southern Africa* agrees: "The beaches are lazy and there's plenty of nothing to do except relax." *Malawi — the Bradt Travel Guide* notes that, at the peak of its popularity — the early 1990s — Cape Maclear "was described as Africa's answer to Kathmandu or Marrakech, a place to which travelers would flock in the hundreds to enjoy a *chamba* (marijuana) and Carlsberg-enhanced atmosphere that for most people was thoroughly irresistible."

One of those to visit in that decade, one of those who found the Cape thoroughly irresistible, was Billy Riordan, a boy-band handsome, easygoing tour boat operator and hostel employee from lush, rural West Kerry, Ireland. He was a traveler. One with a well-worn backpack, a global network of drop-everything-and-go companions, and a craving for destinations along the world's lesser-known roads. The fact that Cape Maclear is smack at the end of one of those roads answers the biggest "What are you doing here?" that might be posed to his mother. Answers why she left her career and home and family back in that lush, rural Kerry to relocate 8,702 miles away and spend her days in a whole other world, searching, bargaining, arranging, boiling, rushing, driving, washing, reviewing, lecturing, phoning, worrying, defending, meeting, not being met. It is because Billy Riordan loved Cape Maclear, during his third visit, in February of 1999, writing in an e-mail, "This is paradise. Mum. You have to come, you have to come, you have to come."

Two days later, on Feb. 20, 1999, after stepping into the waters of Lake Malawi, twenty-five-year-old Billy Riordan drowned.

"What are you doing here?"

When it comes to this life on this earth, it would be natural to imagine Mags Riordan might answer, "Just trying to get through the day." In the space of twenty-six years, she has, in this order, lost her first child — a four-month-old daughter — when the brakes failed on the family car in which mother and infant were seated and the vehicle plunged from a pier; suffered the death of her second son, also at four months, to a crib death that occurred in the back seat of Mags's car while she sat up front reading a paper in a beachfront parking lot; and lost her surviving son to drowning in an African lake. That she is seated on the porch of her flat in a Malawian village she warns prospective visitors and volunteers is no modern Starbuck-strewn hotspot, rather what's known as "deepest, darkest Africa," and that she is not curled into a corner back home, can mystify.

Her survival is never a topic mentioned by the woman an *Irish Times* reporter once wrote could be considered "A mother of sorrows." If asked about how she's survived what life she's been dealt, the answers are brief — "It's an Irish thing" and/or "I was born like this" — and given with the focus of her blue eyes that to the new acquaintance might seem brusque, but that is a trademark of this person who certainly has suffered and who fails to suffer fools, something she practices again on the porch of the chief's sister. She seethes at the time wasted in making this trip across town, and at the absence of any promised participants. Mags simply wants to return to what she is doing here in this village: running the Billy Riordan Memorial Trust, the non-profit umbrella over the clinic, the wards, the feeding program, the HIV/AIDS clinic, the scholarships, and the volunteer center that is her Malawian headquarters and eight-month-a-year home. Today there is another sponsored student to meet. E-mails to return now that the power is back on. An elderly watchman must be gently assured that being let go from his job due to infirmity and age isn't the same thing as what he fears it is: the shame of being fired. A donor needs to be contacted. A group of visiting relatives of a volunteer doctor from England hopes for her presence at a dinner. With luck, the electricity will hold tonight for a Skype session with family. Right now, here on the chief's sister's porch, she is told via the translator the obvious fact that the meeting with the chief's sister must be postponed. The translator awaits her reply.

"He doesn't want to know what I'm thinking," she snarls quietly.

The chief's sister's husband might not want to know, but the comment grabs the imagination, winding the bystander down the lanes of possible reasons for not only how this person has survived what she has, but why she's accomplished what she has, and where she has done it, despite the raging failure rates of non-government organizations, despite being an outsider, despite being one single person, and one single female person, one single white female with a very big idea in a very small country and culture dominated by black males. Then, inevitably in the presence of someone like Mags Riordan, the question turns the listener inward, to ask the self a wider version of what the chief's sister's husband wondered. What am *I* doing here — on this earth, in this life?

But if you are in Mags Riordan's presence, there is little time for pondering. Instead, there is the race to gather your things from the woven straw mat on the chief's sister's front porch and catch up with her as she marches off across the sand of the lane, hoists herself into the boxy white 2009 Toyota Land Cruiser that doubles as one of the Trust's two ambulances and her personal vehicle, and jounce over a rutted road edged with huts and the handful of stalls that constitute Cape Maclear's "big market." Fueled by a press to the gas pedal, and

Mags's disgust about the loss of an hour that could have been better used, there is a swift drive home to launch into the next litany of tasks.

The brakes are ignored in the ambulance's descent of a cratered hill that threatens every joint in the vehicle, and in its occupants' bodies. Yet, at the wheel, Mags breaks into a smile as she calls out an energetic "Hang on!"

It is, you suspect she has learned, sometimes the only thing you can do.

TWO

To understand Mags Riordan's life here, in Cape Maclear, know her life there, in Ireland. Settle into the passenger seat of her decade-old silver Renault McGann coupe on a May day in 2010 and buckle in for a morning-long tour of the place where she holidayed as a young girl, fell in love as a teenager, started married life and motherhood in her early twenties, and where, at an age when, she once predicted, she'd be concerned mainly with babysitting grandchildren, began spending much of the year a continent away to lead a charitable effort that has changed innumerable lives. Including hers.

The coupe shuttles the quaint side lanes of Dingle, then covers six miles west along the main road leading back west, to rural Ventry and on the knife-edged cliffs of peninsula-capping Slea Head, the point in Europe closest to America. Then it's back to town again to touch Dingle's borders north and east, crisscrossing a lush swath of the area she knew so well as that child, that teen, that bride, that mother, that high school guidance counselor, that traveler who once left only for carefree holidays. It stops finally, as it must if the tour is to cover all the facts of Mags Riordan's life here in this place, at the graveyard.

But first, after a breakfast of scones and coffee at Benners, an upscale and normally bustling center-of-town hotel that's all but deserted in a flattened economic climate that since 2008 has swept cash-bearing tourists from the streets, the coupe's key is turned. The manual transmission is engaged and Mags heads for the first of many of the twenty places she lived in the first twenty years of her marriage, when she and ex-husband Richie moved whenever finances, or landlords, dictated they must, or when the wanderlust and wonder of life sparked them to relocate, to the states, to England, to Scotland. In a 1970s Dingle where, Mags notes, "everyone was related to everyone — I learned early to keep my mouth shut about people in front of people," the family's frequent mobility was well known. She affects a mash-thick West Kerry accent to recall the comment by an old woman in the post office who years ago likened her life to that of the itinerant Irish Travellers and the horse-drawn caravans in which they once roamed the countryside: "And where are you living now, Mrs. Riordan? All you need is the piebald pony."

Indeed, like the Travellers once did, the Riordan family often moved on a second's notice, sometimes for a reason as simple as a landlord's relative needing the space they were occupying. "Sure, I'm still onto it," she says of the up-and-go practice that since 2000 has had her frequently flying between Ireland, America, the United Kingdom and Africa. "Forty years later."

Mags laughs as she shifts the car into the next gear, praises its economy ("It goes on the smell of an oil rag") and speaks of the kick she gets from occasionally being able to drive with the top down. The ever-present silver butterflies studding her earlobes catch the light as the car begins its journey. Its driver, wearing cuffed jeans, blue suede flats, and a light blue fleece vest over a white jersey, bears a light mood. The wedding of the younger of her two surviving children, Jennifer, took place the previous weekend at a hotel just north, in the seaside town of Sneem. The couple is about to head off to their honeymoon in Quito and on the Galapagos, and Mags's new purple cell phone, the one she's yet to fully figure out how to operate, will ring frequently this day as the final details of their departure are settled.

The wedding is the main reason that, after five months in Malawi, Mags is back in Dingle. During her three or four visits each year, she occupies three rooms on the second floor of a house she co-owns just past Dingle town, but uses only one — a small vaulted-ceilinged bedroom — for herself. The second room, unfurnished, holds donated goods including a dozen trash bags full of sheets received after she did a radio campaign asking for linens to be used at the clinic. The third room, half the size of the others, is the office from which the Trust is run in Ireland. Mags will be in the office today to work on the logistics of a blues festival to be held over the weekend at the end of the peninsula, a Trust benefit thought of by and featuring the music of the father of a former volunteer.

In the relative calm after the wedding and before the fundraiser, she zips around the area in the snug coupe that's a big change from her wheels back in Cape Maclear, the boxy white Land Cruiser she refers to as "my trusty steed." The car, which Mags drives with the same urgency she utilizes on the unpaved lanes of the Cape, handily does the job of helping to provide a tour of this place that figures so largely in her life.

Mags doesn't remember her first impression of Dingle, a town she visited regularly starting at age eight or nine and where she has made her home since 1972. When she was a child, her family rented a summer place in the village of Castlegregory, seventeen miles away, on the northern side of the peninsula, at the base of the t-shaped Maharees Peninsula that's home to much wildlife and wild surfing, and where she one day would work as a guidance counselor. The family often made the drive to Dingle to purchase fish and lobsters fresh off the boats in a town then a much different place than the current hotspot that, with its restaurants, shops and fifty-two pubs for a population of 1,500, has come to regularly make travel editors' annual lists of "don't-miss" destinations.

In 1585, Queen Elizabeth incorporated Dingle, a village then called by the Irish name *Daingean ni Cushy* — the castle of Hussey — for a British family given a sizeable amount of land by one of the FitzGeralds, Earls of Desmond. Dingle made its way into the world's consciousness 385 years later, with the 1970 premiere of the film *Ryan's Daughter,* most of which was shot at the end of the thirty-mile-long Dingle Peninsula. Brit David Lean directed the critically crunched but dual-Academy-Award-winning film based on *Madame Bovary* and telling of a married woman in a rural nationalist Irish village who enters an affair with a British officer in the wake of the historic 1916 Easter Rising that attempted to end British rule and establish an Irish Republic. During the filming, from 1968 to 1969, Lean was enraptured by the desolate, surf-crashed cliffs and beach, the endless patchwork of green fields that decades later would lead *National Geographic Traveler* to call it "the most beautiful place on earth," and he was fascinated by the looks and life-styles of an agrarian native-speaking people he termed aboriginal. The film's audiences agreed with the critics, hating the picture, but loving the pictures Lean had shot, the grandest advertisement for and lure to a place few outside the country had known existed.

Neatly tarred roads have replaced the single dirt track that forty-five years earlier was the main thoroughfare Robert Mitchum, Sarah Miles, Trevor Howard, John Mills and the rest of the cast and crew used to get to and through Dingle. People now choose to relocate to this wild western place, rather than live here for the duty of carrying on the family farm, and in the boom before Celtic Tiger turned toothless house cat, they constructed grand ocean-view homes in areas that just a few decades earlier enjoyed little access to modern utilities.

Tea-smoked, pistachio-encrusted filets of wild salmon are served in restaurants lining streets where Mags the child would have been hard-pressed to locate the one brand of peanut butter carried in the one grocery store of any size at the time. A handful of the fifty-two pubs still sell dry goods along with their wet fare, J. Curran's on Main Street — Mag's choice of pub, her "local" — among those stocking Wellingtons as well as whiskey behind the counter. In other shops, visitors to Dingle these days can purchase locally crafted or, more commonly, imported versions of the country's trademark thickly knit sweaters, but must work to search out the couple of locations that sell actual skeins of yarn in an area where sheep dot the hills like manna. A stretch of land at the eastern entrance to town recently became the site of a long-awaited approximately $22 million sixty-eight-bed hospital that in late 2010 finally replaced the 162-year-old facility on The High Road overlooking town.

Fishing boats still bob at the docks, but now share space with a sprawling pleasure-boat marina that attracts annual regattas, and with the eleven tourist boats carrying visitors to deeper waters for a guaranteed glimpse of the famous Fungie, a bottlenose dolphin who's been a harbor fixture since 1984 when, according to one legend, his beloved mate washed ashore. On the lane across from that new marina and up a short dead end Mags calls "the colony," a bed-and-breakfast named Baywatch B&B now sits across from the small apartment the family occupied in 1973, the year sea-loving Billy was born. A quarter mile away, on John Street, the building in which the family subsequently lived is adjacent to the storefront for The Curtain Call window-dressing shop.

There were, Mags notes, no such cute names or places back when she first knew the town. "Dingle was very different then, just somewhere we went on holidays every year," she says. "I can't really say that I thought it was in any way special, other than it was a nice place and I liked it. I suppose we did think it was backward and rural and undeveloped, but, I mean, at that stage Ireland wasn't hugely developed anywhere, really, once you left Dublin. If you weren't from Dublin, you were from the country. Whether from Cork or Tralee or Dingle wasn't a huge difference."

One hundred miles south east of Dingle, in the "country" that the county and city of Cork was at the time, Margaret Mary Dillon was born. She and her four siblings born to Katherine "Kitty" and general physician Victor Dillon were raised in a comfortable home in the Shanakiel section of the Republic's second-largest metropolis, now home to 123,000 and a city Mags says always has been a small town.

She, the two brothers born just after her, and their two sisters daily walked the same route home from school, stopping first at their father's surgery — the Irish term for doctor's office — and waiting for him to join them on the final leg of the trip home. Mags enjoyed chatting with the patients and playing with the scale in the waiting room. That setting could have been hers for life, and she initially did not balk at the idea of becoming a physician. What eventually did stop her was the time the track of study required.

"I know my dad would have liked me to do medicine and I think I would have done medicine, but at the time it was seven years studying, and when you're sixteen or seventeen, seven years seems like forever," Mags says as she navigates the coupe around a solitary group of shoppers who've strayed onto Main Street. "My father was a doctor, and we had several other relations in the medical world — I have a brother in medicine, a brother in dentistry, the next girl is a nurse, and had a couple cousins who were doctors, dentists, nurses — a lot of medicine in the family. So, I remember thinking at the time I would do medicine. But no, seven years seemed too long. If they'd said it was five years, I'd probably have done it. It seemed like too long a wait to earn money and, as you think at that stage, have a life."

Sports interested her. She applied to college to become a physical education teacher and was placed in a class, but decided to study English instead.

"I really took a degree in English," Mags admits, "because I didn't know what I wanted to do, and to take a general degree in English is a good general education. I did a three-year degree in English, and after that decided I'd go back to school. Again, the motivations were sort of terrible. I decided I didn't want to finish in university, do another year, get a teacher training diploma, do post grad, which you need for teaching secondary school in Ireland. I said 'I'll stick around for another year, no more.'"

Mags turns into the driveway of a stretch of townhouses on upper Main Street, points to another door that was the family's, not far from where widowed Kitty moved into a small apartment three years ago. When she's in town, Mags sees Kitty often — that is, when Kitty, perhaps the source of familial wanderlust, is home from one of her frequent travels. Their relationship is easy — a fact that was not always the case.

"I would not have liked to have been my parents," Mags says. "I misbehaved all along the line. I was very headstrong, very determined, quite revolutionary."

Mags clarifies the term by describing participation in marches and parades. The specific causes? "Oh, anything. Anything I thought was worthy enough, basically, I did that."

The list includes taking part in a march from Dunquin, on

the tip of the Dingle Peninsula, 223 miles northwest to Dublin in the spring of 1971 to protest the government's closing the national school in that County Kerry village.

"There was a photograph on the first page of the *Irish Times* of me being hauled out of the department of the Gaeltacht, by two policemen, being bodily lifted by the cops. You can imagine my parents. They read the *Irish Times*. That didn't go down too well."

She picketed at Carnsore Point, also in the early 1970s, objecting to the government's proposal to build the country's first nuclear power station there. In those same years, she stood with a placard to protest plans for the country to join the European Union, which it did in 1973.

"Anything," she repeats. "I was up for it. I would have had a strong position. I joined the Labor Party at one stage. I was the (University College Cork) delegate to the All-Ireland Students Union at one stage. That was really combined with being very sports-orientated, swimming and tennis . . . I got my degree, but study didn't get a whole lot of attention."

Other attention was being focused north, to Kerry, and to a young transplanted Dubliner named Richie Riordan. They'd met in 1970, when Mags spent part of the summer in one of the annual *Coláistí Samhraidh,* or Summer Language Colleges, aimed at increasing the use of Irish-language speakers (currently an estimated and scant forty to eighty thousand in a country of 4.5 million) by lodging college students from across the country with families in the country's handful of Gaeltachts, areas where Irish is regularly spoken. To learn the language via total immersion in rural enclaves far from the pulls and familiarity of urban areas, Mags lived with a family in the village of Fionach, just up the road from Dunquin, in a house she can't drive past because it no longer exists. Unlike some students who balk at the idea of such removal from contemporary cul-

ture, she didn't need to be pushed into the summer study experience. "I was very interested in Irish, even though I wasn't doing Irish as a degree subject," Mags says. "I was just into the
language, wanted to keep it up. I met Richie there, in Dingle, at
the end of school. I was very young."

Mags was familiar with Richie from spotting him while on
trips to Dingle, and had gotten friendly with another group of
Dubliners who were his friends. Richie was working on a fishing boat at the time, an émigré from the Dublin business scene
who'd gone straight to an office job after school.

"It was like a collar-and-tie job, he hated it," Mags says.
"He was miserable. His father had died the year before he did
his leaving cert and that had a huge effect on him emotionally.
There was parental pressure to get a respectable job or go to
college. He got a job and stuck with it a year, maybe, then literally took a tent and went to Dingle."

That was Richie's home for a year, a tent in a field near the
lighthouse a short walk from the center of town, in Been
Bawn.

"He just wanted to get away," Mags says, "from sort of the
conservative stranglehold that he saw had happened in his family."

So he became a fisherman.

"He'd no experience. He grew up in suburban Dublin, had
no fishing background, just decided he would do it. He ended
up having his own trawler. He became a very experienced sea-
man and fisherman, obviously, but he came from a very middle
class, conservative Dublin family."

The coupe slows, then swerves around an open-bed truck
off which a pile of auditorium chairs — undoubtedly bound
for the blues festival marquee — has just fallen. Mags navigates

back into her lane. Continues: "Richie was unusual in that there were few people from outside Dingle in Dingle at the time. It was very insulated, very isolated. To have the young Dublin guy living there, fishing on boats with the old guys, he stuck out. I supposed really, too, I was not from the area, either, and kind of stuck out like a sore thumb. I wore way-out clothes, student hippy-type things, I was probably a bit of an oddball as well."

An oddball soon living in her oddball boyfriend's tent.

They were twenty-one when they married in County Adare, chosen for its location halfway between Cork City and Dublin, at a church in Rathkeale with a name she can't recall. Mags wore another way-out hippy-type selection, a long-sleeved, high-necked white dress with thick, geometrically printed, purple horizontal stripes ("flower-power stuff"). A snapshot from that sunny day shows her with curly shoulder-length hair, a yellow flower tucked behind her right ear, her right arm jubilantly waving her bouquet skyward.

"When I think of it now, if one of my kids said they were getting married at twenty-one, I would have had apoplexy," Mags says, quickly ensuring, "I would. But different days, different things. You kind of go with the flow at the time and, you know, anyway, I wouldn't have listened even if my parents had said, which I'm sure they did, 'This is ridiculous.'"

The reason would have been age, rather than any grand plans, as the couple had none. Their first home was a trailer — caravan in Irish parlance — owned by a friend's mother.

"You can imagine how that went on really well with my parents. It was not considered a done thing. When you're so young, you don't really think — I didn't think — about way down the line. It was kind of you lived each day as it came and sort of had a good time, basically."

As she maneuvers the coupe to the neighborhood of

Cooleen, down a lane adjacent to the harbor, past another former home, this one a single-storied yellow-painted cement sprawler just before the Coast Guard building, Mags recalls an early adventure enjoyed by a five-year-old Billy, who went missing while they lived here, only to turn up playing at the pool of the nearby Skellig Hotel, where his granny now swims for exercise several times a week. Mags turns the car around at the small harborfront building that constitutes the town's office park and says she's never thought ahead. "Even today I'm still not like that. I just kind of think 'What happens, happens.'" She recalls a friend recently making plans for a holiday in the following year. "And I said, 'Next year? I don't even know what I'm going to be doing in a month's time, never mind next year.' That's not to say I'm completely stupid, that I'm completely irresponsible. I'm not. I just don't ever kind of plan things and say 'I'll do this and I'll do this,' because you just never know. I've had that feeling all my life."

That trait, she thinks, might have been a factor helping her get through the deaths that have so impacted her.

"There must have been sort of an advantage in it because most people think I'm out-of-my-mind crazy," she says as she steers counter-clockwise at the roundabout just before Cooleen. "I don't think I am. I happen to think that, despite all that's happened in my life, I'm very well balanced. I think when you're born there are certain things genetically in you. Some people are born worriers, some people are born procrastinators, some people are born practical, impractical. Maybe I was just born with a certain predisposition to being able to cope. That's kind of the only thing I can really say."

She stops to peer up a driveway along the stretch of road just past the Dingle Oceanworld aquarium, another tourist destination that would have been considered a hallucination in the isolated town she knew as a kid. "Geez, I forgot we lived here.

Did we live up there? I forgot we did! It's knocked down — a bigger house there now." Her voice drifts as the car idles.

"I have to say, thinking about it, a lot of it had to do with my upbringing," Mags continues. "The environment in which I was raised, which would have been very strict but at the same time very steady, you know, rock-solid, rock-steady. Like, as a kid, I never had to worry about the adult things the way some kids have to worry. I was very fortunate to be raised in a very strong, steady environment. There was never a crisis in my family as a child. I never remember sensing a feeling of instability or uncertainty as a kid. I've a lot of very strong childhood memories of nice things happening. In fact, I have very few childhood memories of not-nice things happening. I think maybe that gives you a mental strength that you can call upon in later years. It's amateur psychology, maybe, but I just think that if you're raised in a strong and supportive and loving family even up to the age of fourteen or fifteen, you're at a huge advantage. I know certainly from the time I was fourteen, fifteen, I was constantly at loggerheads with one of my parents — I would rock the boat, like. But at the end of the day I suppose I never ended up going to prison or any of that kind of stuff that would have brought serious disruption to the family. I did just kind of silly things, things if a kid did them today nobody would raise an eye over it. Times were different, certain expectations were raised by parents. If a child didn't come up to par, the parents let the child know about it — that kind of thing. I think that, yeah, I definitely think that having a really rock-solid childhood stands to you."

When it came to raising her own children, Mags had no dreams about that, either.

"I never really thought about how many kids we'd have, not really," she says.

"Though I always wanted kids. Absolutely I had, but I

mean I hadn't specified how many or anything. Richie was one of six. I think when you come from five, that is a relatively large family, and especially if you've had a nice experience of being in a family, I think you probably want to go and have kids yourself."

In the cottages, houses and apartments Mags points to as she drives, their children were lovingly celebrated and cherished. They napped on beds inside this place, played with trucks in that front garden, ran to the arms of aunts and uncles and cousins who drove to that gate in the best of times, and in the worst.

In 1973, Mags and Richie's first child and first daughter, Niamh Elizabeth Riordan, drowned when the family car plunged off a pier in Dingle.

Mags had driven into town on an April Saturday afternoon to await the end of Richie's workday. The four-month-old baby was in a carrycot in the back seat.

"We had an old banger then," Mags says of the car. "I was turning on the pier, put the car in reverse, put my foot on the brake, but nothing happened. We went over the edge and backwards into the water. I can still remember thinking 'This is it. We're not going to survive this.' But I was a strong swimmer and a trained lifeguard."

Her skill carried her through the shock, and to air.

"The next thing I knew," she says, "I was on the surface. It's all a blur after that. I do remember being on the pier and Richie and the others diving into the water. But it was too late for Niamh. I was told later that I was shot through the windscreen, but I had no marks or bruises. I was in complete shock for days. I don't remember the funeral at all. Nothing."

The unimaginable loss had an unknown counterweight: Mags was two months pregnant at the time of the accident.

"I didn't know I was pregnant, so I suppose once I realized that I was pregnant, one has to decide, 'OK, you're going to see this pregnancy through or you're not.' I suppose you know that if you're sort of in good health yourself, the chances are the child will be fine. You have that protection thing, wanting to protect the unborn child. That had quite a bit to do with it, one of the reasons why I did stay on the straight and narrow at that stage. Because the accident happened in April and then Billy was born in November, seven months later. I think that had a lot to do with it the first time. I think it was a gift and I think it was, as I said, it almost seems like he was sent to kind of pull us through the first loss.

"I can't remember exactly but I obviously must have discovered I was pregnant shortly after the accident. I do remember thinking, 'It's amazing this child has held on.' I was in the very early stage and it would have been so much more expected that the baby would have miscarried. That was Billy. That was the irony of it. He was a huge factor. You couldn't really take to the drink or whatever, any form or kind of substance abuse, because once you knew you were pregnant you weren't going to be going down that road. I also think when you're pregnant you go into I won't say autopilot, but you're focused on one thing — the pregnancy. I suppose, having lost Niamh, like, I was determined I was not going to compound the problem by running the risk of the other."

Billy Coleman Riordan was born whole and healthy on November 12 that same year, and was given his paternal grandfather's name as his first, and his father's middle name for his own. Early photos show him to be an adorable blond in a straight-banged, bowl-cut hairstyle. In another, he is nearly three years old, dressed in dark short overalls and a white shirt, crouching on the grass next to a car seat in which lies an infant wearing aqua pajamas and smiling. His brother, Luke.

When Luke Victor Riordan was born in June of 1976, two

and a half years after his big brother, the family was living in one of the places they occupied over the years on John Street, which runs down a formidable hill leading to Dingle's Main Street. That October, Mags drove some friends and Luke for a walk on Ventry Strand, about seven miles west of Dingle Town. Once there, she decided it was too cold to leave the car so she stayed inside with the baby while the others walked along the shore. As Niamh had been the day she died, Luke was in his carrycot in the seat behind his mother.

"So I just sat there, reading the *Irish Times* and keeping quiet so as not to wake him," Mags remembers. "When the others came back we drove home, and as I lifted Luke from the carrycot, I suddenly realized he was dead."

She rushed him to Dingle Hospital but couldn't bring herself to remain inside the building, instead waiting in the parking lot while the unsuccessful attempts to save Luke were made.

"He was within a day of being the same age as Niamh was when she died," she says. "Sixteen weeks and four days, and sixteen and five. Only a day in the difference."

Mags tells the story as the coupe idles not a quarter mile from Ventry Strand, in the driveway of a modest white cottage that also once had been a Riordan home, though they had not lived there when Luke died of what was determined to be a cot death.

Recalling the horror for an *Irish Times* reporter in one of the many newspaper stories done about the Trust years later, Mags said, "I joined the cot death association after that and learned that Luke's case was a classic one, based on research at the time. I remember going to the funeral. Going to the graveyard. I never thought I'd be there again, not so soon.

"Richie and I were devastated and people wonder how we

27

coped with another death. They still wonder if I grieved. People grieve in different ways. How do you define grief? Does it mean accepting it, fighting it, burying it? You can't control grief, because it's a necessary part of one's existence. I feel that I have grieved. I don't fear grief anymore."

Mags's eyes remain dry, and her voice does not waver as she says, "It was very difficult — it was very, very difficult. I think unless someone has been through something like that, it's hard to comprehend how completely, how catastrophic losing one's child is. Then to lose a second in a relatively short period of time, it's unspeakable. The world stopped that day. It's hard to put it into words. It's really hard to describe. I think nature takes over in one sense and you just go into automatic pilot, for lack of a better word, and you just go through the motions. That wasn't just me. I'm not unique in that. Anybody who's lost a child has the same experience. Disbelief, denial and, eventually, resignation."

Luke's death immersed Mags and Richie in an ugly, familiar place, and this time the horror was set against the sweet presence of a child who was very much alive.

"It was harder with the second, for several reasons," Mags says as the car nears town again. "It was the second one. And Billy was only two and a bit, but at the same time, you were kind of experiencing the loss for him, as well. Kind of seeing him saying, 'Where's Luke? Where's Luke?' This kind of stuff was going on, you were feeling for him and you had your own stuff to deal with, as well. It was not that you loved him any more than you loved the first child. It was probably that you kind of felt, 'This is me, again. Why is it happening a second time?'" She stops, notes another residence, this one at the top of Main Street, where the family lived for five or six years. "Also the fact that I was sitting in the car when it happened, and I was reading the paper — you kind of think, 'I must have missed something. I must have missed something.' Later on I knew I hadn't. I didn't miss something. The baby's in the back seat. If there's a peep, you'd hear it. But at first, you think you'd missed something. Then, of course, the other thing about it is when you lose a second child, your fear is hugely heightened. Like, we were terrified of something happening to Billy at that stage. Even though I had said, very early on, 'There's going to be a third. I don't know where and I don't know how, but it's going to happen.'"

As terrifying as that feeling — knowledge, as Mags puts it — had to be, it was in her, and she kept watch for the third tragedy. Others tried to dissuade her, but the feeling was cemented.

Daughter Emma and her sister, Jennifer, arrived in the five years after Luke's death. Richie left fishing, and the family opened a restaurant in Dingle. In the offseason, they would travel, including to Scotland, and to the States, where Mags would begin the aerobics teaching that would occupy her for the next decade. But not before a near-tragedy. "And then Jennifer," is how Mags starts that story, in a tone underlining that she knew. This mother just knew something else was about to happen.

Newborn Jennifer was just home from the hospital, her release delayed ten days due to an allergy to breast milk that caused her to become more jaundiced and ill with each feeding. She was started on bottles.

At home, in that Cooleen house just before the Coast Guard building in Dingle Town, Mags gave Jennifer a bottle and set her in the middle of the bed before leaving to wash her hands. Returning, she knew something was off.

"I took one look at the child — she was white. I could see

the color just draining out of her face," Mags remembers. "Having seen Luke, I knew what a dead baby looked like. I just picked her up, started screaming. I just shook her and shook and shook her. She came 'round. She wasn't completely dead. I was on my own in the house. Billy was around, Richie wasn't there, and I thought 'This is crazy, like, this child almost died.' And then I went to the doctor with her and people thought that I was nervous."

Billy and Emma were hale and hearty, but Mags felt she was seen as a panicking mother still immersed in the losses of two children. She would have further reason to panic, two days later.

"This time at night, the last thing at night, I changed her, put her into her carry cot. Richie was down at the (trash) bins because collection was the next morning. I walked back into the room, saw her — the same thing. She was white, white, white. I screamed. Richie saw her. We shook her. I picked her up, she was like a rag doll. I shook, shook, shook her, her heart started, she was alive. We went straight up the doctor, the second visit in a couple of days. He said 'Go to Cork with that child.' We drove straight."

It was a two-and-a-half-hour trip to the hospital in Cork where Jennifer had been born and to which Victor Dillon still was attached. The baby was released only after three weeks on an apnea monitor. At home, Mags remembers, "She was on the apnea mat, and then on the alarm, for months, but she was fine. It never happened again. But I thought at that stage, I thought she was going to be the one, but she wasn't. I thought 'This is it, here we go. This is number three.' It wasn't, obviously, but I still carried that right through for years: 'There's gonna be one more.' I didn't know which one, obviously."

Life kept her doing the sordid guessing, including when Emma was seven and contracted meningococcal meningitis.

"She was out playing with a friend, about 7:00 p.m. came in, complained about being sick, kind of had the flu," Mags says. "She wasn't well. My mother was staying here at the time. We had a big beanbag in the living room and we put (Emma) to bed on it. She wasn't settling, was hallucinating. I remember saying to my mother at eleven, 'This child has meningitis.' My mother said 'Don't be ridiculous.' I said, 'Mom, this child has meningitis.' Emma was hallucinating, talking about Daddy's pink Rolls Royce. She had a huge high fever and in the wee hours of the morning I called the doctor (in Dingle), said 'I think she's got meningitis.' He said 'I'm on my way to the surgery at ten.' I said 'You better be, because I'm really anxious about her.' He called me at nine o'clock, said 'I've got another call, I'll come in at lunchtime.' I said 'No, you won't, you come in now or I'm taking her to Tralee.'"

After a single look at Emma, the doctor told Mags her diagnosis was correct. As had been the race to Cork with Jennifer, the drive to Tralee was frustratingly slow in the day when horse-drawn caravans still frequently took up half the road. En route to Tralee, Emma began showing signs of septicemia, bacteria in the blood that, in her case, were evidenced by purple spots on the skin. An emergency team was waiting at the hospital and immediately got her on penicillin.

"She was out of it for two days," Mags remembers. "We didn't know whether she'd come out. There was an outbreak of meningitis in (County) Kerry that summer, children before and after her in the hospital died. About seven kids in Kerry died. But, she wasn't one of them."

Emma Riordan now runs Richie's business, The Rainbow Hostel, located in the only home the family ever built, long yellow, ochre-trimmed, cement and standing on nearly an acre just past the Milltown roundabout at the end of Dingle Town. A carved sign reading "Welcome to Rainbow Hostel" greets guests as they pull in the driveway, the driveway where one can look across a field of grazing sheep to the red house that is Mags's Dingle home and the headquarters of the Billy Riordan Memorial Trust. With beds for fifty, and camping spots for dozens more, the hostel is a spot popular with backpackers, and fittingly was the main place Billy Riordan worked to earn money for his next big journey. Mags takes a left just before the road into the town center to stop by the hostel for a check on Emma and husband Dave Doyle's first child and Mags's first grandchild. White-blond nine-month-old Cillian is stand-ard- bearer of the next generation in the family Mags and Richie created in the fifteen years before they separated. He'd had a cold at his aunt's wedding reception and is resting in his cot in the hostel office, where Emma slides her chair from the space in front of the computer to allow her mother to scoop up the child and check the heat of his forehead.

"Ah, you're grand," she tells the boy, who demonstrates how right she is, wriggling from her arms and, once set down, crawling with astounding speed down the hall.

Emma, as blonde and fair and as easygoing as her mother, gives a quick tour of the wide-halled hostel where Billy Riordan spent so much of his time. Like her sister and father, Emma did not wish to be interviewed for this book, but she speaks lovingly of the brother who was four years her senior, and whose thirst for adventure seems to have made it to the next generation, his nephew now attempting to stand at the door. It's a door his grandmother uses soon. She has work waiting at her own office, and one more stop to make. Just past the roundabout, headed in the direction of Ventry once again, Mags pulls to the left, parks and exits the coupe at Milltown Cemetery, the resting place of three of her children.

The metal gate creaks as she opens it, and it clanks when it closes behind her. She walks the concrete path snaking to the right, next to the thick cement wall enclosing this graveyard a little more than a mile west of the town center. The footsteps of her flats are softened by tufts of grass and small rugs of lichens as she walks deeper into the sprawling cemetery sloping down to the harbor where Crystal Spirit, the blue-and-yellow boat on which Billy once worked, still bobs, the charcoal-tinted Slieve Mish mountains hefty and protective far beyond.

The grass within the graveyard's walls is green in some patches but nonexistent in others. Mags notes stones bearing surnames familiar to her. Reads them aloud. Doesn't know by heart the order they're in as she says she doesn't come to the cemetery that often. "I don't feel the need to," she says, falls silent as she passes a few more stones, then next adds a contradictory "I come often enough."

That's when she takes the sudden left off the path, through an empty plot, stops at a stone in the second row, touches it from the back as she passes. She steps to the front of the marker and begins to tend the garden before it.

"I would come a couple times a year, to pull out weeds like this now." Mags points to the greenery that covers a space the size of an adult's coffin. "I'm trying to get the whole thing to cover with ivy. I don't like the kind of stone they put on these," she says, referring to the popular Irish practice of filling plot rectangles with gray or white pebbles. Throughout the cemetery, square yards of pebbles cover antiseptic spans in front of stones often polished to an aluminum sheen, some of the markers ancient-looking and timeworn, so many of them modern and American-shiny but touched at the bases with the poignantly personal — rosaries, statues of Saint Thérèse, a heart made of plastic flowers — set against their bases. The stone at the head of the plot Mags tends is noticeably old-fashioned, unfinished and arced roughly on top. A hole has been cut just above the *D* in the name RIORDAN, and a sun with a bird has been carved in the center.

Below that:

> Niamh 1973-1973
> Luke 1976-1976
> Billy 1973-1999
>
> *Fly for us*
> *Birds of The sun*
> *Fly high*

At its base, visitors have left an angel figurine. A small lantern with green glass. A collection of crystals. A sister's bridal bouquet.

A wind blows, a bird chirps, a mother pulls at the weeds on a grave. Then she rises, standing on the slim cement border of the plot. Trying, as always, to balance.

THREE

Eight thousand seven hundred and two miles away, in sub-Saharan Africa, stands another stone.

Depending on the day, Mags might pass it eight, twelve, twenty-six times, starting first thing in the morning, when she exits her one-room second-floor flat, descends the thirteen unpainted wooden stairs, and walks to the kitchen or the office or the carport of the lakefront volunteer complex that is her Malawian home. Three yards to the right of the stairs' landing, in a small raised garden maybe three by four feet and edged with clusters of low-growing pink flowers and a palm tree, is the stone Mags delivered here two days after the first anniversary of her son's death, in the year 2000, ten years before the year in which the African leg of the research for this book was done. A foot and a half of gray stone from the West Kerry village of Inch protrudes from the soil, its top edge naturally ragged above the neatly carved words "This is Paradise."

That quote from the final communication from a son to his mother, and two dangling fuchsia shapes bookended by Celtic knots hover above the inscription:

Remembering
Billy Riordan
1973-1999
DINGLE – IRELAND

A two-foot-long path from the rocks edging the garden to the base of the stone is clear between the two plantings of greenery, but unless someone is weeding you probably won't see anyone near. The image of Mags passing the monument with her usual fast-paced walk and without a glance at the memorial at first seems odd until the viewer realizes it would be ridiculous for her to stop and reflect each time. Death is a fact of life for this woman, and the speed with which she flies about and passes the stone a dozen or two or four times a day hits home the fact that she is not here to mourn in the expected manner.

But on the first visit Mags made to Cape Maclear, grief was still a raw-edged wound, and much time was given for pausing and reflecting. That was the point of the trip made both to deliver this stone marking a young man's life, and to heed the request he made the last time he e-mailed.

"This is paradise. Mum. You have to come, you have to come, you have to come."

Mags nods as she recalls the passion in that message. "Paradise," she repeats as she slowly sets a mug of tea on the coffee table of her flat's porch, from which can be heard the soft private songs of a woman washing laundry at the shoreline just below. "He never said that about any other place. He thought it was fantastic here."

The opinion wasn't the unblinkered love of a first-timer. Billy had holidayed in Cape Maclear twice before — in 1996, then in 1997. The following year, his major trip was a backpacking holiday in Morocco with Mags and Jennifer. The next year, he returned to the Cape.

"He loved Africa," says his mother, who held no fears regarding his traveling there, that last, or any, time. "Obviously, when your child is going away, you'd always worry, but you can't hold them back. So, while you worry, you can't clip their wings. You can't make a mammy's boy out of them. Billy had traveled when he was a student, he'd done a lot of stuff while he was growing up. I supposed he was given itchy feet. A wanderlust. I didn't worry specifically about him traveling, no more than I'd worry about anybody else."

Billy's solo adventures began when he was seventeen and headed to Europe for a summer.

"It sounds like you're being neglectful — even nowadays seventeen sounds really young to be letting him off — but he was a very mature kid," Mags says. "We'd lived in America, lived in England, Scotland, (he) had been in and out of several different schools. He was a very mature, savvy kind of young fella, really on the ball. He wasn't a kid who'd grown up in the same place all his life. He was well-traveled at seventeen, had been in ten or twelve different schools. That either makes kids confident or very unsure, but with him it worked that he was just a very confident kid."

That characteristic was coupled with a rather old-fashioned desire to regularly touch base with the folks back home, no matter what far corner of the world was his landing place.

"He was always very good about keeping in touch," Mags says. "Initially when he was away traveling, there was no e-mail, no mobile phones. He kept in touch by fax. I still have loads of faxes from all over the world. He went to endless trouble to find fax machines all over South America, Southeast Asia, Australia, Sumatra, all over the place, and he would always make a point of staying in contact."

Any mother would appreciate that. The relationship Mags had with her surviving son meant the notes and messages were all the more important. "There are people you truly can be yourself around," Mags says. "For me, that was Billy. When I was with him, I was most myself."

To his grandmothers, he sent postcards. "Every square millimeter," Mags says, "written on. They would treasure these."

When Billy could, he'd dial.

"I'd get phone calls from the weirdest places," his mother remembers. "He'd say 'I'm just calling to say I'm fine, I'm grand, don't worry, I'll be in touch.'

And whenever he was able to ring from Cape Maclear, Billy never failed to mention it being like home.

"He kept saying 'It's really like Dingle,'" his mother recalls, her eyes widening. "In one sense it's a town, a village on the end of a peninsula." She imagines the trip a visitor would make into Dingle, and points out that it's not unlike that of coming into the Cape: "You come over a mountain pass, like you'd come over Conor Pass and down to the shore, but this is a lake and in Dingle it's obviously the sea. It's a fishing village, everybody knows everybody, everyone's all related, it's just very similar to Dingle. I'm sure a million places around the world are. But he always used to say Cape Maclear is like Dingle. Like Dingle in the sunshine."

One year and two days after Billy Riordan's death, his mother stood in that sunshine for the first time, concluding a five-day trip that began on a British Airways jumbo jet bound from London to Harare, Zimbabwe. Finally, she was headed to Malawi. She was headed to Cape Maclear. She was headed to paradise. And she was not traveling alone. A one hundred-pound slab of stone was going with her.

Mags had flown coach. The stone, and its legend, had not. It had been swathed in cloth and cardboard and shut behind the plastic door of the closet in the first-class cabin — a courtesy extended by the airline as an alternative to the hold, where the stone could have been damaged.

When the jet landed in Harare, a taxicab was dispatched to its door. Not for any dignitary on the plane, not for any human at all, just to transport to the terminal the legend wrapped in cloth and cardboard. Another courtesy. The taxicab drove the stone to the terminal while the mother made her way on foot.

From there, the mother and the stone began the trip to Cape Maclear. Four days later, as does most every first timer approaching in daylight the flat head of the Cape via the one and only road leading in, she was struck by the wide vista that comes into view just before the village and just a few dozen yards before the downward sloping span of farmland upon which the clinic now rests. But the lake is what Mags Riordan noticed first. Flat, cerulean and ocean-big. Standing with a small party of others important to Billy — including his best friend and frequent travel partner, Ronan Doherty, and Dipali Shah, his last girlfriend — she took in the scene, and the reality. As she had been urged to do a little more than one year and two days before, Mags had come to paradise.

Cape Maclear has known several moments of change in its few hundred years of casually recorded history in a country represented — if found at all — on maps and globes by a slim vertical sliver squeezed against Tanzania to the northeast and Zambia to the northwest, the rest of its border nearly surrounded by Mozambique to the east, south and west. That border encompasses roughly half the shore of 8,683-square-mile Lake Malawi, which had been in Malawi's control by a British decree during its colonial times (1881 to 1964), and further was cemented when African states agreed to keep their colonial borders after becoming independent. The country was first settled in the tenth century, but on a continent where that baobab tree over there could be five thousand years old, a thousand years seems miniscule, making the span in which outsiders brought their ideas for improvement seem that much more a blip.

First was the mid-nineteenth-century arrival of Scottish explorer and Presbyterian missionary David Livingstone. He's said to be the Livingstone of the "Dr. Livingstone, I presume?" question posed by a reporter who at Lake Tanganyika in 1871 finally tracked down the man who helped drive the craze to discover the source of the Nile and inspired many more Europeans to explore — and claim — Africa. But it's a certainty that Livingstone was the first outsider to find the Cape, which he named for his friend, Irish-born South African Sir Thomas Maclear, then Royal Astronomer at the Cape of Good Hope and someone who would never lay eyes on the place bearing his surname. Like Billy Riordan, Livingstone was captivated by the Cape's natural beauty. Over the brachystegia woodland flew white-breasted cormorants and majestic fish eagles, two of the 650 recorded species of birds still found in an area colored by no less than four hundred orchid species. Livingstone redundantly named the fish-filled waters Lake Nyasa, the word for lake in several local languages, romantically nicknamed it the "lake of stars," and openly deplored the slave trade abounding on its shores, saying, "It is against this gigantic evil that my own mission is directed."

Fourteen years after Livingstone arrived in the area, Livingstonia Mission was established at the western edge of the Cape in memory of David Livingstone, whose death in 1873 had resulted in a wave of British support for East African missions. Another son of Scotland, pastor and medical officer Robert Laws, oversaw the rousing start, in which buildings were constructed and farming begun, and an influx of new residents from around the region settled to take advantage of the mission's promise of safety, schooling and the area's first semblance of modern medical service. Whatever that service was, it was helpless against the area's rampant malaria, which pushed Laws to move his mission two hundred miles north, to the town of Bandawe. Thirty-five years after Livingstone's arrival, the mission at the Cape was deserted.

In 1946, Malawi's very first tourist hotel was built on Cape Maclear, near the former mission site, and saw its boom in 1949, when the British Overseas Airways Corporation started using the Cape as a port for the Solent passenger flying boats it operated between the United Kingdom and South Africa. But the flights commenced toward the end of the craft's popularity, and ended after a single year. That also meant the end of the hotel, which was shuttered in 1951 and then dismantled to be moved north by barge to Senga Bay.

Resulting in a longer-lasting change for the Cape was the news in 1984 that the entire area — over fifty-eight miles, including three mainland parcels, a dozen islands, and water up to one hundred yards from the Cape's granite-bouldered shores — had been declared Lake Malawi National Park, the world's first national park created primarily to save freshwater fish. A United Nations Educational, Scientific and Cultural Organization (UNESCO) World Heritage Site, the park is home to the largest number of species of fish found in any lake in the world. Of the three thousand identified here, and easily seen by simply peering into the crystal waters, eight hundred species hail from the cichlidae family and all but five are endemic to the lake.

As for a project meant to save humans, there was one effort before Mags came to town. In 1995, the sixty-one-year-old Washington State-based Christian organization World Vision, which focuses on the needs of one hundred million children in one hundred countries, decided to build a medical clinic in

Chembe Village. A large rectangular building was constructed of concrete blocks on a plot of farmland almost adjacent to that on which the Billy Riordan Memorial Clinic one day would be built. Funding dried up and the project was abandoned two or three years later. The cobalt blue-painted concrete shell now is used as a church school.

That's it. Not even in a nutshell. That's simply it for a list of the outsiders and their events and creations that have affected this community since anyone began writing down such things. The day Mags first arrived at the Cape, what has been the most recent and most successful project — the Billy Riordan Memorial Trust — wasn't a thought in anyone's mind. But it nevertheless began that day, because that day was the start of the spell the village, the Cape and the country cast on her.

However, like her son, Mags saw the place with clear eyes. First stop after descending into Chembe Village, and to the shores of the lake itself, was The Gap, then a hostel where Billy Riordan had rented a bed the night he arrived, left his knapsack unpacked, and from where he set out for a night from which he would not return alive.

"It was a wreck of a place," his mother says of The Gap, recalling the complex's shoddy construction and unreliable plumbing. She'd initially stayed there for the equivalent of fifty cents a night, but found that price criminal: "It had no proper toilet, no shower facilities, the roofs leaked like strainers, the beds were manky. Shortly after we stayed there, it was closed by the Malawi Ministry of Tourism, found to be unfit for human habitation." She adds with a knowing smile, "You have to be really bad to be closed by the Malawi Ministry of Tourism."

But the group that arrived to mark the first anniversary of Billy Riordan's death wasn't there for a holiday. Other than setting the stone in place — as Mags would on the grounds of The Gap, initially in a shaded area with a reed fence as a backdrop, there was no agenda.

"It was a whole jumble of emotions, really. Very different," Mags says and looks out at the water. In the beachfront clearing to the left of her porch, a volunteer enjoying a day off settles into a hammock and begins to strum a guitar. "I met people who'd been with him the day he died. People who had helped him. I was feeling a lot of things, and then there was, of course, the whole thing of being in Africa. I'd been to Africa, but not really Africa. Morocco is Arabic Africa, not deepest, darkest Africa."

And she'd never had a connection to a place on that continent. Certainly not as she now had, all because of her son.

But Mags once before had been to a place of great need. Watching television coverage of the war in Bosnia back in 1995, she felt compelled to help with the relief effort.

"The Bosnia thing," as she refers to her work then, came about, Mags says, "from seeing the dreadful images on TV and feeling distinctly uncomfortable in my cushy life in Dingle. I realized that we had such a surplus of the basics which they so desperately needed, that we should get some of it to them."

She found an aid group in Cork that was amassing necessities, including food and medicine, and joined a friend in making a local plea for donations to fill a forty-foot container. They ended up stuffing three of them.

The following year, Mags traveled to Bosanska Krupa in Northern Bosnia and saw the supplies get into the hands of those who desperately needed them. She calls the experience unbelievable. As the hostilities continued, she rode past devastated homes and villages, the remaining occupants women and children, as the men were fighting or buried. One woman begged Mags to take her son and give him an education. "She was prepared to make the ultimate sacrifice," Mags says, recalling the interaction that took place three years before she herself would part with another of her own children.

Shortly after their arrival in Cape Maclear by matola on that February Friday morning in 1999, Mags Riordan's son and his pair of traveling companions checked in at The Gap hostel. ("The rooms are all divided differently now so I don't know where he was," Mags notes. "Everyone says something different.") The group then walked east on the beach, to Fat Monkeys, a popular and lively open-air waterfront bar and restaurant, and the only lodge in the village at the time. They stayed late, and as they finally walked the beach en route to their rooms at The Gap, Billy decided to take a swim.

"Somewhere one hundred yards down the beach from here," Mags says, "he and the other guys were messing. He took off his shoes, took things out of his pockets — swam out there. Roy and a couple of friends sat on the beach, didn't go in. They heard him swimming. They were chatting, then they didn't hear him. They called out for him, starting out in a dugout canoe. The others thought they'd go out there and he'd upturn them. But they couldn't find him. He loved to have fun, so the boys decided he was hiding behind a boat, or had returned to shore — he was a trained diver and knew how to swim. They went back to their rooms."

She looks up the beach. A parade of children and a scrawny dog are following a pair of white tourists, nearing the portion of beach where Billy went for his swim. Her eyes remain there as she says, "In the morning, he wasn't in the bed. He hadn't even unpacked."

A search party of one hundred villagers searched for Billy's body. It was found nearly forty-eight hours later, fifteen meters offshore, near what is now the tourist company Kayak Africa, two hundred yards west of where he'd stepped into the water.

His mother received the news that Monday. She was in Dingle for the weekend while taking a postgraduate course in counseling at University College Cork and answered the door very early in the morning to find Billy's best friend, Ronan Doherty, telling her someone had phoned the Rainbow hostel, where both he and Billy worked, to say Billy was missing.

Mags knows her response: "I immediately said 'He's not missing, he's dead.'"

Mags knew nothing about the Cape, including how remote it was or the lack of modern conveniences, the nearest landline all the way in Monkey Bay.

"I wanted to come out there," Mags says. "The (Irish) Department of Foreign Affairs said, 'I wouldn't advise it.' The travel was very bad. The (Department) was absolutely brilliant. They kept us in very good contact."

Billy's body didn't arrive home for nearly three weeks, making the slow trip to Monkey Bay, then to Blantyre, then to Johannesburg, London, Dublin. The family convened in the meantime, including Emma, who'd been in Australia when the news was received. They had decided against an autopsy in Malawi, after being told the results could be inconclusive, and the procedure would delay the body's return.

"My brother's a doctor," Mags says. "He reckons it must have been a catastrophic event. Billy was a good swimmer. He had been a diver. He had been here two occasions before. There were (fishing boat) lights on the lake. People were saying he must have been swimming to the lights of the village, but I

45

don't think so because he was a clever guy, he was no idiot — there were no lights in the village at that stage. I think he swam out, probably swam partly to shore. There is a history of aneurysm in my family. He was missing from Friday night to Sunday afternoon. In fresh water for forty-eight hours. There was no embalming. A post mortem was a waste of time. It would have been inconclusive, so what's the point? The end result is the same."

Where it happened is the known fact, and for the majority of the mornings each year, Mags Riordan opens her eyes, parts the mosquito netting shrouding her low-set double bed, walks to the door between her one-room flat and her porch and gazes across her wide view of the lake in which her son died. The water is an everyday reality for her, one she at first tentatively took in, and into which she now often dives for refreshment, relaxation, peace.

Had Billy Riordan drowned in Dingle Harbor — or anywhere a whole lot closer to home — his mother's involvement in the community where he died might seem more understandable. Had the location been a few towns east or west on the Dingle Peninsula — or even in England, a quick plane ride away — one easily could imagine Mags making frequent visits to set up a charity, appear annually at a fundraiser, stop in when she could. Or she could have worked longer-distance to fund some effort in Chembe Village, collecting money, sending checks, perhaps visiting once a year to see how the donations were being spent. Choosing instead not only to start a new project in the village, but to literally move there and oversee it, was a life-altering decision.

Flying from Ireland to Malawi itself is a costly two-day ordeal, and from the airport in Lilongwe to Cape Maclear a jarring and also expensive and lengthy drive. Culturally, there are worlds of difference between the Ireland she originally called home and the place Billy called paradise. Its brochure slogan, "The Warm Heart of Africa," is delivered by the easy welcome extended visitors, but Malawi's realities include corruption, frequent famines, one of the highest rates of malaria in sub-Saharan Africa (in 2011, approximately six million cases — closing in on nearly half the population — annually), an AIDS/HIV population estimated at 14 percent, and antiquated laws that include homosexuality being punishable by imprisonment and hard labor. Of one hundred women who become pregnant, eight will die before the child is born. Of the children who are born, one in ten will die before its fifth birthday. At Cape Maclear and its enclave of Chembe Village, residents rely either on subsistence farming or fishing an overfished lake in order to eat. They bathe in, wash clothing and dishes in, and drink from that lake, a breeding ground for bilharzia, also known as schistosomiasis, a potentially organ-damaging parasitic infection transmitted by snail larvae found in waters contaminated by human waste. They hope their homes can hold out in seasonal floods. They hope their families can hold out through "the hungry season," when household food stores run low and the staple crop of maize is nowhere near ready to be harvested. It's to this place that Mags Riordan made the trip anyhow — five times in the first two-and-a-half years after Billy's death — connected with the people, the area, all the while mulling and reshaping plans to do something in her son's memory.

Not surprisingly, this guidance counselor's first idea was to build a school.

"I think I went twice in 2000, three times in 2001? And it was on one of those trips I made arrangements to work at the school when I'd come back in 2002," Mags remembers while a fishing boat holding an overturned craft motors past The Gap. "I went back and spent three months teaching in the community. The reason I went to teach was because I decided I was going to do something for Billy in the line of education, or build a new school, and you just can't walk into a place. You need to do your spadework, find out how things work. That was the idea behind working at the school, I wanted to just get an idea of how things worked there. "

School buildings exist, but the primary school is attended by nearly two thousand children, one class holding approximately four hundred students. Only 7 percent of the boys and 5 percent of girls continue on to secondary level.

"Children aren't required to go to school and there often isn't the parental push," Mags says. "High school costs 2,400 kwacha a semester – about twelve dollars – and often is too prohibitive. So, if a child hasn't gotten into school in the early grades, he or she often will never go."

Mags credits Cieran Begley, principal of *Meán Scoil Nua An Leith Triúigh* in Castlegregory, with enrollment of 131 in the school year 2012 to 2013 one of the smallest secondary schools in Ireland, for giving her time away from her position in career guidance so she could spend longer stretches at the Cape. Mags certainly took her three-month summer vacations, but also would travel to Malawi during the Christmas holidays, then extend her trip — at times up to as many as four months, thanks to her former boss's help. "He was absolutely super," she says. "He used to say 'Look, take whatever time you really need. You can catch up when you get back.'"

The reason for the latitude given?

"I knew she'd be at this forever," Begley will tell you if you sit with him for a cup of tea back in Dingle. "I always let her off when she needed to go. I knew it was for a good cause. I also knew she'd leave the school one day."

Newly retired, the father of three boys plans to substitute teach and travel. "I was never in Africa or Australia," he says. "In the next five years I hope I'd make it out to the two of them. Who knows, I might be teaching there for six months."

Mags made good use of the months he gave her. Investigated the education situation at the Cape, and how to go about creating a school. Then, the idea to do something very different literally appeared on her doorstep.

During a trip to Cape Maclear in 2001, she was staying in the village, at Gaia lodge, the very beachfront backpacker's place from which a door was removed to carry her son's body from the shore. A man rushed toward her, carrying a boy eight or ten years of age, one with the name of her own father: Victor.

"This child had a huge gash in his leg," she remembers. "He'd been knocked down by a bicycle, and whatever way he'd fallen, he must have fallen on stone. I could see his knee through his skin. There was no doctor, no nurse, so, in desperation, the man brought him to me. He knew that white people generally travel with medical kits — at least a couple of antibiotics, whatever — and he was smart enough to bring the child in to me. I took one look and knew the child would die of septicemia. Two or three weeks, he'd die. Or he'd be taken to a witch doctor who would pour engine oil into the wound, and he'd definitely die. I had loads of plasters and dressings with me, so I put him on a course of antibiotics and pressed the wound together, dressed the leg."

The man brought Victor to Mags twice a day for the next two weeks. The wound healed cleanly. It was during those two weeks that Mags first was hit by the fact there wasn't so much as an aspirin available in the village.

"I didn't realize until then," she says. "You go into a village like that, a big village, and, coming from the environment that we come from, it doesn't dawn on you that there would be no medical treatment. You know, no big fancy hospital, no army of doctors. You'd expect there would be a clinic of some description for people who get sick, but there wasn't.

"I found there was no access to doctors, nurses, medication. People were getting sick and dying of eminently curable diseases. A child with gastroenteritis might die. I found that very, very unacceptable." She speaks the last truth firmly.

The following year, Mags's visit to the Cape coincided with a famine that killed an estimated one thousand to three thousand people.

"Victor gave me the idea to build a clinic. The famine really just confirmed it," she says. "I went to the village and people were dying on the streets of hunger-related diseases. Dropping dead in front of me. Only then I realized what was the point of building a school when people were getting sick and there was no one to treat them? Initially it seems a crazy, crazy idea, but I decided that's what I was going to do."

On the shore below Mags's porch, children run, splash, laugh. As usual, even when a group of them includes toddlers, they are on their own, any nearby adults minding their laundry, toothbrushing, scraping the day's wear from the bottoms of their feet by rubbing them on the odd large stone positioned along the shore. Mags thinks back to that first trip to Cape Maclear, when the only goal was to visit the place Billy had loved, and to leave a memorial bearing his name.

"I just thought I'd like to come here and see the place for myself, and put the whole thing to rest," she says. "In one way I was putting it to rest. In another way I was starting something completely new and different."

FOUR

T he waiting room at The Billy Riordan Memorial Clinic isn't that different from those found at the Mayo Clinic. There's the same snaking line at reception, the same vibe of nervous anticipation, the same craning of necks toward the doorway leading to the consultation rooms, the same sound of children fussing, of conversations held in low tones. Here, though, the waiting is being done on a wide porch open to the weather on two sides, and frequent are the glances from that porch to the path along the side of the building, checking for any sight of the doctors and nurses walking over from The Gap for the start of their workday.

Words of greeting pop into the air when, at ten minutes to eight on this particular Monday morning, the two doctors, two nurses and three medical students round the corner of the building's far wall and walk the final yards to the stairs beneath the word CLINIC. "*Muli bwanji?*" they offer, asking the basic "How are you?" as they weave around the nine people in line at reception, through the crowd of twenty-three seated or standing on the square cement yellow-painted porch, its far wall decorated with a floor-to-ceiling circular mural of Thumbi Island kissed by a setting sun, the words BILLY'S MALAWI PROJECT arcing above.

Those who are waiting glance at the plastic-covered, hand-lettered numbers they were given upon arrival and sit up straighter, smooth sleeves or skirts, attire that is probably the best their wardrobes hold. As is the daily norm, the women wear skirts, most of them the waist-tied *chitenje,* but today's are spotless and unwrinkled and probably the same pieces worn to services at any of the fifteen houses of worship serving the Cape's fifteen thousand souls. The lengths of fabric comprising the skirts include those imprinted with images of Pope John Paul II, marking his 1989 visit to Malawi, and others wishing "Merry Christmas" and "Happy New Year". Most of the men sport freshly laundered T-shirts that at some point in time found their way here from the other side of the world. "CHICAGO," reads one. Another, "DANCE." Yet another, "MUSTANG SOCCER – THE ULTIMATE KIND!!!" Baseball caps are popular. Rosaries drape a few necks.

"It shows you how important they consider this, that they wear their best clothes," says nurse Sheila Byrne-Harte, an Irish nurse who became a volunteer after taking early retirement from her post in Kilkenny.

At the window of reception, next to the carved wooden sign giving the clinic's hours (Monday through Friday 8:00 a.m. to 12:00 p.m., and 2:00 to 4:00 p.m.) and the costs per appointment, two patients hand their documents through a pair of spaces in the opening that are not protected by small-gauge chicken wire. Seated at a beaten-up wooden desk on the other side of that window, Sofina Katumala accepts from each of them the thin booklets titled "Health Passport, General Health Profile" that patients are required to bring to appointments. She searches through her files (similarly beaten-up open-top wooden containers the size of shoeboxes, a letter of alphabet Magic-Markered onto the ends of each), locating the white cards bearing the individuals' data from all past appointments.

Sofina checks the name, age and address of each patient, and reaches to deposit in the top right-hand desk drawer the payments that also are handed through the window. She tugs the drawer, which is angled off its tracks, and adds to the pile of paper money already collected today, some of it folded, some of it crumpled, all of it increasing in wear the lower the denomination.

At the current rate of kwacha to a dollar, a local adult pays approximately one dollar per office visit, including medication and inpatient care, if needed. More than a steal in many other parts of the world, but in this region, that's near a day's pay — if a day of work at the minimum wage of 105 kwacha daily (approximately seventy cents) can be found. The Billy Riordan Memorial Trust is the second-largest employer at the Cape, with thirty-two people on its payroll, a few less than the thirty-five employed by land and water safari company Tourist Africa down along the beach. Therefore, half of those who best could afford anything on the Cape are those employed by the Trust, the staffers of which include certified nursing assistants, laboratory technicians, receptionists, maintenance workers, cooks and night watchmen. The goal is one day to have the clinic operated solely by Cape residents, but that day isn't on any calendar yet printed. Hurdles include basic education not being mandatory in Malawi and, too often, not a priority held by parents; high school fees beyond the reach of most locals; and the fact that most medical students leave the country after graduation for better pay and better facilities. Hastings Kamuzu Banda, the dictator-like first president of Malawi, whose self-proclaimed "president for life" status ended after thirty-one years with a 1994 failed re-election bid, once said there are more Malawian doctors in the English city of Manchester than in Malawi. He wasn't exaggerating. That makes all the more promising the presence of Malawian medical student Donnie Mategula in the current band of volunteers. If one future Malawian doctor chooses to spend his break volunteering, perhaps others soon will. And, they might eventually stay.

But right now, the reality is as hard as the red-painted cement floor beneath Sofina's feet and the waterstained white ceiling above her head. On the cement wall behind her hangs the rota for the clinic's fourteen local staffers, a list of first names including Enoch, Iwell, Chiku, Charles and Wilson, along with both a Dorothy and a Big Dorothy. A nearby sheet of paper holds the number of the hours the clinic's generator has been used. Below, a fan twists on a table occupied by four cell phones of the ubiquitous Zain brand, a giant telecommunications provider in both the Middle East and Africa, whose name spans the length of the lonely billboard at the top of the half-plowed cornfield adjacent to the clinic.

On the road behind that sign and just above the clinic, a baboon lopes. Three women walk toward the village, firewood piled on their heads, machetes in their hands. A boy scrambles after the rolling tire-free bicycle wheel he's guiding down the road with a long stick. At the edge of the road, seven men sit in the shade of a tree. Beyond them is a mountain, tall and rocky and soft-focused in a haze of dust at this tail end of the dry season. Two more women climb the stairs to reception. They lean on the sill's worn patch and hand Sofina their health passports.

Sofina is clad today in matching silky beige-and-black blouse and skirt. She's worked as registrar Monday through Friday since the day the clinic opened. "I like to help the people in the village," she says, and notes that she came to the job after working with a privately funded food program that assisted the area for four years. Between that and living right in the village, "I know everybody," she says. She also knows what life was like before. "Mags is very important. Since they opened the clinic, most of things improved. When Mags come here, most of things are fine. Getting medicine for free, also supply the food, nutrition people, porridge and milk. HIV patients getting medicine."

She smiles. Nods. Turns her attention to the window and the next health passport being held out to her. While she remains busy, those she's already checked in do little but observe the passing scene, or chat with a neighbor, or sleep. The only reading material visible is a copy of a paperback titled *Rooted in Christ*, strapped behind the seat of a bicycle leaning against the mural.

"Sometimes we had some things to read," says Justice Chiphwanya, administration assistant in reception and owner of both the bike and the book. "But just a few people can go for that. Not many people read."

So the Western-world complaint of dusty four-year-old copies of *Time* and *Newsweek* being the only option for amusement isn't heard in this waiting area, where the illiteracy rate is the same 90 percent as that of unemployment. In a village where televisions can be counted on the fingers of one hand, and are located in lodges or in bars frequented mostly by tourists and, if by the few locals, only males, no flat-screen TV offers patients an episode of *Jerry Springer* or *The View*, or one of those pharmaceutical company-sponsored quizzes on medical facts. A child clambers onto the porch sill and attempts to further dismantle the carcass of an old palm-sized radio that is his toy. A few feet away, Mercy Kambwiri, dressed in flip-flops and a pair of green scrubs with CELTIC HEALTHCARE printed below the pants' back waistband, points patients to a digital home-bathroom-model scale she's placed in the waiting area. There she weighs them, inserts a digital thermometer into an armpit of each and records all data on a sheet of paper. She then wheels a hanging scale over to a young mother and assists her in settling the child into the scale's cloth sling.

Patients fan themselves, peek down the hallway hung with a few framed certificates, including one proclaiming the site a non-government organization (one of 3,494 NGOs on the African continent, 108 of them in Malawi), another the clinic's mission statement:

> "The Billy Riordan Memorial Trust works to improve the overall health status of the village of Cape Maclear (Chembe Village) through the provision of a medical clinic and health centre. The trust provides educational opportunities and support. It is the objective of the trust to provide relief of suffering and deprivation in this community."

The patients watch for action at any of the hallway's doors, which hold both the wonders of a modern clinic located so far from modernity, and makeshift solutions to problems created by that distance. There's a consultation room, a pair of treatment rooms, a main pharmacy in which a nurse's iPod is queued to Bruce Springsteen and in which, high above the neat rows of medications, a shelf is dedicated to the bottles of sunscreen distributed to the few locals who happen to be albinos.

In what formerly was the lab, an emergency room includes a maternity cupboard and a lamb-warming lamp to be used on newborns. There's also a bucket of disinfecting Cidex solution, as there is no way to sterilize equipment electrically — autoclaves burn out the power supply (in a pinch, and in what Mags calls a form of bush medicine, staff will wrap equipment in Reynolds Wrap and boil it on the stove at The Gap kitchen). Another door leads to a storeroom for more medications and supplies, and the next opens to a close observation ward of two beds and three cots, where patients are watched overnight before release or transfer. A doctor's consulting room is next, equipped with a bucket and disinfectant due to having no running water. A final storeroom is behind the last door before the one that opens to the path leading back to The Gap.

56

At the other end of the hall, nurse Sheila and medical student Donnie emerge from the pharmacy and begin to check the line for patients with dressings that need to be changed, the first order of the day. Without ceremony, the clinic is open.

Three more women arrive at reception, holding umbrellas to shield themselves from the increasingly hot sun. Babies sleep on their backs, snug in the yards of cloth tied around their mothers' shoulders. One woman has just finished feeding her baby and, though the child is back in the sling on her back, the mother's right breast remains in sight as she holds a conversation with a man who looks nowhere but into her face. Babies are everywhere at the Cape, the average Malawian woman having five children; the mere idea of a childless couple is met with incredulity and suspicion, and the westerner soon learns that female breasts are other facts of life here, often displayed as casually as an elbow.

On a bench a few feet away, Lauren Finlay, one of the two Australian medical students currently volunteering, consults on the porch with a father concerned about his young son's hand. The boy won't be the last child seen today — October to December is known as broken-bone season, due to mangoes ripening and kids climbing high for the fattest ones. Justice, who often serves as an interpreter for doctors and nurses, listening to the Chichewa then standing back to say, "You are free" so the speaker can ask other questions, stands by as Lauren crouches to the child's level. She's twenty-five and in two months will graduate from medical school. The following month she'll begin a year-long internship at Royal Darwin Hospital back home, and the rounds — general medicine, general surgery, general emergency — required of all interns in her country. Between now and then, she'll enjoy six weeks of travel in Kathmandu with her friend Kate Brennan, who also started the five-week medical studies elective at the clinic a few weeks before. "We'll stop being students at the end of this," Lauren says with a smile of anticipation.

Short and pale with hair worn in long strict curls, Lauren talks quickly and can be both funny and intense. She originally wanted to be a teacher but says she lacked passion for the job. Then she considered a career as a physiotherapist, "rubbing the backs of strong men," she'll detail with another smile once the workday has ended, "but I thought it would bore me." She was sixteen when her mother died at forty-three from breast cancer that metastasized to her lungs and brain. "That might have contributed to the reason I wanted to do medicine then," Lauren says. "Now it's different. I like learning, talking to people — sometimes too much." She laughs nervously. "I didn't want to work nine to five. I wanted to be able to work anywhere."

Right now, anywhere is a porch of a clinic in Chembe Village, where she and Kate share a room located just before The Gap's ambulance bay, their rear wall facing the main lane threading through the village. "I made Kate do this," Lauren says of their adventure, placing definite emphasis on the verb. "Kate originally suggested we go to South America. I said 'No, Africa.' I love Africa. I've always wanted to come work here, I've always been obsessed with Africa."

In exchange for Kate's agreeing to come to Malawi, Lauren will accompany her in 2014 to the World Cup in Brazil, where Kate once lived for a year. But right now they are here, in teal scrubs, and in the trenches.

"Yesterday I saw a woman who had a fever," Lauren says. "She'd been three times to Monkey Bay. Nobody (there) tested her. She was HIV positive, had obvious Kaposi's (sarcoma) on her face. I was saying 'Would you go back to Monkey Bay?' She said 'No, no, I'll get treated a lot better here.' She was in shock (about her results), but very grateful."

A patient with a hearing problem also went to Monkey Bay,

Lauren says. "They clicked here (she snaps her fingers on the right side of her head), then here (snaps on the left), and then they said she was deaf." The patient was not deaf, and next came to the clinic. "She told me, 'I know you're here to help us.'"

Lauren had to agree.

"Here, there's time for patients," she says. "What I think I'm all about is the nicety of medicine. The best doctor is one who can talk to the patient. Let them know they are welcome to come back."

An earlier patient, an emergency case accompanied to the clinic by many family members, has stuck in her memory. "I talked with her a lot, got her to the hospital, but then I realized I hadn't talked to the family. I didn't like that. But most would think you don't need to include the family."

Lauren's doing that now as she converses with the father and engages the child. Justice watches. Approximately five feet tall, with a round, smiling and friendly face, he wears jeans, a checkered short-sleeved shirt and flip-flops. At twenty-four, he has been working at the clinic for a year, and likes helping both the community and his family. "I was interested in the experience of a clinic," he says. "I like promoting the lives of villagers." A Cape resident lucky enough to have a regularly scheduled paying job typically supports an average of eleven people, and Justice is no exception. "I like the income for my life and my relatives," he says. "I'm supporting my child and two brothers for school. I volunteer my life for them now."

Fortunate to have work and a mode of transportation — the black multi-speed bicycle that is the sign of a person with a job (bikes go for 20,000 to 30,000 kwacha — sixty-six to one hundred dollars) — he pedals a third of a mile to the clinic from nearby Chiwisi village, which, like the others on the Cape, is named for a local family. Justice attended secondary school in the village then did some teaching. A member of the River of Life Evangelical Church, he has planted two churches in the area, with a combined congregation of fifty. He would like to become a minister but right now is involved in another kind of ministry — working at the clinic — Monday through Friday and weekends on an emergency basis.

He's been on the receiving end of the clinic's services "many times," he estimates, treated for respiratory infections and malaria. Before the clinic opened, Monkey Bay would have been Justice's only option — if he could afford the matola or private car.

"That's what happened in those days — the mortality rate was high," he says.

Wellings Kamwaza sits nearby in dark slacks and white shirt, his feet bare, in his second hour of waiting for one of his four children to see a doctor. He's the owner of the silver five-seat 1998 Toyota sedan parked next to the empty cornfield and beneath a tree that's a rare source of shade at this end of the village. The auto is a rare source of transportation, and a portion of the 110,000 miles on its odometer were added when the ambulance was unavailable and his transfer service was needed.

Wellings isn't a Cape native, but moved here before the clinic opened and knows what life was like then for anyone in need of medical help. "We had to go to Monkey Bay for any disease. The problem with Monkey Bay was financial, getting transportation."

He's solved some of that, and is paid that 4,000 kwacha for a round-trip in the car he purchased by saving half his salary from his government job as a ranger at the National Park.

Similar economic ripples from the clinic extend to a young woman in a black T-shirt and brightly printed skirt sitting on the porch windowsill and using a length of wire to spear samosas from a plastic container. Giving her name only as Ruster, she walked here this morning, as she does every morning, from her home on the road to the National Park, to sell the food she's made. The samosas, along with the small packets of peanuts she's roasted in oil, and the bottles of water, Coke and Fanta that await in her cooler, are priced at ten kwacha each.

The one hundred samosas Ruster made this morning are popular on this porch devoid of the usual hospital waiting-room vending machines, and with no eatery for a good mile. "Everyone who comes in buys them," she says, a statement evidenced by the steady trade throughout the morning.

Ruster, twenty-one, says she has been a patient at the clinic for what she calls ailments, but never has made the journey to Monkey Bay. "No, it's very tough, kind of a long way if you're very sick. Clinic is important. It has saved a lot of people."

"Before the clinic she would not have had this business," Justice says, adding that Ruster's prior option would have been to sell at the big market in town, a collection of stalls and small shops that, despite their limited wares, would be nothing but competition, something that doesn't exist at the clinic. "Now there is high demand. She can sell lots."

A motorcycle can be heard long before it's spotted, so quiet is the road along the clinic. Only three other vehicles pass by all morning, two of them Kayak Africa's heading to and from the beach, and one the ambulance in which assistant program manager Dave Clancy delivers sacks of porridge for the clinic's weekly feeding program. From her seat near the door to the clinic hallway, Violet Nkhoma, twenty-six, watches Dave unload the ambulance. Violet this morning walked over from her home near the National Park, dressed not unlike Ruster in printed skirt and black T-shirt. Her open face regards a newcomer intensely at first, then shyly. She's the only person on the porch unwilling to disclose the reason for her visit on this day, but will offer that she likes the treatment she receives. "Because of the medicine itself," she says, "you get well." Violet has five family members and says their health would be very different if Monkey Bay were the only alternative. There have been illnesses not tended to, due to the distance, "Even deaths," she says.

By 11:00 a.m., fifty-two patients have been seen. Eighty-six new cases and fourteen reviews of old cases will be tended to by the time lunch break begins at noon, when Sofina draws a white curtain across the reception window, signaling that no more registrations will be taken until the two-to-four afternoon hours begin. Everyone registered but yet to be examined will be taken care of before the lunch break, even if it means the doctors don't get to eat. Mercy has removed the baby scale from its holder, and its metal stand is tipped over to further mark the break in the day. Thirteen patients still wait, including an elderly woman holding a cane, her bandaged foot and ankle propped on the bench on which she rests.

Between the porch and the road, Aufi, a Trust watchman in a baseball cap reading "Belmont Shores", inspects the new garden area that will provide a different kind of waiting room for patients and visitors. Twenty by fifteen feet, and located on the incline that eventually meets the road, it includes a mature mango tree shading a bench around its trunk. On that shaded section of ground, a carved-out piece of wood rests on the sand, the board for the game of bao that, with nothing more than handfuls of stones moved between two sets of four depressions, looks elementary but can be as involved and as complicated as chess. Aufi would love nothing more than to give another drink to the plantings he's surrounded with larger stones, but has been asked not to use any more water from the clinic's well. Today his lunch break will be occupied by shooing away the goats from the chest-high wire fencing meant to keep them from leaping into the garden area, and away from the plantings that were supposed to be ones goats did not favor.

Ruster walks from the porch to the addition behind the clinic and sets up her offerings near the group of four people standing outside the door. Gap dogs Bo and Ulemu head to shady spots beneath the bushes across from reception. Their routine is to follow the volunteers on the walk back to The Gap, but today there will be no midday trip home, as the doctors and nurses will work straight through the two hours of lunch.

Add to the already busy Monday is the fact that it's one of the three days of the week on which patients are seen at the government-sponsored antiretroviral program held in the addition built in 2007. Made of bricks mixed and baked, as is the practice here, just yards from where the structure now stands, the original clinic building was constructed by hands holding shovels, wheelbarrows, hammers and nails. Not a power tool was in sight, though the plans included creation of a generator house that eventually would shelter such a machine donated by the Galway Rotary Club. Separated from the clinic by a series of clotheslines currently hung with bed linens that sway inches above the red dirt yard, the extension was built with a bit more modern technology in that post-generator era and holds a men's ward with six beds, shower and toilet; a female and children's ward with six beds, a cot, a shower and a toilet; a laboratory; a kitchen; a laundry room; a room for the children's feeding program; and the ARV counselor's office. In that last room on the left, HIV/AIDS clinics are held four days per week, serving more than eight hundred patients per month at a clinic where, since March of 2008, tests for the disease were done for

6,473 patients, and in a country where the oft-seen slogan "Live Positively" means a lot more than having a good outlook on life.

Across the hall from that office, in the first of two eight-bed wards for overnight care, tiny two-month-old Chifundo Nychafunya lies listless on a small blanket that's been smoothed across an adult-sized bed. Admitted this morning due to vomiting after feeding, he's watched by his mother, Stella Nychafunya, thirty-two, who sits next to him in a long red-and-white dress. He is her second child — a seven-year-old is at home. Stella is pleased with the care Chifundo is getting, and says she would not have been able to afford transportation to Monkey Bay. Had the clinic not existed, her son's health would be more in jeopardy.

The addition has one other room for overnight care, each holding eight beds. Four are occupied today, with two adults and two children admitted. Across the room from Chifundo, twenty-two-year-old Farison Roben leans on an elbow as he stretches out in bed. His wife sits next to him, a child on her lap. A bottle of Coke and another of Fanta are set on a nearby table, as is the small cooler in which the family had brought lunch. (If a family doesn't deliver food, porridge is provided.) Farison, strapping and long-limbed, will say only that he's ill, and that he's in his second day in the ward at the clinic he calls "a very good thing for the community."

In the next room, Livinston Justin, nine months old and suffering from malaria, lies across the lap of his mother, Martha, thirty-two-years-old. It's also his second day in the clinic. At the end of the bed, Martha's mother, Olive Banda, a woman bearing a surname Mags says is as common here as Murphy is in Ireland, stretches out on her side, watching her daughter and grandchild, Martha's younger child by five years. Both women are dressed in bold tropical prints. The baby lies on a piece of green cloth printed with leaves. Against the soft yellow bed blanket and the white brick walls, the colors bring life to the room.

Adjacent to the ward, five women waiting for a patient sit on the dirt beneath a blue gum tree and next to low bushes on which diapers dry. The oldest of the women, wizened and skinny with gaps in her line of teeth, wears a pink T-shirt that proclaims "Thank God I'm Cute." Through Justice, the women say they often use the clinic. "It was very tough. The people could hire cars for Monkey Bay," says one. "It could be taking a long time even for the preparations to get to the hospital." Many they knew well, Justice says, died here, or en route to the hospital.

He's not translating when he offers, "Some of that is due to bewitching." He's referring to the practice of casting spells, not uncommon in a culture where witchcraft remains an age-old tradition, despite remaining controversial. On this day in 2010, approximately fifty Malawians are jailed on accusations made under the country's Witchcraft Act, created by the former colonial power in 1911, in which the professions of witch doctor or witch finder carry a life sentence.

"There is a lot of reliance of people on culture," Justice says. "Most of the ill (are ill) because they believe in old values. They would rather go for what their ancestors were doing. Myths and folktales are transmitted through the country. There are good effects: because of values, the ethnic values and moral values, there's a goodness of a moral life. These concepts make them kind and hospitable. But sorcery and witchcraft beliefs cause them not to believe in science."

As for his own appointments with a witch doctor, Justice says, "I cannot run away from that. Maybe my grandma brought me, but when I came to school and began spiritual formation, I cast that aside."

Dave moves the ambulance from its parking space near the group of women, who are asked if they know how the clinic came about. None have any idea, nor do they know anything about Mags, but a few feet away on the sloping concrete walkway between the clinic and the addition stands a man who does.

"I always give very much thanks about the introduction of this wonderful thing in the community," he says, then adds quietly what is almost an apology for the group on the ground: "Here, the number of people who are illiterate, who don't go to school, it's quite difficult for them to understand things."

The man's name is Steady, the English translation of his Chichewa name, and his broad smile makes him a walking illustration of Malawi's slogan. Steady, thirty-five, lives south of the village and once left here for work in Lilongwe. "When I landed in Lilongwe, it was like in a dream," he says. But it didn't turn out to be a pleasant one. "My mentality tends to go the other way around without support." So he returned to the village.

He's stopped at the clinic en route to the National Park, where this self-taught specialist on local birds and trees often guides visitors for hour-long tours costing the equivalent of ten to fifteen dollars. Two months ago, Steady was diagnosed with bilharzia, as have been two hundred million people worldwide, including many who live in very populated communities on the lake. He knows what the clinic does in a place with such prevalent problems, including malaria that will flare in the upcoming rainy season of November through March.

Steady switches topics, offering, as he does in his job, the name of the peak across from the clinic — Nkhunguni, which translates to fog. He says the mountain is home to a host of creatures, including serval cat, civet cat, bush pig, and baboon, one of which soon clambers down Nkhunguni to sit near a tree and gaze at the clinic for a few minutes before moving on.

Twenty patients fill the waiting area at 2:00 p.m. as Mercy rights the baby scale and Aufi brings out the adult scale. A crash jolts the crowd as a child rolls down the stairs a metal cart on which Mercy had stacked the waiting room numbers. Aufi carries it up from its landing place as two white women, one in T-shirt and shorts, the other in a fun gray minidress and ankle bracelet, walk up the stairs and past him. The one in the dress speaks to Sofina through the window, pays the foreigner's fee, then is directed to Mercy, who asks her to step on the scale and accept the thermometer. Justice says the clinic might have a foreign visitor once a week. "During the World Cup," he says, referring to the championship staged in June and July of 2010 in nine South African cities, "there were lots of Western people coming for that. They came to see the lake 'cause South Africa is close to Malawi."

The patient, who arrived at the Cape two days ago and who'll give her home only as the UK, has come for a malaria test. "I'm not feeling great," she says.

Because of the shorter line this afternoon, medical student Kate soon invites the two women into a consultation room. A blood test is required to determine malaria, and the visitor's sample will be examined by Wilson Adyela, a thirty-four-year-old local who has run the lab since the clinic opened, and who now works in the lab room that is part of the extension. Wearing a blue-and-black-printed scrub top and blue pants, he smiles widely as he gives a tour of the department that's roughly the size of a restroom's handicap stall. The fact that the clinic has a lab of any dimension is a wonder in itself. Normally at a remote clinic, those needing tests must visit a large hospital. "We don't presume malaria, like some clinics who do, and give medication without knowing whether the diagnosis is certain," Wilson says. "We have our own lab." There, he performs tests for malaria, as well as those for HIV — fifteen a day — and other sexually transmitted diseases, as well as pregnancy, tuberculosis and diabetes.

"'Twas horrible," he says of the village's health situation prior to the clinic. "Lot of people were dying from no treatment. In 2001, we had an outbreak of cholera. A lot of people lost their lives."

Wilson completed some studies in Mangochi, forty-six miles south, and now works what he terms "busy days" Monday through Friday, often performing more than thirty tests in one shift. One test was on himself, as he had malaria back in May.

His connections to the clinic go deeper. Ever since its opening he's been on the village committee that has met to discuss issues between the clinic and community. It's a body he calls an illustration of Mags's attempts to keep lines of dialogue open, to make the clinic truly a part of the village rather than a thing established by and run by foreigners.

"Mags is good," he says as he moves a tray of slides toward his microscope. "A straightforward woman of great courage."

At 3:40 p.m., the ambulance pulls in again, this time bearing Dave, Mags and Project Manager Steve Free, Mags's right-hand man. But to call him that is only the starting point. It's hard to imagine the Trust functioning as well as it does without his constant presence, hard work and quiet humor. Steve's nursing background gives him extra insight into and understanding of the clinic and its work, and the fact that he's become Mags's good friend and treasured counsel adds another layer of connection and investment in what she's trying to accomplish.

On this day, Steve is here with Mags to reinforce to Aufi that no one is to take water from the well. They greet him with the area's usual three-part soul shake, which starts with a normal handshake, then slips into each hand encircling the thumb of the other hand before concluding with a traditional shake. The one Mags shares with Aufi is quick, the intro to a message she delivers crisply: "They're taking water from the pump. Nobody is supposed to do that. If we come in the morning and there's no water, you guys are in trouble. We'll be asking you guys why there is no water. Nobody." Her words aren't loud but they are direct. She moves her hands apart to stress the last one.

Aufi nods. Mags's eyes remain fixed on him for the few seconds before Steve asks her to take a look at the garden.

"That's cool!" she enthuses when she rounds the corner and the neat plot comes into view. Her face is lit. "Aufi is the man behind it," she says. "He said something had to be done here." Behind her, Aufi stands, smiling.

"It was just a green square," Steve adds.

"Aufi is the gardener," Mags says with pride, then lowers her voice. "He was mad for watering. We gave him watering hours. Now we're taking away the hose."

An artist named Fantastic painted the pots holding some of the plantings, Steve says as Mags points to the mangoes hanging plentifully. Then she pulls the rug from beneath the beautiful picture, and makes a lot less inviting the bench beneath the tree. "If you sit under them, you'll get a putzi fly in your scalp," she warns. "They lay eggs. You can only get them out with a naked flame, or Vaseline."

She turns and walks to the clinic, up the stairs to reception and then down the emptying clinic hallway, past the pair of female tourists now leaving, the one who had not felt well hav-

ing been diagnosed with malaria and supplied with the envelope of medicines. Noting their presence in a community
where whites are the definite minority, Mags says tourists of
any shade of skin don't know how lucky they are to have a clinic so far from the beaten path. She's still fuming over the tourist who recently fell ill in the village, utilized the emergency
room at The Gap and then skipped town without paying the
10,000 kwacha bill. "The value is second to none," Mags says.
"We are in no way extravagant. This crowd is going away with
10,000 kwacha — that's fifty euro to them, but here that's a
month's salary for the staff. They can come (to the Cape), drink
cocktails at 4 in the afternoon, but they never paid us. This
guy's life was saved. It might as well have been a different story."

She's walking the perimeter of the building now, switching
gears as she's apt to do, heading behind the building, where a
men's and a women's outhouse stand, the incinerator behind
them. The grounds are neat, she's happy to see. "Unlike all the
other hospitals in Malawi," she says, "we provide patients with
food. In other hospitals, people cook outside, you have charcoal piles everywhere. Here, they get porridge. There are lots of
medications that can't be taken without food, so they need to
have something."

What they have here is that meal, this clinic, this woman so
many call out to as they pass, "Mags," "Maggis," "Moggs,"
"Mother," but who was known neither by first nor last name to
anyone when she first approached the late village headman
Chief Chembe shortly after her experience with Victor, to ask
permission to build a clinic here. She had to make an appointment to see him, and had to be escorted by a local, in keeping
with custom. She recalls the chief's home — brick with a tin
roof, a structure she calls "marginally better" than the area's
mud homes with grass roofs — and she remembers the lack of

anxiety involved in proposing her plan. "I wasn't nervous," she recalls. "No — I was giving him a clinic!"

The chief's approval was followed by granting Mags use of a plot of land on which to set the clinic. Even when her plan had been given permission by Malawi's Ministry of Health, had she no land on which to build, there could be no clinic. In this place that is a national park and cannot truly be owned, especially by an outsider, the gift of land was vital. A very early idea had been to use the abandoned World Vision building on the road into the village. In 2001, Mags had asked if it could be donated to the Trust. An inspection found the concrete to have been mixed improperly and the metal roof rife with holes. "The engineers said to get a nice piece of land," Mags remembers. "The chief gave me this one."

On that piece of land, Mags walks around the corner of the addition and up to the clinic porch. There, the two doctors, two nurses and three medical students who eight hours ago walked to The Gap are offered a rare lift back. Steve and Mags sit up front in the ambulance as Dave and the seven medical volunteers crouch to enter the vehicle through its small left-hand back door. Mags encourages Ulemu to jump in the front seat, and she settles onto her lap. Steve gets out and invites Bo into the van, but he reclines near the side of the addition.

"Where else in the world is there a bus full of white medical people and a dog?" Mags asks over the chattering crowd packed in the back, everyone now noticing Aufi trying to urge Bo toward the ambulance before it leaves. The dog doesn't comply, instead watches the ambulance bounce down the road.

Inside the clinic, Wilson clears his workspace. Sofina counts the kwacha heaped in her drawer. Justice takes a seat behind her at a small wooden desk bearing a worn plaque reading UDARÁS NA GAELTACHTA, Irish for Gaeltacht Authority, a regional state agency aimed at developing the culture and economy in Ireland's native speaking pockets, including Mags's adopted County Kerry home — the source of this donation.

Justice logs the day's patient statistics into a wide hardbound book that must be submitted annually to the government. His neat handwriting states that approximately twelve hundred people are cared for each month, 114 on this day alone. In the previous month, September, 964 people were seen. Malaria was the top reason, with 290 new cases logged, along with forty-nine new cases of bilharzia, and thirty-five of pneumonia. The pages also inform that the government-staffed family planning clinic in the extension saw twenty-eight people that month, all of them female in a village and culture where males are less likely to use prophylactics.

The day was a busy one and a good one, the staff agrees. Sofina adds a nod, and a final note: "A good day," she says while shutting the drawer and standing. "A good day should always be busy."

FIVE

A map of the world stuck with pins marking the many countries an uncle had visited. A priest assigned to a church in Kenya. The woman who inspired Live Aid. A way to spend a first break from medical school. Television coverage that led to "bawlin' my eyes out about the kids in Ethiopia."

The inspirations and reasons are as different as the people telling the stories, but all led to the same result: volunteering for stints of from four months to five years at the Billy Riordan Memorial Clinic.

The two doctors, four nurses, two medical students, one project manager and two assistant project managers calling the project's lakefront volunteer center home base are propelled here by various forces, but all end up calling The Gap their home. There they occupy spartan individual or double rooms large enough for a twin bed or two, a set of shelves and a desk. They share shower and toilet facilities, a laundry room, a kitchen, a common area, and a sandy palm-tree-studded yard hung with a hammock facing the beach and pyramidical Thumbi Island. According to the 1997 *Lonely Planet* found on the slightly sagging set of bookshelves on the far wall of the L-shaped dining and common area, a night at this place cost a mere dollar in the era of Billy Riordan's visits, back when it was a hostel called The Gap. Locals and volunteers still use that name for it, even though the lettering on the big white sign next to the prickly pear cacti at the gate reads "The Billy Riordan Memorial Trust Volunteer Centre" and even though, due to extensive rebuilding and construction by the Trust, which rents the property from the former hostel's owner, a man known as John The Gap, it hardly resembles its former self. Meticulously tended, beginning with a 5:00 a.m. daily sweeping of the sand courtyard by a watchman bearing a locally made straw broom, the mini-village of seven tidy rust-red-painted thatch-roof concrete buildings includes volunteer quarters, flats for Mags and Steve, a beachfront open-windowed kitchen/dining room/common room and a carport for the two ambulances.

The Gap has moved in looks and amenities well beyond its buck-a-night days, and the fee structure is different, too. There are two levels: 130 euros ($169) a week for the medical students on their four-to-eight-week stints, and zero euros for regular volunteers, who in serving a minimum of four months make the greatest commitments of time. But whatever their length of stay or level of skill, no volunteer is spared the hefty amount of charges that begin with the cost of passport, plane ticket, travel health insurance, inoculations, and a land transfer from the airport to the Cape that alone could be an additional $220 one way. For some volunteers, such regular bills as utilities and mortgage or rent must continue to be paid while they are continents away. And once they've settled in at The Gap, there's more to hand over, for gas used in the kitchen, for groceries. The optional meal plan is a bargain at the equivalent of sixty cents a day, which will get you a spread that might include local kampango fish or individual pizzas but often is an homage to carbohydrates, watchmen/chefs Joab or Edward frequently preparing for a single sitting at the dining room's two long tables family-style servings of rice, potatoes and bread.

Temperatures at the end of this particular October climbed to 114, illustrating keenly the need for hydration. There's plentiful water pumped from the borehole down the lane and toted over daily by a woman who ducks as she enters the kitchen with a forty-pound blue plastic bucket balanced atop her head. Though a chlorine bleach tablet is then tossed into each bucketful to make it potable, most volunteers prefer to rely on commercial beverages. Choices are the glass bottles of Coke or Fanta, "a green" (slang for the emerald bottles of Carlsberg Beer filled in Blantyre, site of the brand's first brewery outside Denmark, created after a Danish official who visited Malawi in 1968 found no decent beer), the traditional local maize-based brew Chibuku, Malawi Gin and, certainly, many, many, many bottles of the ubiquitous Sobo-brand water, which are initialed by volunteers and tucked into one of the kitchen's three freezers for the chilliest keeping through the near-daily power outages that last from a few hours to a weekend.

And, given the great distances from the place most call home, there's usually a strong desire to keep in touch, and the resulting fees and complications. The nearest post office is in Monkey Bay. If you really need to receive mail, as the Project does, have it sent to the Bag 7 in Blantyre, but be prepared to wait the one or two months between trips that Mags and Steve make there to purchase supplies and check that mail bag. For quicker communication, if enough bars can be caught, cell phone calls can be made via Zain phone cards, at the cost of roughly a dollar a minute. Unless you wish to purchase a satellite device to go online via your laptop, the Internet can be accessed only at a Skyband Internet carrier hotspot (on the Cape, those are at a few of the lodges, plus The Gap) and only with the password on a Skyband card, available on the Cape at those few lodges. Volunteers can buy cards (the best deal: 5,000 kwacha — $25 — for five hours) from a stash Steve stocks up on at the Skyband headquarters during trips to Blantyre.

Finally, no price can be placed on the relationships put on

hold, weakened or lost while the volunteers are so far from home, or on the inability to be present when a sister gives birth or a grandfather takes his last breath.

Yet, despite all the varied, required or potential costs, the applications roll in.

If Mags wants privacy for work or rest, she will shut the red door to her flat, as she has on this afternoon, in order to have time to herself to read her e-mail. Today, 2,148 messages await reply. She estimates that she receives twenty a day, and on this day, seven of those are volunteer applications from those who visited www.billysmalawiproject.org and clicked on the words "Volunteer Application Form."

Illustrating the type of applicants she hopes someday will come from Malawi, they've been filled out by people living in relative comfort, by people of means, people with degrees and experience. In this case, at this time, the applicants are thousands of miles away. Those who will work for nothing, as volunteer staff.

An article in the March 2010 American Medical Association *Journal of Ethics* stated the percentage of graduating medical students participating in global health electives has increased from 6 to 30 percent in the past quarter of a century. The American Academy of Family Physicians has compiled a list of nearly eighty international programs medical school residents can be part of, some offering rotations in multiple countries. The Massachusetts Medical Society's Global Medicine Network also keeps a similar information bank. According to Dr. Joanne Conroy, chief healthcare officer for the Association of American Medical Colleges, those who practice overseas "learn how to do more with less. They form some lasting friendships. And they often return to give back in those countries . . . Every physician is just a patchwork of the places they've been and the work they've done." Africa always has been a hot destination for those who want to do good in this world. A few months before the 1961 founding of the Peace Corps, through which author Paul Theroux volunteered in Malawi in 1963, President John F. Kennedy shouted to a University of Michigan crowd "How many of you who are going to be doctors are willing to spend your days in Ghana?" Since 1961, two hundred thousand volunteers from America alone have spent days, years and decades in 139 countries, many of them hoping for a posting in a faraway, exotic Africa they've never seen. Via other programs, college students from across the globe these days are skipping breaks spent on tropical islands to help work on reforestation projects in Zambia. They're raising funds for microfinance organizations that will buy sewing machines for Rwandan women. And some of them are writing to Mags Riordan, to ask about volunteer openings at the clinic.

She reads their messages on the black three-or-four-year-old Acer laptop set on the long wooden desk in her one-room flat, which comprises the top floor of an addition constructed in 2008. Prior to that, Mags for eight years stayed in what is now volunteers' quarters, specifically in Room 1, just off the courtyard below. In her new digs, her workspace is to the right of the door she closes in order to work, and it is to the left of the door leading to the porch and a dreamy view of Lake Malawi. She focuses ahead as she sits in a wooden chair before a window, its dark blue curtain raised. Pictures of family members hang on the wall, and music plays from a radio in the courtyard. Mags settles her feet under the desk, next to a plastic tote and the hard-sided lilac suitcase she's emptied of the thirty-five kilograms (seventy-seven pounds) of goods — most of them clinic necessities — South African Airlines allows her on each flight from home, a weight that has increased with the number of miles she's logged with the company.

Behind her is a double bed set low on the floor, made up neatly in dark blue sheets, a carved wooden chest at its foot. A wide white mosquito net bundles the mattress like froth. To the right of the bed sits a knee-high stack of books, the first one Norman Doidge's *The Brain that Changes Itself: Stories of Personal Triumph from the Frontiers of Brain Science* ("Fascinating," Mags says.), then Deepak Chopra's *The Seven Spiritual Laws of Success* ("I carry it with me everywhere — a lot of stuff in it makes a lot of sense."), then the novels *Brick Lane* by Monica Ali ("My mother gave it to me.") and *Strange Fits of Passion* by Anita Shreve ("Just nicked it off someone.").

"By the time you get into bed at night, you're about knackered," she says without turning from the computer screen, but she finds time to read a bit for leisure anyhow, other titles chosen from a selection that fills two shelves to the left of the bed, including Johan Marais's *A Complete Guide to the Snakes of Southern Africa*, *The Penguin Dictionary of Psychology*, David Scott's *The Healthy Vegetarian Cookbook*, John Banville's *The Sea* and John Gray's *Men Are from Mars, Women Are from Venus*. To the right of the bed and the stack of books is storage for her clothing. Beyond that, the bathroom. To the right of the bathroom door is an open kitchen with toaster, mini fridge and the essential electric kettle. Look to the right of that and the tour of the room is complete. There is Mags, at her desk, typing away.

"It's very modest what I've got, but I think it's gorgeous," she says. "I don't accumulate things because I don't have the room. I don't really need stuff, anyway. I have bamboo hooks on the wall and hang clothes there, have two (cabinets) under the kitchen sink, a couple of open shelves. I do have a cooker that sits on the top of the workspace, only use it rarely. It's all I need. I have a lady who comes in and cleans every day, and dusts it and washes it out. You have to, really. When I moved into it first I thought there's no way I'm getting somebody to clean this, but after twenty-three weeks of trying to wash floors every day but getting really bad chest infections from dust, and there's 80 percent of villagers with no job and here I am washing the floor . . ." She shakes her head, both at the thought, and at the computer screen and continues: "Steve wanted ironing and washing done. We got a woman in. She has a job, it's regular, she would consider where we're living palatial. She's delighted. It's a win-win situation."

Today, Mags hopes to hire another worker or two — these as volunteers — but she begins by writing to someone who will not be given a job.

In her hunt-and-peck style of typing, with reading glasses perched on her nose, she informs an applicant with no medical training that there are no volunteer placements for non-medical staff at the time. She changes that to "Non-medical volunteer placements." She ponders the line. Adds that two years hence would be the next openings for such work. Scans her message again. Closes with "Best regards, Mags Riordan." Hits "Send."

Mags is not a fast typist. But when it's suggested that Dave, who knows his way around a keyboard, craft a variety of boilerplate rejections in order to save her time in this ever-continuing process, she has no interest. "Every applicant is different," she says, "I read every one, and respond."

Filling out the form is the first hurdle for a prospective volunteer. The next is getting Mags's approval. She selects the most fitting, depending on upcoming openings and balance of positions, then interviews all the most promising applicants but medical students serving a course elective, excluding them due to the relatively brief time they will be at the clinic. Aside from credentials, experience and references, her main concern is personality. How will someone fit in, how might they fare during what could be the first time in the third world?

Prospective volunteers must be more than twenty-five years of age and must be qualified to fill positions including doctor, nurse, lab technician, pharmacist, optometrist, audiologist, dentist, landscaper and office technician. Along with those medical students serving from four to eight weeks, volunteers completing their final year of an Irish general practitioner program work a total of fourteen weeks. All volunteers are asked to serve their months at a single stretch, to dress modestly, to live only at the volunteer center, to have no overnight visitors, to refrain from publishing information about their experience without Mags's permission, and not to join in business ventures with locals.

Mags says she just knows when someone is right for the job and for the mix of personalities the clinic holds. To date, the majority of volunteers have hailed from Ireland and the United Kingdom, due largely to media attention the Trust has received there. Depending on a travel schedule that regularly takes her through the hub that is London's Heathrow, she holds face-to-face interviews in both the United Kingdom and in Ireland.

Applicants might be given the go-ahead at the end of their interview, or in a phone call or e-mail as soon as the next day. Months later, the reed gate at The Gap opens to admit the newest volunteer. And as soon as the next morning, the work, and what is often the fulfillment of a dream, begins.

She reads an application from Australia. Then another from England, sent by a man in a general practitioner program. She likes what she finds in his resume and writes to request an interview with him between now and the end of the year. Tells him she'll be returning to Europe somewhere in that space and perhaps they can meet up in the United Kingdom during a layover. Her phone rings. She ignores it. Types, "We are currently recruiting medical staff for the recond part of next year." Clicks on the spellcheck to correct the spelling of "second."

Another doctor is applying, also from England. She's interested in him, too.

A medical student in his penultimate year at Kings College in London writes to ask about serving a medical elective next July to September. Mags focuses on the keyboard and types that the following September would be good, then moves on quickly to read an e-mail from a doctor in England who's written to say that "for several years I have been thinking about volunteering abroad and I feel that a suitable point in my training has arisen for me to 'give something back.'"

She stops, ponders. Moves on to see what the next message holds. It's from a doctor in Wales who was offered a placement the following April and is checking in to say the search for flights has begun.

Mags scans the next form, rejecting it because the applicant is only twenty. The next person meets the age requirement, and has some unusual experience. "Here's someone who breeds pigs in Ireland," she says, reading the full form, then states, without making any particular connection, that he might be a good candidate for assistant project manager.

A fifth-year med student from Edinburgh University writes that he is coming to serve an elective at Kamuzu Central Hospital in Lilongwe and will be in the area. Might he be of help during that time?

She replies. He might be. She closes with her regards and her name.

All who are accepted are emailed pamphlets outlining the basics of living at The Gap and on the Cape. They're given a list of recommended items to pack, including mosquito net, insect repellent, rainwear for December through April, and jacket and jumper from June through September. They're told that inoculations are their responsibility, and that a rabies shot is advisable. They're warned of frequent power cuts and the high cost of international calls on pay-as-you-go phone cards, of the absence of an ATM machine at the Cape. A separate sheet tells of the founding of the Trust in 2002 in Dingle, and the number by which it is registered with the Irish Government as a charity, but other than in the name of the Trust, there is no mention of Billy Riordan or why this effort bears his name. Instead, the sheet gives information on accommodations, the local social life, languages, and safety concerns. ("Malawians are open and welcoming and personal safety, while not absolutely guaranteed, is not an issue in the village.") A third document is a "Medicine Wish List," and results in volunteers amassing what they can, tucking around the T-shirts and socks and swimwear packed in their suitcases lengths of suction tubing, tension bandages, intravenous antibiotics, urine dipsticks and suppositories. A final note on the wish list informs that as disposable gloves are extremely expensive in Malawi, all medical volunteers are required to bring ten boxes for their own use.

Whatever the financial and emotional bottom line for making this trip and commitment, and sometimes the physical cost (Who would know better than they the astounding palette of ailments that await in the tropics?), volunteers still say it's a privilege and a joy being a "Billys", shorthand for any non-local living at The Gap, a fast way to identify who they are and what they're doing at the Cape. "She's Beelys" a local might tell another upon a newcomer's introduction. "I'm a Billys" helps dismiss the craft-selling beach boys mistaking a volunteer for a tourist, rather than someone pulling in no salary. The volunteers' tabs, a credit system standard at village shops, restaurant and bars, might be headed BRMT, for Billy Riordan Memorial Trust, but more likely just will be titled "Billys."

British nurse Katie Acheson, three months into a six-month stint at the clinic, describes being a Billys as a "selfish" act.

"Maybe your family doesn't want you to do it, but I think everybody has a responsibility to contribute," she says. "If you're lucky enough to do these kinds of jobs, you can come here and do this kind of work. I think everybody has a social responsibility to do what they can. My whole reason to become a nurse was to work overseas."

Katie is thirty-one but could pass for twenty-one, is model-thin with blonde curly hair, clear pale skin, always a touch of eye makeup, and three macramé pink-and-blue bracelets on her right wrist. During lunch or after hours, her scrubs typically are exchanged for short shorts and a T-shirt with a rock theme or peace sign, the cut of sleeve or neckline revealing a hint of the tattoo of a geisha on her left arm and another of flowers trailing down her back. Even in a community of volunteers big on warmth, the former resident of North London easily could be the resident Miss Congeniality, greeting everyone she passes, knowing most every person in the clinic, on the road, on the beach, in the marketplaces and clubs, calling out names in an accent that neatly minces her syllables. She's sweet to the kids who mill around the clinic, at the back porch of the volunteer center, and regularly takes them into her arms — which is why she is scratching those arms as she sits in the dining room during her lunch break, wondering if she has contracted scabies, a definite possibility.

The prospect doesn't turn Katie Acheson's stomach. She's been exposed to worse in a career that began at age nineteen, much to the initial chagrin of her late mother, Jackie, a nurse whose whole life was her job before she died of lung cancer three years before this interview, at age fifty-two. A nurse who wanted her daughter to become anything but.

"To discourage me from nursing, she sent me to do care work, thinkin' I'd hate it," Katie recalls, then smiles widely at her reaction to being immersed in tending to a patient's most basic needs: "I loved it."

Jackie could place blame only on herself and her husband John, now newly retired from thirty-five years as janitor at a special-needs school that presented him with an award for never missing a day, a man whose daughter calls him "A lovely man, the kindest man I know."

"I was raised to care," that daughter says of the family in which she is the only girl, one with two older brothers. "I find it very hard when people don't care. When I traveled to India, I saw how people turned away from the slums. It broke my heart, I spent a week cryin'. How can people spend money to go there and not care? You have to accept life but you can try to help. It's a human thing. You should try to help other people. I absolutely love bein' a nurse. Even when someone is shoutin' at me, at least I'm trying to make it a better world. You could wash someone's hair, put it in rollers for her — you might not have had time for your tea and biscuits, but you've made someone feel better."

Katie's love of the job overpowered an interest in law, and studying on course to attend law school. She leapt into not only her mother's world but, eventually, into a type of work her mother might have done.

While growing up in Buckinghamshire, ninety minutes north of London and known for its natural beauty and native son Roald Dahl, Katie would hear her mother say she would have wanted to travel to assist those in the Biafran famine of the late 1960s and early '70s, but that marriage changed her plans. Perhaps as a result of her mother's interest, Katie says,

she was struck by news coverage of subsequent similar tragedies. "I remember being a kid," she says, "and bawlin' my eyes
out over kids in Ethiopia." Years later, while enrolled at the
prestigious London School of Hygiene and Tropical Medicine
for a parasitology class — required for those who wish to work
in refugee settings or set up clinics — a prominent figure from
that relief effort was her teacher.

"I was taught by the lady behind Live Aid," Katie says with
pride, referring to Dame Claire Bertschinger, who, like her pu-
pil, was fueled to volunteerism in part by something seen on
TV. For Bertschinger, it was a 1960's viewing of the then-two-
year-old *The Inn of the Sixth Happiness* on her family's newly purchased first set. Watching Ingrid Berman play an English missionary in China, Bertschinger said, "I could do that," and did.
The year 1984 found her in Ethiopia as a field nurse for the
International Committee of the Red Cross when she was fea-
tured in a BBC interview eventually seen by not-yet-then-Sir
Bob Geldof. Bertschinger told reporter Michael Buerk of the
two feeding centers she was running and how they could ac-
commodate no more than seventy children despite the thousands starving. Her duties included marking the foreheads of
the children who would be fed, and leaving blank those who
would go without a meal.

"In her was vested the power of life and death," said Geldof, who later that year created Band Aid, through which a
group of English and Irish musicians recorded the now-classic
"Do They Know It's Christmas?" The song raised $144 million
for Ethiopian relief efforts and led to the 1985 Live Aid concert, which raised another $283 million. It also began to a wave
of similar grand-scale musical fundraisers around the globe that
included a star-studded group of performers who'd gathered in
1984 under the umbrella of USA For Africa to record the "We
Are the World" single, which raised more than $63 million for

aid in Africa and the United States.

That world was of great interest to Katie, who watched one of her two brothers regularly leave for trips abroad, and who each childhood summer while holidaying at the home of an uncle outside Belfast took note of one particular wall decoration. "He had a map with pins in it showing where he'd been. I'd be at his house, he'd be off somewhere."

Katie eventually went off somewhere, too — went off to many somewheres, catching a severe travel bug that has resulted in adventures, some solo and as long as eleven months. "Traveling is massive for your confidence," she says. "You hear all these horror stories of what happens when you travel, but you get out of it. I went away for seven months two years ago, back to Asia, India, Nepal, South Asia. I can't settle. I don't even have a TV back home. I move, travel, work. I'm the opposite of a lot of people. I love change. I thrive on that. I get bored very easily."

One antidote to the boredom was a trip to Africa four years ago that took her to Tanzania, Kenya, Uganda and Mozambique. Though she'd always meant to get to Malawi, she finally arrived via an unintentional route.

Yearning to work in other lands, Katie last year applied to Voluntary Service Overseas (VSO), a London-based organization that since its founding in 1958 has disbursed to developing countries volunteers with skills ranging from farming to healthcare to marketing. The organization requires that an applicant's significant other must come to the interview, to make clear what the applicant faces, as one of the biggest reasons for volunteers dropping out is a problem at home. Katie's significant other refused to attend. "That put an end to that," she says, meaning VSO but not the relationship. Then a friend who'd volunteered at the Cape told her Mags was amenable to shorter stints than the VSO's usual two-year commitment, which might go over better with the boyfriend.

It did, so Katie applied, and she is here, ten months after traveling to Newcastle to meet Mags for an interview and learning of her acceptance that very day. Though delighted to be heading back to a continent that enthralled her, she was heading to a setting not as intense as she would like.

Sierra Leone, a West-African nation staggering back from an eleven-year civil war that between 1991 and 2002 made it one of the world's most dangerous countries, is one place she'd love to work. Add to that a refugee camp. "Something extreme. Long-term development or teaching," she says. "It's not that I don't like it here, but I would want something for a longer term, and not a job that a Malawian could do. I do really love the hands-on stuff because it has a longer-lastin' effect on the community. That will happen here, and I'm really happy I've been a part of it. When I apply elsewhere, it will be good to have the experience, and it's invaluable experience because nothin' prepares you for not havin' facilities you take for granted. You do the best you can and that's all you can do."

Katie doesn't miss dealing with staffing, budgets, audits or any of the less patient-centered responsibilities her old job held. "Back home, you're in charge of a unit," she says. "Here, it is more restful, in a way. I work, then I might be on call. I'm almost like a doctor, doin' what you'd do if you were a nurse practitioner."

For her next step, Katie might consider working for organizations like Oxfam and Save the Children, perhaps becoming a regional health advisor, the person who organizes a health facility following a major outbreak or other crisis.

"This is all I've ever seen myself doin'," she says. But, in an echo of the choice her mother made, she glances at the kids playing soccer on the beach and she adds, "because of the age I am, I'm fifty-fifty about where my life is goin'. You can't have a family if you go too far down this route."

But for now, for the next three months, this is the route, this is her home, this is her focus. "What my life's like in the UK?" she asks. "I can't even remember."

Ask Siobhan Cogan about life back at home and she'll pause before answering slowly with a wonder that hints this might be the first time she's spoken this answer: "I suppose here is my home now."

The twenty-seven-year-old native of Castlepollard in Ireland's west-of-Dublin County Westmeath is in her second stint at the Cape, this time a two-year commitment made all the more serious by the fact she has resigned from her job back home.

Though the daughter of a general practitioner father and a midwife mother, Siobhan was like Mags in not instantly gravitating toward medicine. She only was certain a desk job wouldn't suit her and, with an interest in sports (she ran track and played field hockey and camogie, the women's version of the Irish sport of hurling) might have taught physical education, but around age sixteen, after two years of working in a nursing home and a hospital, began to think about a medical career.

With a younger brother in engineering and a younger sister in science, Siobhan is the one to follow most directly in her parents' career footsteps. She studied nursing at University College Dublin then at the Mater Misericordiae University Hospital. She knew the city well as, since age thirteen, Siobhan had boarded at Alexandra College in that city a two-hour drive from home. In adulthood she was living in the Dublin suburb of Rathgar, working as a staff nurse in the city, when she decided to move much farther south.

An interest in volunteering led to scanning the possibilities, but the requirements of many programs — including multiple years of experience, a tropical nursing degree and age restrictions (often a minimum of twenty-five to her twenty-four at the time) — didn't go with what she had to offer. She collected a folder full of information, read listings, made calls, made no progress. Then she heard from two friends who'd been Billys and who assured her she'd love it. The application was filled out.

Siobhan's interview with Mags took place in May of 2008 at an inn on Dublin's Baggott Street. "One of the friends who'd volunteered had told me briefly about her, that she was great," Siobhan recalls. "I'd kind of looked up to her as well — through the story I was inspired by her quite a bit. To be able to continue to do what she's doing, having gone through so much. We had a chat. It was lovely. But I was kind of overwhelmed — she said there was availability in August and for ages I'd been looking, looking, looking, suddenly it's 'No problem, we'd love to have you!' My God, I was so happy!"

Siobhan grabbed the invitation and served at the clinic from August of 2008 to February of 2009. She was enamored enough to return to Cape Maclear in August of 2009 for her annual four-week leave from work. During that visit, she attended a reunion of volunteers from a variety of charities. Their enthusiasm renewed her interest in volunteering again, with the Cape being her dream destination.

She's back with the help of the Volunteer Missionary Movement, whose bases in Ireland, the United Kingdom and the United States recruit volunteers for postings worldwide in health, education, community and diocesan efforts. Benefits include financial help with transportation and living expenses, a boost for Siobhan, who'd worried she wouldn't be able to afford to return to the clinic.

"I'd wanted to get out of Dublin for a long time," she says.

"I was there since I was thirteen. It was just a city I liked, I had a job there, but I got sick of it. It was very repetitive and I kind of felt a bit lonely at times. I had my friends, but I was ready to move on. When I went back, I didn't want to go back. Saying that, I had a great year being home, but it just wasn't the same. I enjoyed the work, but it simply wasn't the work I wanted to be doing."

Or where she wanted to be.

"I loved it here and I loved the work and" — here she stops to smile and push back the bangs of her black shoulder-length hair — "I suppose I met a guy here who I cared about as well."

It's not mentioned on the website, but volunteering can lead to love, and, to date, has resulted in two children born in relationships forged via the volunteer experience. In Siobhan's case, the relationship is with a man named Snoopy — birthname Danson — a local landscaper. Just as she's living in his town, Snoopy visited hers last winter, leaving his country for the first time, seeing snow for the first time, seeing Siobhan for the first time in half a year.

Now seated in the dining area, wearing a black tank top and olive capris perfect for the Cape's steady October temps of between 90 and 95 Fahrenheit, Siobhan continues her list of what makes this place right for her, including the chance to take the antiretroviral course that will enable her to work with HIV/AIDS patients.

"At home, you're power tripping, the doctors are overpowering you. Here, we all work together as a team, have fun together. You're never really lonely. There's a lot of autonomy in nursing here. At home, there are so many rules and regulations, which is fair enough because everything at home is so legal. Here, you write (information) on a piece of paper, but people don't even ask what's wrong with them. Even the pain threshold is different here. You'd have to get a general anesthetic to do something at home, but here they have such a big pain threshold. And if someone dies, the feeling here is 'It's the will of God, get on with it.'"

Tonight, Siobhan will be on call, a shift that begins at 4:00 p.m. and continues to eight in the morning. Emergency cases are brought not to the clinic itself but to The Gap and its after-hours clinic, one small room at the end of the building in the center of the square. A watchman will summon Siobhan if anyone arrives. Should she need additional help or consultation, she will alert the doctor on call. Right now, nine patients rest in the clinic's two wards, including one suffering complications of HIV, another with pancreatitis, another with malaria, a baby who was severely dehydrated and a woman with pneumonia. To check on them, the on-callers grab the ambulance keys and drive over the hill.

As with any emergency room, nights can be still or hectic. "You don't know what you're going to get in," Siobhan notes. "Fevers and vomiting, they're the urgent thing. If you come in with a sore leg you've had for four days, a cough you've had for two days, you can go to the clinic the next day. They don't know what an emergency is. They're not educated enough to know."

Siobhan says a volunteer on call might see anything and everything. "Nothing's going to shock you. Some nights you could see a drunk guy with a machete through his head. Or a little kid might fall off a mango tree and break his wrist or arm. Two nights ago we had a kid who had a stick go through his foot. They have no shoes, can't afford them, and they have such a big pain threshold — the kid with the stick through his foot, it was like that for two days."

There's a good chance Siobhan will next see that child at her very own back door. The Gap's dining room and common area opens to a large concrete porch of sorts with stairs leading to the beach, and to the water a dozen steps away. Children, including those right now calling "Balla! Balla!" as their soccer ball bounces up the stairs and through the open wall of the dining room lounge, frequently congregate at the stairs. They wait for the ball to be returned — children are not allowed to enter the building — or for the attention of Siobhan and Sheila Byrne-Harte, the two volunteers who regularly spend their lunchtimes and hours after work on those steps, handing out pages from coloring books and pens for drawing. Mags frowns on distributing candy and other edibles to the children, feeling The Gap is not the place for that, but Siobhan has been known to break the rules, on city trips purchasing sleeves of biscuits to distribute to the kids who've come to know they have to form a semi-orderly line in order to be served. Siobhan is working on her Chichewa, and also uses time with the children to practice words and phrases, asking the few whose names she does not know *"Dzina lanu ndani?"* and trying out the verbs she's been picking up during work. The image of her sitting on the stairs within a circle of children is something that easily could be found on one of the volunteer websites she visited before learning of the clinic. But it's not for show.

"A lot of people who do go off to volunteer think they're going to become Gandhi," she says. "But I think with healthcare, you really can make an impact. You're treating people the whole time, helping people. It's sustainable. The local people are involved. It's the local staff and us, working as a big team. Which is lovely."

Dr. Nora Murray-Cavanagh joined that team by being a patient first, a decade back and many miles away.

"I had plans to go into education. Then I was sick for a few months toward the end of my high school career. That changed things for me," she says. "I thought health was fundamental to being the best person you could be."

In that way, the glandular fever/mononucleosis that knocked out Nora also knocked her into the next chapter of her life. Raised in Derry/Londonderry, Northern Ireland, she moved to Scotland for college, enrolling at the University of Edinburgh for six years of medical studies. She then took two years of a foundation program and progressed to a general practitioner training scheme before leaving for the Cape.

As for why she's a Billy's, Nora reflects on the question as she sits one afternoon at the dining table nearest the kitchen door. "It's probably no different from everyone's answer," she says. "We do what we do, feel we can help people. Here, where need is greatest, it seems like a good and worthy use of my time. There are also personal benefits for me. I see a lot, learn a lot — not just medical stuff. Cultural, teamwork.

"I chose to come here for a couple different reasons. First, myself and my partner, Dave, wanted to go volunteer together. That's not always possible — certainly, with a bigger organization it isn't. They can't guarantee placement for two, certainly not today. We were drawn to the scale, the impact. Finally, a real consideration was how well set up the project was, how well established it was for GP trainees. I knew those at my level of training would come here, and I knew I wasn't going to be in a mud hut in the middle of nowhere doing a cesarean section by myself. I wanted to make this a positive experience for me, and I wanted to make a positive impact."

"Volunteering was always on my mind to do," says Dave Clancy, Nora's partner of nine years, and one of two assistant project managers currently working with Steve. "When I was a kid I knew someone who had a brother in Africa doing work. That might have inspired me early on — it just seemed far away and exotic. It was on my mind when I first met Nora. I'd wanted to do it a few years back, but life gets in the way."

Dave, thirty-five and newly resigned from his job as risk analyst for a major asset management firm in Edinburgh, learned about the project from a list compiled by *Comhlámh* (Irish for "solidarity"), a thirty-five-year-old Dublin-based organization concerned with social justice, human rights and global development.

"This one jumped off the page," Dave says during one of the several breaks for the Malawi-grown Chombe–brand tea a day at The Gap might hold. Tall, lean, pale, dark-featured, the Dublin native is unfailingly smiley and polite, and unfailingly in shorts, a short-sleeved shirt and sandals, usually holding one of the project's cell phones. "We wanted to find (an opportunity) with a medical component because Nora would be taking time out of her training and we'd go together," he continues. "And I liked the story of the clinic. Obviously tragic but very human and that drew us here — to make a difference in a small village."

The couple applied the previous February or March, met Mags in Edinburgh in June. "We got a very positive response in an e-mail," Dave says. "We had the interview, and received another e-mail a week later. It all happened very quickly after all the thinking and planning we did."

"We didn't know Mags," Nora notes, "we just looked up the website and read the articles and watched the video interview with her. I like the way that she tries to meet all the volunteers, and it's really personal. That's one of the things that drew us, the personal feeling. I find her really a remarkable character. I think of what she's done and achieved. I think the setup in the clinic is wonderful. And that's to do with Mags and the people she has selected to have here."

She singles out Dr. Jeannette van Os, a native of The

Netherlands who met Mags in 2001 during a medical studies trip and has been a medical director at the clinic since 2005. "One of the things I really liked about Jeannette is, when I came here, of course, I had a hundred questions a day. She said 'If you can think of a better way to do something, tell me.' Everyone is really approachable."

As is Nora. Short, sturdy, rectangular glasses, chin-length dark hair parted on the side and held back with clip or hair band, she bears a ready laugh and, after-hours, a full repertoire of Joni Mitchell delivered in a recording-ready voice she accompanies with her guitar. She mentions a party game that asks which celebrity would best portray you in a film and gives her answer of Molly Shannon. Both she and Dave are welcoming and helpful to any newcomers, figuratively making sure there's a place at the table for all, and doing that literally during the shared lunches or dinners, Nora moving over to create room for someone who might be alone at the other of the two tables, Dave always relied upon to have the kettle going and the pot full of steaming tea.

They arrived at the end of August and will be at the Cape until the end of February. Nora thinks it's taken about six weeks to get into the swing of the culture and routines, and the realities of the life in both the village and the country. There's poverty ("If a kid is wearing shoes, you automatically think the family is wealthy — that's something you would just never think at home.") and there's the lack of options for helping some patients of any means.

"We just had to send a man with severe HIV and pneumonia to Monkey Bay," Nora says. "We couldn't support him, and I knew they wouldn't, either. But I couldn't leave a patient here to die."

Nora's voice is layered by the frustration she felt over the inability to help. Striving to do her best for a community is not just her job, it's in her blood. She's the eldest of three kids and the only one in medicine. Her medical connections are a general practitioner grandfather and various relations in the field. Her parents, Anne Murray and Colm Cavanagh, have led the movement for integrated schools in Northern Ireland, an effort that began in 1981, the year Nora came into the world. Anne helped establish and was the first principal at Oakgrove Integrated Primary School, the first school in the northwest of Northern Ireland founded to educate children from Protestant and Catholic backgrounds, as well as those having other — or no — religious affiliations. She's still at that desk.

The July before she left for Malawi, Nora was one of twenty-four hundred people selected from twenty-six thousand applicants to stand on the fourth plinth in London's Trafalgar Square and, for an hour, to become a piece of art. For her moment in the four-month-long One and Other project, she wore a yellow T-shirt printed with a large number six, noting the fact that only 6 percent of Northern Ireland's children attend integrated schools.

"Everyone can do something to make a difference," Nora says. "People don't have to come to Africa. They can make a donation of their weekly salary. We all have the responsibility to help when we can. We're all Africans."

When she says it, the line doesn't sound like a slogan about Africa being the birthplace of humanity, but a truth.

"I am so much more lucky than lots of people I speak to," Nora continues. "I don't see any limit to what I can do. I won't live here in Africa for the rest of my life. I might want different things for my family. But now, I can come here and do this."

Donnie Mategula is not unusual in being a medical student pitching in at the clinic, but is in being the first Malawian medical student to do anything at the clinic. He could be enjoying the sheer fun of the break between his first and second year of medical school. Instead, he's elected to come to the Cape and spend five weeks volunteering.

Donnie has five more years at the country's one and only medical school, nineteen-year-old College of Medicine in Blantyre, part of the University of Malawi. Approximately sixty students are admitted annually to study with 110 faculty members. Two hundred and fifty doctors have graduated from the college, the mission of which is "to be an academic centre of excellence, responsive to the health needs of Malawi and its neighbours within the Southern African region in training of professionals, provision of clinical services and medical research."

Donnie already looks like one of those professionals. Tall and thin, white doctor's coat daily topping his shirt, tie and dress pants, hair cropped closely and glasses Hollywood-casting large, stethoscope slung around his neck, he's newly twenty — turned that during his time at the Cape — but due to his formal manner comes off as ten years older.

Though from Lilongwe, he's no stranger to the Cape, or Chembe Village, having visited a friend here several times. While volunteering, he's staying with that friend's family, a few doors down from The Gap, where he arrives each morning to join the others in walking to the clinic he learned about through its website.

In his coat pocket nest both *The Oxford Handbook of Clinical Medicine* and a paperback titled *Christ in His Sanctuary*. In the back pocket of his trousers sits a white-covered copy of the New Testament bound with the Book of Psalms and the Book of Proverbs.

"It explains my existence right here on earth," Donnie says of the second title. He talks easily about his faith and of being a

Seventh Day Adventist, one of the largest churches in this country where British colonizers popularized Christianity.

"I always have to believe God is helping me through," Donnie says. "Why do we exist? Why war? Why suffering? Why are some happy, some not? Some have no food. There has to be something behind the scenes going on. There are so many unanswered questions. Being an atheist doesn't really answer them." He looks at Bo, Ulemu and Lisa sprawled nearby on the dining area's concrete floor. "We are different from animals," Donnie says. "We have a soul, and purpose for living."

He is the only volunteer you'll hear readily speaking about spirituality, and he's doing so on this day while, because his religion prohibits its members from drinking anything caffeinated, he sips from a mug of hot water and milk.

"Living a life with faith is interesting, having the belief in some supernatural power behind everything we do," Donnie says. "It is an awesome experience being with Christ every day. It's like a close friend with you each and every day. Looking forward to him taking us home someday."

Donnie's desire to become a physician was a career choice, but still not all his decision.

"What compelled me was what I feel was some kind of calling. The reasons for going to medical school, especially in Malawi, are it's where geniuses go. Or to fulfill a lifetime dream. I'm going to answer a calling to serve my people. In my case, I didn't think too much of becoming a doctor. At a certain time, I could see people suffering, with diseases, and I thought, 'I could help.' It's also the best place to provide hope in a person. A person in a certain state of suffering is in need of hope and assurance."

With a father who's an auctioneer and mother who's stayed at home to raise five children, this fourth of those five (three girls and two boys) has no medical role models. "I grew up different," Donnie says. "Being in boarding school for secondary school, I was exposed to different things. My parents were happy with my choice to become a doctor. They left me to make every choice. The way I passed the (Malawi School Certificate of Education Examination), I could go to any course I wanted. I had to choose what life I wanted. I'm glad they allowed me to make my own choice.

"I don't know what really to expect," he says of his time at the clinic, and in his career, and could be speaking for all the volunteers when he says that, and then adds, "I'm just ready to meet whatever is there."

SIX

Other than a medical clinic, the Billy Riordan Memorial Trust has created something else very unusual for Cape Maclear and the country in which it's located: employment.

Once a person lands a job with the Trust, he or she does everything possible to keep it for life, so openings are rare and postings unnecessary. Word of any possibility spreads quickly through the village and gets dozens and dozens of locals mobilized for this rarity of a chance to work and earn, has them finding looseleaf and pen and sitting down to write a letter of intent in their neatest hand, getting out their finest outfit just for the delivery of that letter to The Gap's gate. And those letters might start as do these from the inches-thick file of pleas from prospects:

> *"I shall be very grateful if my application will meet with your favourable consideration."*
>
> *"I promise to work with keen interest and efficiency if considered for the job or consideration."*
>
> *"I apply for the topic above. I apply for that because I like caring sick people and giving them an extra getting well son."*
>
> *"I need a job in your project if possible sir, I have been attending your interviews almost twice without being successful, that is why I am coming again for the third time now and I hope I well be employed (27 years)."*

"I am person which can cure sick peoples."
"I hereby write to apply for any job."

For the hour or two it takes to look over these letters, to reacquaint Mags and Steve with older ones and consider the newest, Steve's office in a row of volunteers' quarters just before the kitchen becomes the Human Resources Department. On the table are the openings the Trust faces. A part-time personal care attendant is being moved up to full time so a part-timer is needed, and a full-time watchman's retirement and replacement by a part-timer means a part-time watchman vacancy. Behind that table — Steve's desk — Steve, in his comfortable and usual checkered short-sleeved shirt, capris and sandals, sits beneath a large poster of Jamaican reggae artist Burning Spear, a gift from a poor man who befriended him as he sat vigil day after day for a hospitalized friend several years back. "He had nothing, but he gave me this," Steve says while Burning Spear hovers behind him. To the right of the poster hangs a front page of the British paper *The Sun*. Its headline, "STEVIE FREE," refers to some other Steve in this world, a celebrity one who was released from jail, but Steve Free's mother thought it would be good for a laugh and sent it to her son. The right-hand wall of the dorm-room-sized office is home to a set of shelves packed with labeled boxes holding screw-in light bulbs, bayonet lightbulbs, mosquito nets, tape, glue and WD-40. An adjacent bulletin board is hung with a map of Malawi, the number for the Irish ambassador, contacts at Mangochi Hospital, and the Trust's Bank of Ireland account number. A photo of volunteers in goofy glasses hangs on the side of the next set of shelves, which holds binders of information on clinical policies, malaria, monthly medical reports, and those job applications.

Dressed in yellow capris, flip-flops and a blue tank top,

glasses atop her head, Mags sits next to Steve and his Packard Bell laptop and recites the background of one applicant, another villager she knows so well she doesn't have to check the CV. "He wants to be a driver," she says. "That's the haven of refuge, to be a driver."

"He's a bright spark," Steve says of another as he looks over a different letter.

Mags scans a third piece of paper. She says only, "Ah, but if I could write half that page in half-as-good Chichewa."

She also knows by heart the names and occupations of one candidate's family members: "He works in the lodge, he has a minibus, you won't see him in the bar — he found God a few weeks ago . . ." And she reads on:

> *"So I would like to thank that clinic because he protect my parent and relatives so that suffered a long time."*
>
> *"I am a woman of fourty years of age and I have written this piece of monography in application for any kind of job you might have at your hospital eg — hospital clearner/patient assitance."*
>
> *"I would like to work as a sweeping boy or garden boy. You can use this number for talk to my friend."*
>
> *"May I please on the behaf of the family and to my own behaf I hereby ask you if you can kinly employ one member of my family who is the bearer of this note who in person giving you."*
>
> *"I am apply this letter for looking the job for your company. I have been stayed at home, nothing I can do, but it is good to me to have the job. Please am looking job any job even night/day watchman. I am able to do so I have job I promise I am to best as employee please help me, my family we are in trouble some for the problem of money. I cannot manage to feed the large family without getting job. Please help me. I try my*

best to manage my family but am felled. I try any business no
responsibility come out. That's why am apply this letter. Please
help me, help me."

"I hate doing this," Mags says, exhaling with exasperation and expressing a version of what Katie Acheson's teacher had to have felt when choosing what children to feed, a paycheck here often meaning the difference between meals for a family or going hungry. "It's always a difficult decision. You want to give everybody a job. But we only have so many."

She recalls greeting a villager one day and asking how he was. The delighted response: "I got a job working with white people!" That is the situation — that is where the work is. Other than through the Trust, or at Kayak Africa, establishments indeed operated by white people, the only employment opportunities are at the village's few lodges, bars, schools and shops. Farming is evident in the fields currently being tilled by men and women bearing rudimentary stick-and-metal-triangle hoes, but it's not an occupation here, done only for subsistence. The reason why it has never increased on the Cape, Mags says, is "People don't do what they're not used to doing — or what they've never done." To encourage agriculture, she ran a farming education scheme in the village a few years back, but it ended when the landlord became problematic.

For those who find work, minimum wage in Malawi is 105 kwacha a day. The average Trust employee makes between 14,500 and 20,000 a month and is paid overtime for every hour or more of extra work. For thirty-three-year-old Little Dorothy, assigned to the HIV/AIDS clinic, the job supports the ten children she looks after, three of them her own. You can see her at midday, dressed in green scrub top, blue skirt and leather flip-flops, the pocketbook over her shoulder full of books as she strides along the village's main lane at midday. "I have to go home because none of the children are old enough to make their own lunch," she'll explain. So she cannot tarry. But if you do ask how long she's worked at the clinic, how long she's held this job that supports this extended family, she'll call back to you as she rushes forward, giving the exact date: "Fifth of May, 2006."

The next two people who might soon be reciting their date of hire have yet to be determined. Steve sets a stack of letters on his desk. "Let's put the kettle on — prioritize!" he suggests to Mags, and the two head out the door, turn left and walk the few yards to the dining room.

Tobacco is Malawi's greatest export, though tobacco farms — also run by non-natives — recently created in Mozambique have meant competition, and in 2011 a drop in annual trade from $350 million to $178 million. Included with cotton and sugar in the tier of lesser exports is tea, Malawi being second only to Kenya in growing the continent's greatest amounts. With the proliferation of Irish, English and Australian volunteers, gallons of it flow freely at The Gap, brewed using loose leaves and water boiled to a scream in one of the two electric kettles standing at the far end of the kitchen.

A DVD of the first season of Larry David's HBO series *Curb Your Enthusiasm* is on the first table in the dining room, not far from a copy of the World Health Organization's *2010 Guidelines for the Treatment of Malaria, 2nd Ed.* Both are moved to make room for the teapot, cups, sugar, a box of Parmalat Long Life two-percent low-fat milk and a sleeve of Kwality Cream Crackers.

The applications are set nearby.

"We don't generally advertise for jobs," Steve says. "It's word of mouth. When people come around asking for work, we say, 'Fill out an application.' So when we have the opportunity to hire, we'll call. And when we call, we'll have a flood of applications because word gets out about the job. You go for periods without applications. End of school is a big time for them."

The clinic receives such letters of application thrice weekly, both when a job is available and simply when locals want to make sure to be in consideration for the next ones. Some are attached to CVs, some are just a letter stating that the writer once worked at Fat Monkeys or Cape Mac Lodge down the beach.

"I hate doing this," Mags says again.

Already today, she's had several in-her-face reminders of the area's poverty. Already today, four people have come up to her and made pleas for money. One was the man who, back when she was transforming The Gap hostel into The Gap volunteer center, swiped CDs from the windowsill of Mags's room, and took all the laundry from the lines. Authorities picked him up, beat him up. It could have been much worse. When the clinic was being built, a local man got drunk, pulled a sink from the building's wall and ran off with it. He was caught and sentenced to four months in the Mangochi jail, three hours away.

As is the case in most hospitals in Malawi, in jails in Malawi, occupants eat only if someone from the outside delivers a meal. The sink thief did not starve. "We ended up bringing food each time we traveled to Mangochi," Mags says, then shakes her head and says, "the irony of it." As for the man who stole the CDs and the laundry, he left all the items on Mags's doorstep upon his release by police the next night. Today, more than six years later, he just came by and told Mags he was hungry. Told her of a chance he had to buy a fishing boat, but the deal didn't go through. She now is considering asking him if he'd like to work as a watchman. His English is good, she knows him well by now, and she wants to help him. But today he wanted only money. She shrugs before she tells the end of that story. "So what do you think I did?" she asks Steve before spilling that she went up to her flat, put some kwacha in an envelope and handed it over.

Steve says he knows the deal. A watchman the other day asked him for 15,000 needed to buy a new roof. "If he'd gotten me on the right day," Steve says, "I would have helped."

Mags recalls that when she first started renting The Gap property, landlord John The Gap had three children. "I told him that, in addition to paying rent, I'd pay him money per year to educate them — at 2,500 a term — in secondary school," she said. "It was better than giving him a lot of money he didn't know what to do with. He had one wife at that stage. He has three now. Seven kids now. I was an innocent. I had no concept then!"

Steve pours the tea and says that's normal for a newcomer.

"The longer you're here, the more cynical you get," Mags says. "The other thing is, you come to another place with a European mindset. My first trip here, I had a Walkman. The guys here were so envious — the beach boys — so I'd bring a few back each time. Weeks later, they'd be in bits, the doors open, wires pulled out. I was so stupefied. It didn't dawn on me that people wouldn't take care of their things. You're bringing things to people who wouldn't take care of it. When you're first here, you swallow it all."

There were no others in the village who fell into the category of *mzungu,* so she was an easy target. "Nobody else ever robbed me," Mags says, "but I was scammed left and right. A few years down the line, you look back."

"And after all these years, you still fall," Steve says, and both of them laugh.

Steve's years at The Gap began in 2008, and they've been his second volunteering experience in Malawi. Born in Hertfordshire, England, in 1957, Steve grew up with, as he puts it, "absolutely no idea what I wanted to be or do." Somehow, from the age of sixteen, he ended up working for the post office. First at the counters in his hometown, then at the chief office in London, then at branches within the city, then it was on to administration, working in the Stores and Buildings Department, and then the Wages Department.

"I worked there for many years because it was 'money for old rope,'" he says. "Then along came Margaret Thatcher and productivity. I was expected to 'earn' my wages. Also, at that point I decided that I did not like what I was doing but did not know what I wanted to do. Some friends of mine, one of whom worked as a operating department assistant, and his girlfriend at the time — now his wife — who worked as a nurse, suggested that I might make a good nurse. They thought that I had the qualities needed. I said that I may as well give it a go as I could always leave if I did not like it. That is how my nursing career started at the age of thirty-one."

Steve trained at a hospital in Essex from 1988 to 1992. He first worked in a National Health Service hospital, in general medicine, general surgery, and later, accident and emergency. Then it was off to a private hospital before returning to the NHS for a position as senior nurse in a private wing. It took him a decade to reach the salary he'd been getting at the post office. "That shows the differences between a female-dominated profession and a male-dominated workforce," he says. "But I was happy in my work."

He had always wanted to volunteer, so in 2005 he began, as did Katie, through Voluntary Service Overseas.

"I'd wanted to work as a volunteer with VSO for many years, even before going into nursing," Steve says. "I had visited a bus belonging to them at a music festival, World of Music Art and Dance, which was set up by Peter Gabriel from Genesis. The bus toured around and showed what VSO was trying to achieve around the world and that appealed to me. One day while looking through the *Nursing Times*, an advert from VSO jumped out at me. I was in my late forties by then and thought that I should give it a try because I would hate to have regrets wondering 'What if' or 'If only' in my later years. A few people encouraged me and a few cautioned me, saying that I was mad — at the peak of my earning capacity, giving up a chance of promotion, et cetera. Anyway, I decided to take a leap of faith and go for it and have so far not regretted my decision. It may yet come back to bite me in the arse, so to speak, but not so far."

He was posted to Nkhoma College of Nursing, where he worked as a nurse tutor. He describes the work as "challenging, frustrating and fulfilling all at the same time. There were many times that I considered giving it all up because I felt that nobody seemed to care about standards, things being done properly or with any sense of urgency but then, just as I was losing heart, something would happen or a student would say something to me to restore my faith. I ended up extending from two years to three years. It was during my time at Nkhoma that I met Mags, through my friend, Dr. Nick Metcalf, who ran the Nkhoma Eye Hospital. I was amazed by what Mags had managed to achieve out of such tragic circumstances."

Steve returned home in May of 2008. Back in Malawi, Mags was asking Nick how Steve was doing.

"Nick said that he didn't think I was that happy," Steve recalls. "I did not have a job and anything which seemed interesting was either in London or some other major city. I had lived in London in my twenties and didn't want to live there again. Neither did I want to commute. I'd done that in my post office days and, believe me, it is not much fun. Mags asked me if I would be interested in returning to Malawi as her project manager, but I would have to commit to a minimum of four months."

On that day in the dining room, as Steve and Mags conferred over tea about the applications, he'd been there two years and was thinking of applying for another two. At this point, he's a veteran of both volunteering and being an assumed wealthy white person living in Malawi, and cracks up knowingly at Mags's description of a T-shirt she once saw in the city.

"It says, 'Yes, I am a mzungu, but I don't have money for —' and on the back it was ticked off: 'school fees, mother, bag of maize.'"

Pouring himself a cup, Dave joins the table and tells of a train trip in Thailand for which he was charged first class but ended up nearly in baggage. "A friend said, 'If you haven't been scammed, you have not traveled."

"You're on an emotional merry-go-round," Mags says.

"Every day you get a story," Dave answers.

"You're lucky," Mags counters, "if you only get one."

"It's a different story for some," Steve says softly of those with genuine hardships faced.

"Then, Steve," says Mags, pointing to the stack of applications, "what do we do about this?"

When the calls for interview appointments are made later that day, one goes to Kenet. As he enters the gate at ten the next morning, he passes a young man who's been standing there for an hour, and will wait one more until his eleven o'clock meeting, mopping his brow in the hot sun and in a white short-sleeved, button-down shirt, a short vintage-looking, gold-striped necktie, and pressed dress slacks secured by a belt with a broken buckle.

Kenet is admitted by the watchmen, then shown to a seat beneath the thatched roof in the clearing. On the other side of the long table sit Steve and Mags. Steve asks Kenet if he knows Mags, which he does; if he has been to school, which at first elicits from Kenet a nervous laugh, then a "No," and then the detail that he completed Standard 4 — roughly four years of elementary school. Has he ever held a job? "Fisherman, then watchman, Cape Mac," he says, referring to the lodge.

Steve wants to know why he left that position. After a long wait, Kenet, who's in his mid-twenties, asks for the question again. "Why did you finish," Steve asks, "you were there April to July — a short time." When Kenet looks puzzled, Mags offers the same line in Chichewa, then in English says, "Many people are looking for this job, many people are coming to us. Understand? Only part-time work — some days no work. Understand?"

Kenet nods. Says nothing more.

Mags rises. "Today we will speak with many people who want this job and we will let you know."

Like all applicants who are called for an interview, Kenet has been obliged to answer an essay question in person, to prove he is the one writing the material, to prove that he indeed can write. Knowledge of English is key, especially in a health setting. Including for any cleaning positions.

The question for this round of applicants asks why the clinic is important.

In blue ink on notebook paper, one man has written, *"This shows that without the clinic in Chembe we would all die no survive because we can not take a serious disease to Monkey-Bay and get the hospital arrive. The clinic is powerful and helpful."*

Another, in which Mags is called "Marks," says: *"The truly marks is the without your help of chembe village, the people of chembe village would have been died and god continue to bless you."*

A woman in her mid-twenties walks to the table to hand in her essay, thanks Steve and Mags and curtseys with each thank-you.

Next to arrive is a man named Charles, who has a two-month history of work with the Trust so has submitted no application letter. When asked his age, he says seventy-one, but he means the year of his birth. He gives his residence as "this side," meaning his home's location in relation to the center of town. Charles says there are three children in his family, and to answer the question about their ages he holds his hand to their approximate heights.

"One wife or two wives?" Mags asks.

"One, big one," Charles says, and raises his hand to her much taller height.

"One is enough," Mags says, and he agrees with the "Sure, sure" that is the answer for so much in the area, and in a culture where multiple wives wouldn't be unusual enough to spark a reality show, but where setting a limit of four children recently has been considered by the government in an effort to stem overpopulation.

Mags gives Charles the speech about the many people who are interested in the job, and he parts with a nod to both of them.

"I like him," Steve says, "but would get a volunteer to teach him English."

A watchman approaches to tell Steve that a broom salesman is at the gate. Brooms are essential for grooming the grounds daily, so Steve takes a moment to check out the wares, which are piled on the back of a bicycle the broom salesman has parked outside the gate. Steve knows the question to ask:

"How long will they last?"

"Six weeks last," answers the salesman.

Steve thinks for a moment. "I'll take six." Then he returns to the table, where he and Mags next greet a woman who is twenty-three, married less than a year — "only me and husband" — and hoping to support the both of them as he has no job.

"What does a personal care attendant do?" Mags asks.

"I remove the clothes," she says quietly, "correcting the word to "clo-thess" before continuing: "I wash the body. When he or she is crying I can manage to say, 'Calm down, everything will be all right, don't worry, be strong.'"

Forty-five minutes later than he was promised, the man at the gate finally gets his interview. By now he also wears a good sheen of sweat, and an extra coating of nerves is palpable as he looks at the table and says he is Francis, then says, "I am a boy of twenty-one."

"Why are you here?" Steve asks.

"I came here to find a job."

"You came to Cape Maclear to find a job?" Steve's voice all but shouts the question of how the Cape could be considered an employment hub, and what does that say about how bad things are in Francis's village.

"Yes," Francis says, "I came here to find a job."

SEVEN

T ake a walk.

Down the beach, then up one of the skinny lanes that allow beach access between properties. The path is lined with reed fences, and through them you can glimpse backyards, chickens, laundry, an open fire. Cross the main sandy lane that runs parallel to the beach and head along the left-hand side of a small brick house, where a flimsy reed gate is opened for you. Enter the home of Memory and her family.

Step into a backyard measuring maybe twenty by twenty feet. At the far side is a brick structure the size of one of those metal outbuildings you can buy at Sears for storing your riding mower. At the far end of the backyard are two tall and round houses also made of reeds, six or so feet off the ground, reed ladders reaching to the little door at each of their fronts. These are the homes for the two chickens Memory owns, and the four that belong to the family. As for the small brick building, through one door is the family's kitchen. Through the other is the home of Memory and her daughters, fourteen-year-old Faith and ten-month-old Carolyn.

The yard is sand, like everywhere else around the neighborhood, and smells faintly of the reeds that surround it. Faith sits on the ground near the back of the house, writing in a school notebook. A woman steps from the doorway to her right. This is Martha, Memory's mother. Like Memory, she wears a brightly colored chitenje and white blouse, and her hair

113

is wrapped in more cloth. She greets you and invites you through the door, to the table inside, just past a storeroom to the left and two doors to bedrooms on the right. Three chairs await. Memory has followed but doesn't join the two of you. Martha, who has far more English than Memory, tells you Memory has been, and will continue to be, busy cooking.

Martha offers you tea from a Thermos. It's hot and good. Look around. Along the walls, way up near the low ceiling, take in the row of photographs in simple frames or glued to cardboard, and the placard reading LOVE GOD. One picture is of a United Kingdom church group that visited the village, others are of a few former Billys who sent pictures of their own families back in Ireland. "Billys," Martha says as you look at the faces. Nods.

As is the case with most families in the village, those under Martha's roof have been helped by at least a few of the past or present Billys. Most recently, granddaughter Faith went to the clinic for breathing problems. In all, Martha has eight children — six of them girls — with husband Jimmy, who works a coveted job at the resort on Thumbi Island across the lake and comes home once a week. Their boys live in Lilongwe but can't find work there and have little to eat. You want to ask if they get assistance but then remember there is none in this country — no unemployment, no welfare, no healthcare coverage, nothing that you're used to or would need if you were in similar circumstances back home. In Malawi, where forty percent of the nation's $1.6 billion 2013 budget is funded by Western donors, there isn't the money for such things, and, if they do exist, are the work of private individuals or concerns, often religious organizations, and always from another country. Or of people like Mags, driven by passion or by tragedy, or both.

Martha's other daughters live in the main house, too, and two more of them, Rebecca and Henrietta, enter to say hello.

Martha tells you about the three other grandchildren, one of them somewhere out behind the house. Between the six daughters, five grandchildren, and Martha, that's a dozen people living here in a tiny three-room building and one small room in the building out back, neither structure offering water nor electricity. In dry weather — that's about seven months of the year — they prefer to sleep outside, on mats. It's cooler there but the risk of malaria anywhere away from a netted interior bed is greater. You wonder which you would choose on a night when it's 105 degrees.

When you were invited for dinner here, you wanted to know what you might bring. At home it would be a box of candy or a bottle of wine or a bunch of flowers. Mags and Steve remind you this place is far from your home, and make other suggestions. You purchase at a shop down the street a pound of the sugar they'd suggested. You do not pick up the bar of soap they'd said was a popular gift, because you thought bringing somebody a bar of soap would be weird. When you hold forth the plastic shopping bag of sugar, Martha says "Thank you for the gift," without opening the bag, then adds, "You know it costs 5,000 kwacha to send a child to school." There is no segue between the expression of gratitude and the information about the finances involved in private secondary education, as in, "If you wanted to give us something, we are in need of funds for school." Then Martha asks if you have laundry in need of washing, says that Memory and her sister do laundry and they could use the income.

Martha talks about having applied to Mags for scholarship help, and about a former Billys who had been funding some schooling for a few family members. Mags had said you might be hit up to sponsor a child — or an entire family — during this visit, but Martha doesn't go near that more than to mention prices a few times. She's talkative in general, so all of it just sort of flows. She tells you she wakes around five, with the sun, as does the rest of the village. Then she, like most of the village, heads to the lakefront to do dishes and clothes and bathing at the edge of the lake, where the community calls loudly to one another, chants, sings while kids scream, bang on things and start the ceaseless running down the beach and throwing themselves into the water that will continue until dusk, no lifeguard, no adult supervision, no water wings, no one watching.

The sounds are an alarm clock, and also a reason the list of things for volunteers to pack includes a set of earplugs. Just as natural light starts the day, it also ends activity. About an hour into your chat with Martha, you can't see her though she's only four feet across the table. Memory brings in a flashlight and waves it across the serving dishes that she carries in next, metal floral-printed casserole dishes with matching lids, Martha's best dishes, full of white rice, spinach, boiled eggs in a tomato sauce, and a starch called *nsima* that is made of maize and, as one Billys rightfully described it, tastes like Play-Doh without the salt.

There is no tasting allowed, though, until after Martha recites the Our Father. She is a devout member of the local Anglican church and says that she reads, and even owns, a Bible. Martha reaches behind her to the little table holding the flashlight and finds the book, a cartoon version with drawings of stories like Jesus being tempted in the desert, all quotes given in balloons. Other than the cartoon Bible, Martha has no reading materials. A newspaper is published weekly somewhere beyond this town, but there is no way to get it out here, she says, though she occasionally gets to read a copy a neighbor might have been given. During the day, Martha strings small carvings — fish, trees, faces — onto cords, making necklaces and bracelets sold at a local lodge and to wholesalers who sell them to lodges farther afield. After dark, when it's impossible to string anything, she sits in the yard with family and neighbors, then goes to bed around ten. In between, she says, she worries a lot.

Born in 1958, on a day she didn't know was St. Patrick's until you informed her, Martha is fifty-two. That's old for this country, and she's well aware of that. Both her parents have died. Her two sisters are dead, too. She again brings up schooling for her grandchildren, wonders if they'll ever go, and looks to the floor, where Memory has chosen to have her meal, rather than use the third chair. In Memory's lap, Carolyn sits, naked and breastfeeding while her mother uses a hand to eat her meal, using a glob of nsima for a utensil, scooping everything else with it while you use the spoon you just realized is a courtesy given a mzungu.

In the faint flashlight glow, Memory and Carolyn look like a painting of mother-and-child connection. You ask her if she likes being a mother. Where you live, it's a question that usually prompts mothers to tell lots of stories, usually sweet ones, usually accompanied by an iPhone full of the latest snaps from that local baby photographer everyone's going to. Memory's answer to the question is a firm "No," given with a blank expression.

In case you didn't understand, Martha translates: "She say 'No.' She makes only 500 kwacha." That's less than five dollars a week for six days of work at a lodge down the lane, cleaning rooms, washing showers and toilets, raking the sandy yard. Hardly enough money for a woman to support herself, let alone herself and two kids.

They don't want your help cleaning the table. They only want you to go get your rest — it's getting late. Through the open window behind you, figures pass in the dark, accounting for the only traffic on this street. The occasional beam from a cell phone light marks an out-of-towner — local residents seem able to see in the dark. You bring out your own flashlight. It's time to leave. Memory is now against the wall, the baby sleeping in her lap. You thank her and Martha for the meal, and Martha tells you, to come back again to visit. "We are friends," she tells you and she leaves it at that, mentions nothing more. She leads you out the door and past a cluster of family members seated against the house and in the yard. She opens the gate and watches as you head off into the dark.

EIGHT

E very Tuesday morning, thanks to funding by a group of Dutch supporters of the clinic, portions of Likuni Phala, a fortified porridge mix, are distributed at the clinic to mothers who have undernourished children up to five years of age. On this Tuesday in mid-October, they'll be receiving something extra. For the first time, the Trust will be giving out mosquito nets, a key in preventing malaria.

Mags, the porridge, and the large stack of green nets are found this morning in the clinic addition, in the room through first door on the left as you come down the ramp from reception. The space is airy and long, with a desk at the far end of the right-hand wall. The hungry season has begun. It's the last month of the dry season, and rain won't start until sometime in December. Families are preparing their homes for the upcoming deluges, cutting fresh reeds in the forest and repairing roofs and walls. And they're scraping by on the last of the ground maize they stored from the previous harvest, relying more than ever on the lake for their meals — though fish stocks are greatly depleted from overfishing. For families with very small children the porridge can be a lifesaver.

Mothers begin arriving at the clinic, carrying infants and children, and the pots in which they will collect their porridge for the week. But at 8:00 a.m. on this distribution day, they are directed into the empty ward down the end of the hall, where they take seats on beds or on the floor, awaiting a lecture on the mosquito nets that will be distributed. A lone man and his son are in the flow finding space in the room. In Malawian culture, mothers raise children, doing so almost sternly, with little warm emotion shared; fathers normally don't have much interaction with their kids. Mags has seen that changing a bit in the ten years she's spent time on the Cape, but says it still is rare to see a man with a child, and she makes note of the one father when she comes to the door and glances around.

Thanks to a donation by students in a health class at Westfield, Massachusetts' North Middle School, two hundred nets were purchased in the effort to save children from potentially fatal malaria. They are to be distributed today, but not before what Mags sees as the crucial component of education.

"Too many NGOs simply throw donations of goods at people and don't instruct them in the reasons for the items, or how to use them," she says as Wilson from the lab takes his place inside the door and begins to speak in Chichewa to the packed room. Mags translates: "A lot of times an NGO just comes into a village with nets — two days later you see them used as fishing nets, bridal dresses, goal posts for football. They don't realize the value of it and what it can save. We'll tell them, 'If we see you're using them for other uses, we'll take them back.' We hope this new project they built will bear fruit. If the amount of children presenting with malaria shows a decline over the next two years, we'll know."

Those two hundred nets stacked down the hall were a long time in getting here. Two years ago, Mags began a correspondence with the Malawian government regarding a net program. The fact that these nets were funded by pennies collected a year ago by kids in a community half a world away is another statement about government inefficiency here. And about some of the fruit born of Mags's annual visits to heavily Irish-American Western Massachusetts, where she's met many donors by standing at a New England fair booth hung with photos of the clinic and answering over and again their question of "What are you doing here?" with the reply "My son, Billy, drowned in Malawi, and I've built a clinic there in his memory."

What she was doing in New England was trying to raise funds for a clinic that was just getting under way. In 2003, she'd accepted the invitation of friend Fran Ryan, a Dingle knitwear designer who once a year assembles a group of craftspeople from town to sell their wares at the Eastern States Exposition in West Springfield, Massachusetts, one of the ten largest fairs in the United States. Set in an area with a large Irish-American population, "The Big E" has been a natural place to attract interest in an African clinic with Irish roots, and Mags has attended almost annually. Acquaintances made there have led to several locals creating Billy's Malawi Project USA, a fundraising group that meets in nearby Chicopee and that in 2007 obtained non-profit status. Mags's annual presence also has led to connections with local clubs, schools and individuals who've donated funds, and goods including those nets.

Suzanne and Mark Meserve's quaint Cape a few miles from the Exposition grounds became Mags's American home on that first visit, after Suzanne, who'd purchased items from Fran during her first years at the fair, offered to lodge vendors in the bedrooms vacated by two daughters off at college. Fran responded that Mags indeed needed a room, and on a September day in 2003, Suzanne headed to the bus station in Springfield to meet her.

"She had a suitcase full of paintings and jewelry to sell," Suzanne says, "and carried a scale model of what was to be the clinic."

As mothers working in the health field, (Suzanne, fifty-five, teaches childbirth education and breastfeeding classes, and is a doula and a lactation counselor), the two bonded quickly. Mags has stayed with the Meserves many times since, setting up the Acer at a living room table to work, texting overseas over a breakfast of toast and tea at the kitchen island, standing in the driveway to catch a lift to a Rotary Club meeting where she'll speak to a lunch crowd — or to a middle school collecting pennies to buy mosquito nets for kids half a world away.

That stack of nets to be distributed today is the latest step in malaria education with the Cape Maclear community at large. At The Gap, where nets are standard, few volunteers over the years have gotten the disease. Two of the current ones no longer take a malaria preventative, just rely on the net that hangs from the ceiling and is tucked beneath their mattress.

"They can be the difference between life and death," Mags says. "Especially for children."

The blue nets hanging over the wards' beds for use each night have been knotted for the day as the group, numbering approximately seventy, listens to Wilson. The overflow of another eight women and half a dozen kids in the hallway is only somewhat listening, and Wilson pokes his head out regularly, gestures, has them repeat the info he's telling them. They laugh when he does.

The information on the use, and misuse, of the nets, Mags says, needs to come from a local. "So if they see him in the village they'll say, 'Oh, he told me not to use these for anything else.'"

What he told them, Wilson says as the crowd pours from the ward and down the hall to the feeding room twenty minutes later, was the basics.

"First I had to tell them it was a disease," he says. "Especially in Africa, most countries in which malaria is a problem. They need to know how to use it. How malaria is very dangerous. Especially for pregnant women and children under five, they should be protected. Malaria is a prevalent disease, as well. I was telling them how to prevent."

Wilson repeats information about the female anopheles mosquito and the science of malaria. He gives the signs of the disease, likening it to the worst stomach flu imaginable, with extreme fever, headache, diarrhea, vomiting. An enlarged spleen, he says, hints at a worsened case. He explains how to prevent mosquito breeding areas — holes that can fill with stagnant water — and how after six months the repellent in the nets will have lessened, and tablets can be obtained for soaking the nets to refresh the repellent.

"We told them to use it properly," he says. "We firmly told them. Because we do stay in the village. If we see someone using the net in inappropriate ways, we will report them to the police."

"Precious Banda!"

With the formal tone of a man announcing a visitor to a receiving line of royalty, watchman Nathan calls down the hallway line the name of the first child to receive porridge and net. "Precious Banda!"

Precious is given the honor of receiving the first net, due to her health passport having been the first one put in a stack at the desk, where Dave and another assistant project manager, Elaine Cosgrove, tend to paperwork. Mags stands behind them, hand on hip, leaning over their heads to see the list of names, of which Precious is not the most unusual.

Felesita, Grecious, Fledrick, Junior, Trinity, Takeness, Verandar, Mercy and Handsome are yet to be announced this morning. In this culture with a very high infant mortality rate, a baby is not considered a person until six months of age, and those distant fathers are very distant until that point, not allowed to touch their own offspring until they reach that age. When a child eventually is named, it is in Chichewa, but some adopt or are given a mzungu name. Rather than Bob or Mary, those can be Biblical, like Gideon down the beach or Joab in The Gap kitchen, or perhaps pop culture, like Rambo. Some of the names are due to something happening in one's life at the time, hence the choices of Trouble, Gift, Naughty, Innocent, and Memory. There's also Confident, Beauty, Funny, Lucky, John Banana, Dryclean, Military, and Mr. Computer, one of the village's rare old men, who, Mags points out, had to have been born long before the advent of the device. Snoopy's brother is known as Statesman. There's Portia and Juliet, thanks to a father named William who was told about Shakespeare by missionaries. "Batman is my favorite," Katie Acheson says. "There are about three of them here." There has even been a Hitler.

Big Dorothy got her adjective from the Trust, which needed to differentiate between two Dorothys (the other, the more slender of the two, is Small Dorothy) employed. Today, Big Dorothy's navy blue T-shirt and chitenje are covered by a white sheet as she sits behind the giant sack of the porridge mix. At the desk to Big Dorothy's right, Precious Banda's mother leaves the only signature she knows how to sign — a thumbprint — on the log of people who will be served today. Big Dorothy scoops into the woman's plastic bowl Precious's portion of the mix. Dave holds forth a net in a plastic bag imprinted with mother and child snoozing beneath the words *Chitetezo Net, Cha Mayi Ndi Mwana* — roughly Defense Net for Mother and Child. Precious' mother regards the package with a smile.

After an early morning zipping between her flat, Steve's office and the liaison office, and taking time to digest that an Irish film crew that was to have arrived at the end of the month for an update on a piece they did on her several years

124

back now has called to say it's unable to make the trip, Mags stays while the next few women sign in at the table, then heads off to another task. She was here promptly for the 8:00 a.m. lecture by Wilson, despite Steve reminding her, "You know, eight o'clock for a Malawian is ten o'clock."

Now Mags is at the back of the extension, checking out the locks that have been placed on the faucets to prevent further thefts of water. A baboon watches from the lane next to the building as she says, "I'll play devil's advocate," and tries to get her fingers into the metal cap that successfully prevents her from becoming the next person to further drain the well without permission.

She returns to the clinic and has a conversation with Steve about replacing doors in the hallway, then joins him in talking to a cleaner about doing a more thorough job. Passing the close observation ward, she calls in to the woman on the bed, "*Muli bwanji!*" Mags moves on to examine an exposed section of brick behind the plaster facing in the emergency room, from where a baby can be heard screaming. "Sounds like they're crucifying a child in there," she says, then spots a villager headed toward the exit, a tiny infant tied to her back. "How's the baby?" she asks with a wide smile. "Getting big?" Mags illustrates with her hands the child's size increasing. The next second, she turns servicelike and tells Steve again, yes, they need to definitely look at doors, and locks, as well. Turning quickly, near a poster for the MAP (Malawi Against Polio) Clinic, she calls to a woman in the hall, "You were looking for me?" The woman, a staffer, has asked permission to bring her baby to work so it can get a better sleep than it does during the day at home. "No, too many sick people here," Mags says, "and you're working."

Then she's out the door. It's lunchtime and the doctors and nurses have decided to walk home rather than catch a ride back in the ambulance. "They're divils for punishment, so they are,"

Mags says with a laugh.

Without passengers to bring home, she and Steve decide to swing by the village carpentry shops for quotes on doors. The carpenters they'll visit are located toward the eastern end of the peninsula, nearer the big market and primary school, and all three establishments look rudimentary enough to once have had Jesus as an apprentice. Beneath thatched roofs held up by poles, muscle is the power source, the expected ringing scream of a table saw replaced by the rhythmic back-and-forth of a handsaw.

"Going and buying a door here isn't just a matter of cash and carry," Mags says as the ambulance rolls up to a shop where a stack of window frames awaits buyers. Next to them, a fine door.

Hens and their chicks cross the road as Mags and Steve exit the ambulance and look at the piece on display. They ask the carpenter his price for making, varnishing, hinging, hanging and putting old locks into a new door.

"Remember," Mags adds, "it's for the clinic." The man holding the saw gives her a price of 6,000.

At the next shop, in front of a home with a goat in the front yard and a radio playing a speaker's voice at the very, very loud volume that any radio here is played, a carpenter marks a length of lumber with a pencil and then says he cannot give a price for such a thing as a door.

Mags and Steve move on.

At a third shop, located across from Zama Zama Welding and, like the other carpentry establishments, bearing no name itself, Mags asks a price. "Not mzungu numbers," she stresses, "clinic numbers."

Here, that number is 8,000.

The pair heads back to the first shop and finds cook Joab examining the door that first had caught their eyes. It's his, he proudly tells Mags and Steve. The shop made it for 6,000 kwacha, and in forty-five minutes. Mags and Steve place their order, then offer to drive Joab and the door the half mile to his home, to spare him from having to carry it there balanced on his head, as he was about to do.

As the ambulance begins to jounce down the lane, Joab points out the three types of wood that have been used in his door, but doesn't know the specific names. At the top of the alley leading to his house, he jumps from the open back of the ambulance and balances the door on his head, then begins to walk down the alley with a very purposeful stride, to the home where he lives with his wife, five kids, four of his sister's children, and his uncle.

Joab, forty-two, supports all eleven people through his work as a cook. In this maternal-led society, a man moves to the woman's village upon marriage. And anyone in the family who is bringing in a salary is expected to distribute it to family needs. Joab has been employed in the kitchens of various establishments in the village since learning to cook at the National Park, and has been with the Trust for three years. He would like to go to cooking school, he'll say, but then will admit he's not saving for that goal. He can't save. The money he makes automatically goes to supporting his family.

Mags and Steve watch Joab walk away. "I'd say this is a proud moment for him, going home to his house with a new door he bought," Mags says. "That's an example right here of the money coming into this community."

She estimates that, since the clinic's opening, it has infused $1.3 million euro into the village.

"This," she says, nodding toward the receding figure of Joab and his new purchase, "is a spring-off from that."

Because the clinic is a non-profit, with ninety-seven cents of every dollar donated going directly to keeping it functioning, everything in Mags's path today — the complex in which she woke, the ambulance that got her to the clinic, the clinic itself, the porridge and nets distributed, the door Joab took home and the one she and Steve ordered — that, and so much more in the place, stems from the generosity of donors.

Mags says she's not sure how much the Trust takes in annually, but she would like to have roughly $200,000 arriving in its account annually. Recent financial fiascos the world over have greatly reduced the number of donors and dented the donations. "We're not on the brink, or teetering on the brink, or about to fall off any moment, but I still get up the first of January every year and think, 'I hope I'm going to have enough money to keep going,'" she says. "Initially, I had this wonderful idea that we'd fundraise enough to keep going, but you'd have to have an awful lot. If I was to really relax about spending money, we would go through 150,000 a year, but I'm literally questioning every packet of envelopes I buy. I suppose it would be better if I didn't, but I would literally say we will walk from one supermarket to another to buy toilet paper at a better rate. I laughed at Steve recently in the supermarket in Lilongwe, 'Oh, Steve, the toilet paper is on offer here.' He says, 'Mags, it's like 500 kwacha cheaper across the road. We're not buying it here, we're buying it across the road.' We watch everything. Down to the last kwacha, the last timbala."

The Trust's official headquarters, the collection point for donations that eventually are turned into those timbalas, is nothing grand, nothing larger than six by ten feet, nothing more than one of three rooms comprising what is home for Mags when she is in Dingle.

"This is my office. This is where I do everything — well, I haven't been working here for a month now, obviously, because I've been away, but this is where everything is run," Mags said the previous May in Dingle as she opened the door to the smallest of the three rooms that include her en suite bedroom, simple and uncluttered, with its double bed, nightstand, dresser and tiny bath, bright white walls. Across the hall, another door opened to a second room used for storage and donations, then home to a mound of a dozen trash bags filled with linens destined for the clinic, given by locals who responded to a request Mags made during a recent radio interview. This third door, between the two, opens to a space taken up by the Trust.

That it's a workspace is clear from the rest of the contents: a wooden-topped desk holding computer, eight-shelf organizer, a lamp and several stacks of mail and paperwork; the pair of well-utilized bookcases on either end of the desk, one shelf holding a pair of Malawian flags; and, along the opposite wall, the lineup of small wooden dresser and stack of plastic tubs, and a guitar she hasn't played in years. Plastic bottles to be used for collecting donations at events sit empty on the floor next to a CD of an Irish television special on the Trust, folders for income and expenditures from the past calendar year, and seven tags from seven visits made to the Big E. Decorations in the office are few, most of them framed family pictures, a certificate for "World's Best Mum," and a photo of the sun rising over Lake Malawi on the first day of the new millennium.

"Someday when I break my leg I'll get this done," Mags says as she points to the tubs and takes a seat on the office chair covered in gray-blue upholstery that matches the pristine wall-to-wall rug. Above her, a slanting skylight brightens the room. It's the only window in the space, and the view of verdant fields it offers can be enjoyed only while standing precariously on her wheel-based office chair, something Mags invites visitors to do but doesn't regularly practice herself. "I've no view from down here," she acknowledges, "but, on the other hand, it would only distract me. That's the way I look at it."

Mags doesn't welcome distractions. And when they're present, she remains as focused on what's in front of her as if wearing blinders. When in Dingle town, she'll certainly stop in the road to chat with a friend who flags her down from his car, but when she has to run she'll say so, powering on to a stop at the bank, or to lunch with a reporter, or to another visit with a new grandson.

At the Cape, she'll listen to a volunteer's suggestions as she makes her way to her ambulance, but once at the vehicle she'll ask the person to join her for a quick trip to the clinic so the conversation can be continued en route. Few moments are wasted. And when that possibility arises, she moves to a Plan B always at the ready. Today, her laptop, resting open on the desk, is not allowing access to the Internet. The modem had just been repaired and Mags hopes she won't have the additional delay of another trip to the shop.

"The whole operation runs off this computer," she says with a level of remove in her voice. "I have paperwork to get sorted out and stuff to get logged. I have this stack of mail — it would have been accumulated over less than a month. There are letters with checks. I got through some of it a couple of days last week. When did I get back here? Saturday. And I did some of it then — the more urgent stuff. But this is stuff that needs to be looked after now. Hopefully, I'll be able to do it tomorrow."

Those chores and more are the reality of a charity that in many respects is a one-woman operation. Mags has volunteers for the crucial staffing of the clinic, and a cadre of others who regularly run fundraisers, among those events that first annual West Kerry Blues Festival to be held in nearby Ballydavid, at the end of the Long Road, the following weekend, and for which Mags will spend part of her day phoning around to find help with selling tickets. At the Cape, Steve is greatly relied upon, tending to an endless and varied list of tasks including those his post-office days prepared him well for: dealing with personnel matters, keeping track of the payroll, monitoring supplies, answering countless questions spoken through the open office door. But many tasks fall to Mags, mostly by her choice. As much as she wants to have the clinic one day run by Cape residents and other Malawians, and as much as she remarks on the incalculable value of all the volunteers, for now, she is the biggest force keeping the Trust on track. There's the traveling back to Ireland three or four times a year and once a year to the States for public relations-related efforts; reading and responding to applications; and meeting with prospective volunteers when her travel plans bring her near their homes. Then there are the cultural aspects, including dealing with the layer upon layer of bureaucracy in Malawi, where bribery is so common that airport security make no effort to hide the paper money handed them by passengers who don't want their bags examined, and is so expected that a meeting with an official often requires bringing an unmarked envelope containing payment. It also often makes for frustrating memories, including that of the government official who was to speak at the opening of the clinic but who demanded to be paid for petrol to be used on the trip. (There was no government speaker at the opening.)

On this day back in May, back in Dingle, Mags is far from all that drama, but without computer access that will allow her to do the work that awaits. She sifts through a stack of checks from donors, and the notes that accompany them. One is for ten euro. Another, 5,000.

She looks at the stack again, says any amount surprises her. Says she knows the challenges of potential donors. Her own charitable history includes donations to a donkey sanctuary and to Goal, a Dublin-based organization helping the disadvantaged in more than fifty countries. "Whenever I had the money, I'd give," she says, "but I was always broke. I didn't even have a checkbook, never mind writing checks, I wasn't working for years when I was home with the kids. It was only when we separated that I went to work, basically. And then I was a single parent with three kids, so I didn't have a choice, didn't have money to be flashing around."

She decides to give an overdue look at what's stored beneath her desk, specifically a trove of family photos, many of which illustrate the life of the young man the trust based in this room memorializes. She pulls out a green suitcase containing just such pictures and unzips the case in one loud motion.

The images stored inside, unconfined to organized album pages and therefore stacked right side up, upside down, a few dates written on the back of some, nothing on others, resemble anyone's collection: family lineups, people cramming together to fit into the viewfinder, tots collected and caught in the moment the fewest of them are howling, all the dated clothing and hairstyles, all the picturesque backdrops, all the milestones, all the smiles. The disorder of the stacks' state also mirrors the random way memories pop into the mind. There's no rhyme or reason to how our past flashes before us in a given day, and there's none to the order of these photos, and the memories they evoke for Mags.

Before delving into the contents of the suitcase, from the same space below the desk she drags out a small cardboard box holding more such touchstones. She runs a hand through, regarding individual photographs, turning them over, chuckling once in a while, pointing out a face, offering commentary like, "There's me when I went to university," which she announces as she points to a picture of a serious-faced, long-haired blonde holding a guitar. That she resembles a '60s folksinger isn't a coincidence. "I was aspiring to be," she says, "at that stage."

The room is silent but for the flipping of the photos. "Most of these are very old," Mags says after a few moments, and as proof lifts one in particular, of a tot in a woman's arms: "There's Billy outside the first little house, in The Colony. With my sister. Yes, there's Billy."

She says nothing for the few moments it takes to consider the shot of a son so small he sits on the arm of her sister. Then Mags moves on to another, her bits of narration as disparate as the sequence of the images: "These are really old pictures," she says, "ancient things. There are all the Riordan cousins. My God, me on my wedding day."

In the next shot, as if he materialized at three or four years of age the day after the wedding, a tiny Billy Riordan stands in shorts and works on devouring an ice cream cone. His mother flips the shot over but finds no date. On the next, he's leaped twenty years or so and walks with a woman in a headscarf down a dirt lane between stone buildings that look to be from Biblical times. "That's Marrakesh, anyway," says his mother. "Somewhere in Morocco or somewhere. That's when they went to Morocco, with his Dad."

In the next picture, Jennifer looks to be in first grade, wearing a dark velvety dress with lace collar and sitting in the lap of her big brother. In the next, Florence Rossignol, a former girlfriend of Billy's who's remained close to the family, smiles on a rainy day.

"That's Richie," Mags says as she holds a photo of a dark-haired man, the sea behind him, "taken somewhere on a boat, I'd say. And that's Richie's sister, and all her brothers. She's an only girl. That's me, that's my wedding, and my bridesmaid, Marion." She flips the stack to pick out a dapper man standing next to a VW. "That's my dad."

The order of the disorder jumps her life ten years hence, the decade in which two of her children already had died. Only one — Luke — appears in any of the shots she finds, an infant nestled into a carrycot guarded to its left by Billy sporting a Dutch boy haircut and crouching before a stone wall edged with yellow and orange marigolds. "That's a nice picture," Mags says before flipping to the next shot of her second son, whom she thinks resembled a Dillon. "He was more like our side of the family, really. The girls are more like the Riordans, but he was more like our side." With the next shot: "And that's Billy and his cousins, that's quite a nice picture, actually — Billy and his first cousins."

They are indeed nice, but sit with Mags as she studies the images with a half smile and you get the impression her mind is searching for other adjectives. It's one thing to watch a proud parent sharing photos of fondly remembered times with a child. It's another to sit with one for whom those times abruptly stopped, living now only in the heart, as well as in a stack of photos in a box and a suitcase kept beneath a desk.

The next pile she collects from the box isn't hers.

"All these are kids Billy took pictures of when he was in South America," Mags says. Then she unfolds a paper tucked into the collection and marvels at its presence, the only piece of paperwork in a sea of photographs, saying, "I never saw that before."

The room falls silent again as she reads the accomplishment of a life, the page headed by the underlined words "CURRICULUM VITAE" and then the name, William Coleman Riordan.

His address is given as Rainbow Hostel, Dingle. Date of

birth as 12 November, 1973. He speaks conversational French and Irish and is a graduate of the Christian Brothers School in Dingle, as well as the University College, Galway, receiving a bachelor of arts degree in archaeology and English. His work history began in 1991, when he managed the hostel and campsite through the summers of 1995, and from June to October of 1995 he organized, marketed and operated sea-angling trips with a forty-foot motor launch. He skippered that boat and others, operated tourists' trips to visit dolphin Fungie. He worked as a barman in France during his studies there in 1993. Back at home, he also participated in archaeological digs and surveys. His interests were hiking, hillwalking, fishing, shooting, scuba diving, reading and travel.

His mother reads every line, nods, folds the paper and replaces it back onto a stack. Then it's on to the next shot, Billy the traveler in a white shirt, his shoulders draped with a very, very long snake. He holds the neck in his right hand and the tail in the other, and looks very pleased. "Somewhere in South America," Mags offers as she moves that aside and flips the others like they're playing cards. "He would have been twenty-two, maybe." The flipping continues. "These are of him," his mother says plainly. "They're all literally, every one, of him."

It's not a cliché to say that a thoroughly enjoyed life is palpable in each shot. The kind of life friends and family describe as Billy's, a whirl of working at the hostel and on the boat, time with family and friends, and time spent with lodgers visiting his part of the world. Then, when funding and time allowed, he became a visitor in theirs, traveling way beyond West Kerry to satiate some of a great appetite for life and experience. Billy smiles as he floats in a pool edged with rock, poses with sturdy backpack, naps on a deserted beach, dances in shorts, wraps an arm around the shoulders of a girlfriend. His mother narrates the peripatetic's journeys, including that final one to Malawi.

"That was taken the weekend before he went to Africa," she says while studying a shot of Billy raising a glass. With the next, of him and a friend in Belgium, Mags says, "He was en route to Africa when that was taken. He stopped into a couple of places in various parts of Europe before he left, to see people he hadn't seen in a long time. It's very strange. He stopped in France to see some other people. Stopped into London to see some other people before he went to Africa that time."

That time.

Mags reviews the stack again. Puts it down. Picks up another, ignores an image of herself in a fancy dress, saying only a swift, "That was me being presented with some donation for something or other."

There's a shot of Billy and his best friend, Ronan. Another of Florence with her father in France. One of Billy climbing over the side of a boat, emerging from the waters off Ventry, just down the road from where Mags now sits on the floor of her office. Then, in a bright yellow raincoat, he walks a field. "That's somewhere up the country," Mags says, finding no exact information on the back, "up in Galway, somewhere."

Mixed in with the pictures of the living Billy is a shot of a group at one of the first fundraisers for the Trust, held at a horse fair in Dublin. Then there's one of Billy climbing up vertical Skellig Michael, an island off the southwest coast that was one of Ireland's earliest monastic settlements. In the Seventh Century it became home to monks who lived in beehive-shaped stone huts 670 nearly vertical steps above the surf from which they fished. It's easy to imagine Billy living on such an island, but Mags doesn't allow time for that reflection as she moves to the next shot. "And there's Billy's tent." It's a pop-up-style, green, assembled in a garden. His mother notes it wasn't his one and only. "He would have had many tents."

She continues. "That's in Dublin with his uncle and his

cousin and his dad. "And upon finding one of Billy and Richie each hoisting a three-foot-long fish by the gills, she says "That's outside the hostel." Next is a series of black-and-whites that, laid next to the colors of the rest of the collection, look artful for their stark tones. There's Billy lying on a beach. Riding in a boat off Slea Head.

Then, back in full color, there's his mother with a small boy, in a very different world. Again, Mags has no time for shots that include herself. "That's just me and some kid in Malawi. I wonder how that got stuck in there." It's placed aside as she picks up another of Billy. "That's himself and Ronan in there again. There's Ronan again. That was taken in the hostel. I knew I had a whole load of them somewhere."

Then, one of a young woman. "She was a New Zealand girl he was traveling with at one stage. I can't remember her name. That's Ronan again. And Simon and another friend of his. That's taken downstairs in the kitchen."

Some look familiar to anyone who's visited the Trust's website. One of the two photos on the "Billy" link in the "Gallery" section of www.billysmalawiproject.org is of him somewhere in Southeast Asia, wearing a dark T-shirt emblazoned with multi-colored Celtic knots, a backpack slung over his shoulders, and a brilliantly colored parrot resting on his left hand. He looks at the camera with his mother's direct gaze, a small smile on his face. And the one of him on Skellig Michael, leaning on rocks, looking happy. That's the one that accompanies the "About Billy" page on which Mags tells the story with the straight-on first line: "In February 1999 my only son Billy was drowned in Lake Malawi in Central Africa."

In the headquarters for the charity that sprang from that loss, his mother is holding up a photo of herself, Billy and Jennifer standing in an airport. "That's when we were going to Morocco," she says, then with the next one, "That was me and him at the circus when he was a small child. That's him in Spain."

In that shot, Billy wears a T-shirt printed with the Irish words *Slán abhaile.*

"That's lovely," Mags says, reading the legend aloud to its pronunciation of "slan awall," which she then translates. "It means," she says, "safe home."

NINE

That evening, Mags and Ronan Doherty sit at a table in the busy bar just inside the main entrance to Dingle Benners Hotel. Having welcomed travelers for two centuries, and being the oldest hotel on the peninsula, Benners has a history. Mags and Ronan have one, too. If you want to know about Billy, his mother says, talk with Ronan. As she says, "He's the brother Billy never had."

Between the two sways an easy rapport one can imagine existing between Mags and her own son. When asked how he met Billy, Ronan smiles and glances at Mags to ask, "Should I do the X-rated version?"

"Oh, I don't mind," she says in playful tone before standing. "I'm leaving now so you can say what you like."

For those now expecting the salacious, the answer is a letdown: "I don't remember how exactly we met, to be honest," Ronan begins. "I met a lot of people from Dingle."

But only one would become his best friend.

The two shared a strong friendship for the last seven years of Billy's life, meeting when they enrolled in college in September of 1991 and beginning a personal era packed with travel, adventure and growth, so much of that experienced side by side.

They were nearly the same age, Ronan born four months earlier. On this evening, he remains as fit as he looked in the many photos of Billy and him back in those boxes beneath Mags's desk down the road. His hair is short and brown, his face thin, and he would remind any television-viewing American of *Parenthood* star Peter Krause as he appeared in the early 2000s HBO hit *Six Feet Under*. On this night he wears a brown T-shirt and brown pants. His voice is soft, his manner shy, courteous.

Over a pot of tea, Ronan begins to recall all those Dingle kids he first met, the group of them that lived in one house on Galway's Castlelawn Heights, a student-populated area near the university.

"It was probably a four-bedroom house, a semi-detached house. They used to pack them pretty tight," he says.

"Four bedrooms, probably ten people," calls Mags, who hasn't yet made it to the door.

"Seven," corrects Ronan.

By geographic and cultural contrast, Ronan had come down to Galway from County Donegal's remote Inishowen Peninsula, which crowns the top of both Ireland and Northern Ireland. In an accent bearing more than a hint of Northern Ireland upspeak, and speech that includes the Republic's generous use of "emmm" as a placeholder and the concern of "do ya know?" added to the middle or end of sentences, he recalls feeling drawn to Billy despite the fact that 329 miles separated their home villages at far-flung edges of the country.

"I felt like one of the main reasons for going to university wasn't really the academic side of it but to get away from home and to find like-minded people, or to find what I thought of at the time were people of similar intellect that I could start fresh with," he says.

Billy was that.

"I always met him in a group with other fellas from Dingle. But we really hit it off the night after final exams. Good meaningful talks right there, both of us. I think he saw something in me, do ya know, that he liked, and likewise. So that was it. The next day, Mags came and picked him up from Galway."

Mags is enjoying the memories, despite having to leave for an engagement in town. Still slowly moving toward the door, she adds that she arrived at Billy's apartment that day with cleaning gloves. "I refused to hand it back to the landlord in the state it was in," she says, then leaves.

That summer, travelers that they were, Billy visited Turkey and Ronan went to Germany. At the start of the next school year, they picked up their friendship, soon moving into the same house. The like minds continued to mesh and find links in shared philosophies, outlooks and that interest in travel.

"I think a lot of people were more cliquish and into scenes and stuff like that," Ronan says. "We were staying up late and smoking joints and playing cards and talking." He adds with a laugh, using slang for skipping school, "Or was it dossing?"

The pair celebrated an exam that year with a night out. When offered acid by a couple of female friends, they first declined. "We were kind of 'Nah, nah,'" Ronan says, "but, then, we were still young and into trying things out and experimenting, so we got the acid. It was just myself and Billy. We completely clicked. It was one of the best nights of my life and I expect it was the same for him. I don't know what we were talking about but we were talking about something and I just kind of expressed my views and philosophy and struck a chord with him and he kind of realized I had something to say. He kind of said it as such, you know, 'You're a solid fella.' And I said, 'You're the same, like,' kind of thing, so it was from that point our relationship took off. From then on we did quite a bit, traveled a lot together."

Their first shared journey was in 1993 or 1994, to Amsterdam, Spain and Morocco. Ronan had taken time off from school to work in Germany and met Billy and friend Simon Doyle in Amsterdam.

"We were supposed to go to Indonesia but never quite got

141

Suzanne Strempek Shea

enough money together for that trip so we decided on Morocco," he remembers. "I took the train up and met them, spent a couple of days there, took the train from there to the south of Spain, went to Morocco and traveled for six or seven weeks."

On the way back, Ronan and Billy spent a week in Costa del Sol, wandering the beach, tucking into sleeping bags for the night. "We'd light a fire, it was brilliant." Ronan smiles, then recounts the trip made to South America the following year. They saw another continent together when Billy visited Ronan in Australia, where he lived from 1996 to 1997, working an assembly line job, boxing CDs and booklets for a contractor of Microsoft.

"I suppose he was thinking of working there and staying for a while," Ronan says, "but he kind of decided to be off in some less-developed place."

Destinations off the beaten track — often way off — were what the two preferred.

"He was great to go traveling with because you always ended up getting into something different," Ronan says. "It was kind of adventurous, nearly on the edge, we always ended up getting stuck and finding ourselves in good situations."

Visiting Quito, the two had planned to see a bullfight but no tickets were available. The outing that instead just happened: "We ended up meeting some fella in the street and just ended up going drinking with him and a couple hours later we were cycling along and there were ice cream sellers so we borrowed their bicycles and went around selling ice cream in Quito. Just for the craic of it."

Another smile. "He had a lively, alert kind of mind and brain," Ronan says, "so he was one of these people if you go out for a night, he had the kind of endless energy and appetite for it. So you always end up, I dunno, getting into stuff."

Ronan admits to feeling a bit like he rode coattails, but

142

never complained. The second youngest in a family of five boys and one girl, he wasn't looking for another brother in Billy.

"Maybe because I had lots of brothers, I see things from a different point of view and stuff like that is said often — someone's like someone's brother," he starts. "But, to be honest, I'm close to my family and close to my brothers, but friendship relationships and brother relationships are quite different because brothers, when you hang around with your brothers, you could be arguing with them or pissed off with them. It's not necessarily the same as a friendship. When someone talks about somebody being like a brother, I'm not sure it's an accurate description of our relationship. We just clicked. It was a really good, strong friendship. It was unusual. Males seem to have more groups of friends, rather than having something very deep. There was a very deep bond between us."

Ronan sips his tea and begins to talk more slowly. The waiter sorting cutlery at the bar drops the pieces into containers almost musically.

"I mean, I think it even got to the stage where I dunno, it was nearly like we were kind of holding each other back in a way. I know from my point of view, like, I'd say the last year or so that I knew Billy, I really looked up to him and admired him and I didn't feel kind of worthy of his friendship." Ronan makes that sound like a question. "In a way, I think it was because I was really introverted in a lot of ways, especially sort of in my twenties, so I saw him as being really kind of capable and socially capable and stuff like that. Even when we'd go on our big nights out, the way I saw it, I always saw him as the front-runner and that sort of thing. I think even in the last year or so, I kind of felt like we weren't having as many talks. I think I probably wasn't in the happiest place myself, so I felt, I suppose, like I think we both were — how can I say it?"

In a voice that's even softer, he answers himself: "I think like I felt I wasn't giving or offering him enough, maybe, as a friend. To maintain the friendship we always had. But looking back on it, or after a lot of stuff I got to know about Billy after he died that I didn't realize or didn't see, I think I was so caught in that time with my own introversions and different things and I always felt 100 percent sure that Billy was kind of OK and confident and sure of himself. That he could look after himself, he would always be fine. I kind of had a selfish view, when I look back, because I kind of wasn't really looking out for him, if that makes sense. I always thought because I always saw him as a really sure, confident person, that he would be OK."

Billy's hunger for information led him to learn more about computers in the last few years of his life. "He got really into it and really taught himself a lot of stuff," Ronan says. "He always felt that he was gonna be good and successful at things, do ya know? It was kind of safe and comforting to be his friend. But, afterwards, I saw there was kind of, facades and fronts there, as well, so probably he wasn't the happiest person at times. I supposed he was going through what everybody goes through — the turbulent twenties — but I didn't see that or realize that until after he died."

That knowledge came to him. "Even though we were very close, he did keep real big secrets from me. Even though he knew about Luke and Niamh, he never told me about that stuff. I didn't know anything. I remember one fella staying in the hostel at one time and working in town mentioned it to me. Someone had told him, I think, about Luke, and I said it to Billy after and he got sort of angry. Not angry with me, just angry that someone would be gossiping. At the same time, I knew there was something there. Unspoken things that were never discussed with Mags or Richie. I presume, you know, when kids are young, when do you tell them something? Then it goes on and on and it's very hard to say, 'OK, this is the right time.' Because things have gone on too far. That's sometimes how it happens but they — all the three kids — kind of knew about Luke and Niamh, but it was kind of an unspoken thing. I'm not sure if they discussed it with each other, even, or was it just the kind of thing that was never discussed within the family."

When Ronan learned about the two children, he felt a bit disappointed that Billy hadn't shared those facts with him, but had with others. "Maybe he felt more comfortable talking with them. I'm not sure," he says. "I think part of the thing was he was very protective of his family, including his parents. He would have been determined to keep that stuff quiet for their sake. When I thought about it and rationalized everything, I was fine with it. It wasn't a big deal, do ya know?"

He saw Billy for the last time just before Christmas of 1998, when Billy was about to leave for a trip to Africa. The journey was spurred by a visit that year from a Norwegian friend whom Billy had met on a previous trip to the continent. Before long, Ronan says, the friend convinced Billy to return. "It wasn't hard to convince him. He wasn't planning to travel again but Roy whetted his appetite. He decided he'd visit Roy out there."

Ronan's pick for a trip would have been South America. "You get notions in your head, I think," Ronan says, "and I think it was because I never heard much about the place growing up. It was a bit more unknown to me than, say, other places. Not that I had a great knowledge of Africa, but Africa was always on the TV. I always had some kind of, some certain knowledge of Africa."

And he had Billy's enthusiastic reviews.

"He really liked the people he met there. I suppose, do ya

know, he could have gone to some other undeveloped place, but he really loved it, and he loved South America, but when he did go back to Africa again, he e-mailed me something — or else I spoke to him on the phone — but he did say it was *the* place, that kind of thing. He said, more or less, he'd been to South America and Indonesia and all, and had been to Africa, and when back in Africa, he said, 'This is the place. It's my number one destination, like.'"

As for Cape Maclear, Ronan says, "He just loved it there. If you have the means for existence, you can have a great time. It's a lovely place to hang around. By the water, just a real easy-going place."

That was Billy's destination the last time the friends parted. Ronan was going to Donegal for the holidays and asked Billy for a lift to the bus station in Tralee. They'd spent the previous night out together, attending Jennifer's school concert and then drinking pints of Guinness and whiskeys at *An Droichead Beag*, a pub on lower Main Street, their local when the two were living in the hostel.

"That's where the music was on and that's where all the hostel crowd was. We used to go there chasing girls," Ronan says. "I got up pretty early the next day. He drove me into the bus station in Tralee and dropped me off there. That was the last time I saw him. The one thing I remember, I suppose you always have regrets, is like, emm, that we didn't embrace. Do ya know? I know the moment was there. We'd embrace now and then, just kind of a statement, that we're really close, just a warm, affectionate thing to do, and, uh, when saying good-bye it crossed my mind. And then, I didn't do it. We shoulda done it. And I'm sure he probably wanted to, he would have liked that I showed him, just kind of a way to say, 'I'm really fond of ya.'"

Benners is getting noisier. The dinner crowd has descended. Ronan stays focused. Considers that Billy perhaps regretted not hugging. But then says, "The other side of it was, it was a real casual see-ya-later kind of thing. We never would have done anything to hold the other person back, so I suppose that was one big thing about our relationship, that if Billy ever wanted to do something or suggest doing something, I'd never have contradicted him or said, 'No, no, that's stupid.' I would have said, 'Oh, yeah, whatever, let's go for it' kind of thing. So I suppose it was just kind of part of the casual good luck thing that day: 'Great, you're going off traveling, see you soon.'"

There was no pile of bags to unload, as Ronan had only a backpack for the short visit home. He grabbed that, said good-bye and walked into the terminal.

The next month, Ronan sent a note to Billy's Hotmail account. He remembers it as "quite a good e-mail," one he unsuccessfully tried to retrieve from Billy's account after he died. "I wanted to see if he'd read the e-mail," Ronan explains. "It was just a nice e-mail, a close, warm one. I never actually got that far. I just kind of let it go after that. I don't know if he got the e-mail or not. He was in Blantyre at the time. He might have checked his e-mail before he went to Cape Maclear, but I'm not sure. So that was, yeah, that was it."

Between 5:00 and 5:30 a.m. the morning of February 22, the hostel phone rang. It was Roy.

"He was a bit scattered, as you would be, all over the place," Ronan remembers. "He told me Billy was missing, do ya know. He was saying, 'You know, he may have swam off to one of the islands.' I supposed he could have just been clinging to something. I didn't know the geography of the place, but there was no chance that was a realistic possibility at all. Roy did say to me it wasn't looking good. It wasn't very positive."

Ronan's first task was to knock on the door of Billy's father's quarters. "He was just kind of in a state. He was pacing around the room. He asked was it likely Billy was alive. I said, 'No.'" Ronan tried to imagine the body of water. Added to that the word "disappeared." And Roy's saying it was "very unlikely" Billy was alive because no one had seen him since the night before.

He then set out for Mags's house. "I never would have called around to Mags's house that early," he says, "so I supposed she knew something. At the same time, when she saw me, she said, 'Oh, Ronan, how's it going?' So I told her.

"It was hard to do. There was a lot of that over that period, ya know, I suppose I spent a lot of time telling people, friends and different people connected to Billy. I suppose I took that responsibility on."

The conversations drained him, but it was something to do for Billy during a time in which he could do nothing else.

"That was a lot of it," Ronan says. "I suppose he knew a lot of people from a lot of places that you wouldn't always have contact with. We did go through his address book, contact people, but for a while after, you'd get someone who showed up at the hostel looking for him. It's a hard thing to do. At the same time, when you look back at it, you know, it's quite a privilege to be the person in that position, that kind of way, like. I look back on that period and it was incredibly sad, but I look back on it quite warmly in some ways."

Over the weeks until Billy's body returned home, there was much traffic at the hostel. "People were arriving all the time," Ronan says. "People who were close to him and connected. We spent time in the hostel. I don't know, it was just like a big long wake, I suppose, do ya know? Richie was there all the time, Mags was there, Jennifer. Emma was in Australia, she had to come home. But, yeah, it was just really mourning and grieving and stuff like that. The weeks were all over the place."

The body was flown to Dublin. Several cars made the eighty-eight mile journey from Dingle north to Limerick to meet the body there. The family asked Ronan to accompany the body home by riding in the hearse. Though he acknowledges the invitation spoke to his relationship with Billy, the reality of the trip wasn't the highly emotional experience he imagined.

"It wasn't how it should have been, I don't think," Ronan says. "It was kind of funny, like. The driver, so, he's not caught up in the enormity of it. So he was chatting me with me a lot." Ronan stops to laugh. "Part of me didn't want to talk. I wanted to spend that time with Billy. And (the driver) was driving perhaps a bit too fast — wasn't speeding but I think maybe on the main road some of the convoy found it hard to keep pace. So even though it was an experience, it wasn't quite the deep experience I thought it could be. I mean, like, I say that in the hearse journey, your man was talking so there was a few moments of quiet when I tried to remove myself from him, focus on the hearse, but, yeah, mostly it wasn't the time."

Upon the cars' arrival at the hostel, a low whistle played as the casket was set on the kitchen table. Ronan stayed up most of the night. "We had a wake for Billy," he says. "It wasn't quite a traditional wake because of the week we'd waited, but I supposed there were lots of people around, waiting for him to come back. There were a few drinks, a few songs, things like that."

A favorite tune of Billy's was Tom Waits's "Back in the Good Old World", in which Waits' bottom-of-the-barrel voice increases in passion, the clip-clop of a circus band behind him as he sings the point of view of a man no longer in this life and looking back wistfully.

"Me and Billy were huge Tom Waits fans, like," Ronan says. "Another connection we had. At that time we were kind of fanatical. He was the main artist, we used to play him a lot in the hostel."

At the wake, Galway singer/songwriter Tony Small offered the Waits tune.

"It's quite, I suppose, appropriate," Ronan says. "Tony had learned that song beforehand, played it out in the pub. It was probably the most poignant song of the occasion. Other songs were sung, a coupla fellas had a few drinks, wanted to sing all night. Those songs didn't mean a lot to me. But Tony's song did."

Ronan spent part of the night writing what he'd say at the funeral.

"I wanted some time on my own. I stayed up with the casket on my own and just, I suppose, to spend time with on my own with him. I wrote my speech then."

That night, the casket wasn't a casket, he says.

"It was kind of strange because you didn't see his body. So what I tried to do was picture him physically. I could only picture him in sections. I could visualize his feet, I could visualize different parts, but I couldn't visualize him as a whole person. At that time, I would have had not many deaths close to me at that stage. I'd an aunty who died, a grandfather who died, stuff like that. I suppose they would have been waked in their house, but the casket would have been open, you would have seen them. At the time, a part of me thought you really need to see the person to get some finality on it. It's a different point of view when you do see a dead person — they don't look like themselves. They look dead." He laughs. "So when you don't see a person, your last image isn't them inside a casket, dead. Your image of them is as alive, which is kind of, I guess, nicer to have. Wakes are obviously there for a reason. Maybe it is to give you that finality but I think when someone as close as that to you dies, finality comes over years. I don't think you could physically take on board what happened. Your body wouldn't be able to cope with it. You'd just wind up and die yourself if the reality of it hits you in one go."

The mention of the physical, rather than the spiritual, reflects another thing Ronan and Billy shared: "Exactly the same belief in religion and the afterlife and all. We both thought it was the biggest load of horseshit ever."

Ronan was raised Catholic. "He wasn't," Ronan says of Billy. "They didn't do any religion, really. We weren't from a similar background in that sense. He would have had his anti-Catholic religion issues and feelings partly because people tried to force it on him. He was different in that way from other kids in school. He believed just live in the here and now."

In the here and now following Billy's burial, "living and coping without him was a process," Ronan says. "It was very hard, like, I mean very hard for I suppose a year and a half. There were different stages of it. Very gray days, I suppose, for a good while, do ya know? There were other people around Dingle our age who were very good to me, looking back. Some have become really close friends of mine. At the time I just kinda felt like I was a dark cloud, I really felt like they were just being polite. But at the same time, they just wanted to be, because I was just carrying misery around, so you know it was one of those times of real anguish. I suppose one of the things I remember about it is being up at the graveyard, like, in the weeks after the burial. I remember looking back at the hills and they looked alive, do ya know? They looked individual, existing sort of as almost creature-beings out there. There was something more to them that I could see through different eyes. It was almost like something you'd see coming down on acid, but it was kind of funny because it felt to me like a kind of religious or sort of a divine kind of thing was trying to get into my head — but I wasn't gonna let it in. I felt to let it in would be a kind of a betrayal to what me and Billy believed." He pauses, adds rather quickly, "But that stuff passed.

"I did probably develop a few more contradictions that kind of way, but I didn't get religion. I used to go and talk to Billy a lot. Maybe once a week. I used to go when I needed to go talk about something, or when I was getting really down. It used to help me. I think the kind of contradiction is even though I didn't believe he was there, I don't believe he was there, I don't believe he can affect things, I still went there and it still felt like it did something. I still felt like something happened. I still have that contradiction in me. Maybe I'm just lazy about exploring things and I don't want to upset my equilibrium." He smiles. "Just go about my way. I suppose some people would look on me with sympathy when I tell them I don't believe in the afterlife, I don't believe in that stuff a'tall. When you lose someone, you don't think you will see them again. But from my point of voice, I think that my way of looking at things can be a lot more clear in a sense that you don't, you're not hanging around waiting for someday. You take what you have and I suppose, from Billy's point of view, you're gone."

A family occupying the next table loudly catches up on the day, but it's not the noise that makes it hard for Ronan to fathom his current feelings about Billy's death.

"It's hard to know where it all sits with me now," he says. "It is quite a long time. It doesn't impact on my life, do ya know, very much. Every now and then for a small spell it does impact on my life and I do still occasionally shed a tear, do ya know, for him. I haven't been to the grave in a long, long time. I was up there for his anniversary last year, tenth anniversary.

So more than a year ago. It's not something that enters my head to do. I'm sure there will be the occasion when it will, when I'm really down, but it's not something I do or something I feel like I need."

Not unlike the case with Mags, Ronan's grieving took him on the road.

"Again, I suppose I did it on my own in a lot of ways. I did drink quite heavily throughout my twenties, there definitely was a spell I would have drunk quite heavier. One of the things I did was I took off and went traveling. I went to visit friends. I went to Canada. I felt quite — because I was around all of Billy's family — there was an element at the time, do ya know, a heavy weight. They looked to me, kind of as a substitute in a way, or kind of as a window into Billy. They saw me as his closest friend, they saw I would have had similarities, or insight of Billy that they wouldn't have been privy to. Even though, do ya know, I needed them and I needed and loved the fact that I was close to him, and I needed them and there was definitely a symbiotic relationship, at the same time I did feel like, OK, I have to get away and do my own thing and own grieving away from there. So I decided to take off. I traveled, was gone maybe a month and a half. I went to Donegal. So, yeah, it wouldn't have been the biggest trip of my life. I went to visit a girl I knew in Montreal and I went to visit a fella Billy and me knew and met in Australia, in Halifax, and went with him to visit his family in Winnipeg."

Home now is West Kerry, despite Ronan's initially thinking that Dingle was a temporary thing. He'd left the area in 2001 to travel with a girlfriend, returned to live with a brother and sister north of Dublin, worked, did postgrad at Senior College Dun Laoghaire there. Made a visit to Dingle.

"When I left Dingle, I didn't know, didn't feel I was part of the people. So when I came back that time, I got a real sense that I was part of this place. I spent the postgrad year wracking my head, trying to work out, didn't want to live in Dublin, looking for a few jobs and trying to figure out what I was going to do, and I really got this feeling, OK, I do belong here and am part of people's lives here. I did mean something to people. I made the decision, I knew where I wanted to live. I suppose I had to leave a place in order to know where I wanted to live."

Ronan now works at a shelter in Tralee and has married a woman who is best friends with the woman who was Billy's girlfriend at the time of his death.

"So they way back would have been kind of plotting to fix me and Fiona up. Years later, we're together," he smiles.

Some might say Billy is at work getting people together, but not Ronan.

"In your head, he had his life, and life is over. You can have your memories. He's not floating around doing magical things," he says. "If Billy was around now, I'd thank him. In dying he's made me, kinda turned me into a man in a lot of ways. A more independent person. Before he died I sort of felt, do ya know, completely dependent on him. So after he died he wasn't there anymore. There was a journey there. When I kind of came out the other side I kind of came out a stronger, more independent person. I suppose in sort of a fucked up way I'm sort of grateful to him for that. Another one of my contradictions, I suppose. 'Dying was nearly the greatest thing you can do for me. . .' Would I have turned out the same way, I can't tell. But it seems like when he died, not that he did that for my benefit, but it kind of benefitted me as a person, that I was able to develop into this person. Stuff that used to get me doesn't get me. I learned to grow up, cope with those things, deal with those things. I'm now a capable, independent person because of that. So because I've changed a lot as a person, maybe as a result of him dying."

TEN

Florence Rossignol met Billy through his father. Through an invitation to step aboard a boat headed into Dingle Harbor for a glimpse of Fungie the dolphin. Richie Riordan didn't know that the young French tourist often seen hanging around the dock already was well acquainted with Fungie, that she swam with him many mornings in the harbor before the sound of boat engines caused him to swim to deeper waters. Florence told Richie she didn't need to pay to go on a boat to see Fungie. Richie said she should hop aboard anyhow.

She did. Aboard the boat where seventeen-year-old Billy Riordan worked.

This was the summer of 1990. Twenty-one-year-old Florence Rossignol was on her first trip to Ireland, a place that had interested her since childhood. She was studying in England at the time and had talked a friend into hitchhiking around Ireland. "A man left us in Dingle, so we were here," is how she describes her arrival. No plan, no goal, the town was just where she was deposited.

She often spent time on the docks at the base of the town, and eventually became a frequent guest on the dolphin tours, after hours walking up to *An Droichead Beag* with the crew for pints and music. "But I was more talking with Richie," Florence notes. "Billy was very young and I was older than him, so I was not close to him that much."

Florence can see Billy working on the boat, "doing the ropes," but her clearer pictures are from the following summer, when she and a friend accepted Richie's offer of summer jobs in the hostel he'd just created in the family home. "I lived in the hostel, we had the kind of people who live in the hostel, and friends of Richie, fishermen and things, and we liked having dinner every night together," she says. "I'd go out with them and their friends. Eventually I'd be with Billy."

She recalls that unexpected start, and the subsequent three-and-a-half-year relationship, over tea in Benners. Silverware clangs again in the background, but now is accompanied by flutes from the classical music track playing. Florence is seated not far from where Ronan told the story of his relationship with Billy earlier in the week. Her table is set before a stained-glass window, and the midday sun throws colors onto Florence, whose surname, to many the name of a ski company, means nightingale.

Billy was only her third boyfriend, and was the first with whom she lived, though initially the cohabitation at university was a challenge. "The first year was kind of different because we were from different cultures and it's these Irish young people, they were all living the day-to-day kind of thing, they drove me crazy," she says. "I don't know, it was very different from what I had known before, so the first year, it was hard . . . so much different from my previous studies in France. And he was trying to explain how it was for him. It was his first year studying and being out of Dingle and all that. For me, I had already left my mum's place two years back and had my own flat, was sharing as well with other girls in Brittany, so living with somebody, you have to find a balance anyway."

Laughter got Billy and Florence through and beyond. It

was, she says, what brought them together in the first place. "I think we were laughing a lot together. When you spend time together and you get along well and you have a bit of a laugh, I don't think there is any other explanation. First of all, he was good looking."

She smiles recalling images of Billy over the years, with hair long or short. Her preferred hairstyle for him? "I liked him all the time, so that made no difference," she says.

"He was a very kind person. Very careful, especially when you're a foreigner, like me. He was very kind to tourists. He would be good to a foreigner, to not make you feel apart. He was a well-balanced guy. Easygoing, curious about everything, so that's it."

As she remembers Billy two decades later, it's clear from the slower pace of her words and the tears in her eyes that the effect Billy had on Florence was large, and remains so.

"He made me feel comfortable with myself because I was like many young ladies, young girls or how you call it," Florence begins. "I was full of 'I don't like this or I don't like that about my body' and he actually was very important, made me feel comfortable with my body. Because, I suppose, when you love somebody, you want them to love themselves as well."

And you might hope they'd share your interests.

"Between his travels, he was telling me all about them, and he was the only one who made me realize that I really wanted to travel," Florence says, "and told me to not fear being on my own. He made me discover Ireland and the Irish. He was very good company and he was a very good friend, a close friend — it was very important to have somebody to rely on."

Next, Florence asks herself a question. "What did Billy do to me?" Her answer is swift: "He broke my heart."

She stops to wipe a tear. She sighs. She says, "Well, but, ah, everybody has that once in their life."

But most are unable to carry on as close friends after the romance is over, as Billy and Florence did.

"Wherever I was, sometimes he'd showed up — at least twice a year — and we'd go somewhere and have a couple of days together," she says.

She saw him for the last time in January of 1998, before she made a lengthy trip to Asia — solo, thanks to that long-ago encouragement from Billy to not be afraid. She was working in a pub in the County Mayo town of Westport and took a few days off once Billy drove up.

"We stayed in a small hotel, walked around, drove around, went to pubs, talked a lot, we were still good friends," she recalls. "He had his own life and I had my own but it was good to see him now and then."

Their parting was just another one of their partings, except this time it was the last.

"Like every time, he just had to go and I had to go back to work so we went back to Westport and he left." She stops, thinks. "Yeah, he got to see the place I lived, anyway." She stops for a few more moments. "He was always turning up without saying. And he'd send a couple of postcards when he was traveling. He even sent me a ring from Africa, and an ankle chain made out of seeds."

Florence still has the ring, which features a moonstone, said to be inspirational, and a protector on land and at sea. It's a reminder of Billy and his travels, and of the way he used wandering the globe to learn about it.

"I think it was his way of exploring different things, meeting different people. He was very curious of everything," Florence says, "so I think he just would have been bored, here at that age to settle down. It's an Irish thing. Many Irish people do travel a couple years before they settle down."

Is that what she has done? Florence laughs to begin her answer. "That's what actually came between Billy and me. When he wanted to travel, I wanted to complete my studies. I had another year to go. So I stayed and he went."

Florence was in India when Billy died. The trip had been fantastic and great, in her words. She had planned to spend a year there but had contracted a parasitic illness.

"I had two months of being sick and I tried many kinds of cures," she says. "Nothing worked so I had to go back. Actually, I felt sick about the time I learned about Billy's death. I was in India. They deal with death differently than in Europe, so it helped me a lot. I was in Benares and you have the Ganges River and they burn the bodies there. I spent maybe three hours watching that, because it was such a shock to see. When I learned about Billy's death, I was in a place totally different so actually it helped me, not to understand (but) to admit it — well, not to admit, but to cope with it."

Word came via an e-mail from the sister of a good friend. "I don't know who told my mother, I don't know how things went, but my mother didn't want to ruin my trip so she was against telling me," she says. "But my friends were for telling me, so I was told by this person."

That was at the end of March. "Everything was done by then," she says in a low voice, "the funeral, everything."

Florence weeps. Then recalls the only previous loss in her life at the time, her grandfather, when she was six. "I'm usually OK," she says as an apology for losing her composure, and she looks at the still-empty tables to her left and right. "But it's just picturing the moment in my head. I was coming back from the few days in the desert when I found out. I was alone. I packed and I left for another place, where I stayed for two months. I met nice people there at the time that I could talk to, and I was in this small town, which was very colorful — in Rajasthan, very lovely. It's just I felt really bad to have been told that late, but, actually, maybe it's better I didn't go to the funeral."

Like Billy and Ronan, Florence belongs to no religion. She was raised Catholic, had believed in God, but says, "I don't know what — growing up I kind of thought, 'I'm not into that.' I feel like that not only about the Catholic Church but in any monument dedicated to any God. I feel the respect, I respect people that believe, and I have people around me that do believe in God and it's fine with me. I realize everybody finds his own balance but for me the main thing is to respect the other and to be tolerant and try not to argue, and try to talk about all these values. That would be the value of religion. That's the way I live, as well, but I'm not attached to any kind of god in particular. I believe more in nature."

She visits Billy's grave each time she's in Dingle, which she tries to get to every two years. The day before she tells her story, Florence had gone to the cemetery with Jennifer and her new husband, Greg, to leave Jennifer's wedding bouquet at the grave. "That was actually my first time there with people," Florence says. "Usually I go there on my own." She can't sum up the feelings she has during the visits, and she's weeping again. "I sit and talk with him. I go there on my own and just look and see the changes and talk."

She's quiet for a few minutes. The front door of the hotel opens, and closes solidly.

"I don't think you get used to it," Florence then says. "It was a definite limit in time, which is over. It's kind of odd when you die so young — it's so unnatural. There have been a couple of times, like meeting with Ronan and Jenny, or at Richie's place, we don't talk about that but it's not that we never talk about Billy. With Ronan, something will happen and he says, 'It's like in the old times. We're all together. He's not here but he should be here, but he's not here.' It's very kind of odd now and again, but of course most of the time we're here to be together. Special times. Like I remember a few years ago I went up to Jen and Greg's and had a barbecue and singsong in the garden and even she sang a song she wrote for him and said, 'I have to sing that song when we're together.' That was sort of emotional." A few more moments pass and Florence adds, "But most of the time it's OK." And she laughs. A little.

Florence likes West Kerry enough, she says, "but I love my friends, now that's why I'm coming back. The Irish way of life. Laid back. True people."

She's lived in Paris for the past four years and now is with a boyfriend who bought a restaurant in the city. Their life is hectic, she says, and includes her job teaching French to foreign students. "They're from all over the place," she says. "I love it. I don't travel any more so it's kind of a way of keeping in touch with traveling."

She's yet to go to Malawi and hasn't been involved in the Trust. "Because," she explains, "Mags has her own thing and I have my own life now. I think if I was single now, well, if I was single I would probably be living in Ireland anyway, but probably not in Dingle, but I would be involved. I would have gone already to Malawi. But it's just that I went through so many different things and now that I'm settling down I can't say to my man, 'OK, I'm going to Malawi for three months, being a volunteer in Africa.' He would probably understand but you can't just take three months and say 'Bye.' So if I go it will not be as a volunteer, just as a visitor."

She thinks back to when she first met Mags, who then had an intense fear of flying.

"I met her a couple of times after the Trust started and I said 'Now you're fine with the flying.' It's amazing what she's done, really, but at the same time, it's as big as all the loss she had in her life. With the loss of three kids. I'm not a mother but it must be the most dreadful thing to happen to a parent. Not only to the mother but to the father. So I think what she's done is as great as the loss, like, and I think it's the only way to survive, kind of. To have done this, of course in memory of Billy, but also to keep doing something good because how can you survive all that?"

ELEVEN

Anne Clarke has some idea.

Find her on Grays Lane, a few blocks up the hill from Dingle Harbor, in a 1930s attached house down from the new cheese shop near the corner. She'll welcome you into a sitting room cozy with simple furnishings and wood floors. She'll settle onto a couch with a beige printed throw tossed over it, across from a big fire in the stove on a chilly late-summer night, and she'll talk easily, needing no prompts to launch into her thoughts on the woman she's known for many years.

Anne, fifty-three, has operated the Old Forge Internet Café down the road for six years. The work can be slow in the winter, so at that time of year she knits teddy bears to help pass the time. It's a different life from that as restaurant operator, which she was on the Dingle road called the Mall from 2000 to 2006. She looks more the laid-back café operator these days, dressed in flowered long-sleeved jersey, jeans, white sandals bedecked with flowers, a pair of blue ball-shaped earrings swaying beneath her curly brown shoulder-length hair as she speaks rapid-fire about the friend she considers a sister.

"I have lots of friends but nearly only three I'd tell everything to," she starts. "You know Mags won't tell anybody. Be it good news or bad, if you don't want her to. She is a very private person herself, so she knows. I'd do anything for her.

What she's done after Billy died is really amazing. I don't think local people realize what she's done. That's her life."

Mags's and Anne's life as friends began through the local restaurant world in which they worked when Anne moved to Dingle from County Cavan years ago, and it grew through the shared schedules of their children, including Anne's two daughters. At the mention of Mags's visits to Emma and Cillian while in town, Anne says, "It's funny to see Emma with children — I remember all them as children."

Billy stands out in Anne's mind for being what she terms "the most adorable child." She smiles and adds, "I thought he was the most gorgeous little fella. Big blond beautiful hair. I can remember him when he was very small. At Jenny's birthday party — she would have been three, a small little red-haired thing. Billy was this little face with blond, blond page-boy hair. Actually, the last sight of him, he wasn't that much different. Whether he was in his late teens, he wasn't like most fellas that age — he would say hello. I wouldn't know him well. But any memory of him was a nice one."

The same is true for her memories of his parents together. "As a couple, they were fun," Anne recalls. "They would go more to people's houses, wouldn't be in the pub or going to the cinema. They were always working. Mags was a good cook, made the nicest meringues ever."

Anne remembers Mags and Richie running a pair of restaurants at the same time, always on the go. "They were never the kind who did nothing," is how she puts it. "Mags was very family oriented, yet able to work, teaching part-time. Talk about multitasking, she's the expert. She was mad about those kids. She went with them if they wanted to go to dances, went to other children's houses. She was always good with children. I don't remember her being cross with them. They were always happy. That's my recollection of them, that they were happy chappies. And she was always fit. To see her after having babies, in a flat skirt, she didn't seem to have a pick on her. That I can remember, seeing her in the bank, thinking, 'How'd she lose the weight?'"

Credit the aerobics classes Mags led at night and in which Anne enrolled. Her verdict: "She always was faster, way faster than me. She'd be a good person to have on a deserted island with you."

Niamh and Luke had died before Anne ever set foot in town. Somewhere along the way, she overheard someone say of Mags, "She lost two babies," and learned of another facet of her friend's life and story. "It had all happened by the time I came here," she says. "I would hear people talking, hear them say, 'They were so young.' How do you go on after that happens?" When Mags and Richie opened the restaurant, Anne recalls, "People said things like, 'Do you remember, about the children?' And then Jenny had something similar to cot death symptoms. You're like, in the name of God, you're just like, 'Why does one person get all that shit, like?' Maybe it's because she can cope?"

Anne never heard what she'd call gossip regarding the deaths or the family. "And it's a small town," she notes of a place where so many residents are related that, as local hairdresser "Marie The Yank" Galvin says, "If you pinch one person in Dingle the whole town screams."

"If they did gossip, they wouldn't have been doing it around me," Anne says. "But I wouldn't say they gossip around here. And Mags would have kept to herself. The kind of friends she had wouldn't be the kind that would do that." Thinking of a woman she knows whose baby died in the fourth month of pregnancy and who to this day remains depressed,

Anne says, "You see someone like Mags, and she keeps going, says, 'I have other children to look after.'

"She has a good reason to be down but I never see her down. When Billy died, there certainly were reasons, but she never moaned the way we all have a good moan once in a while. She never used to cry. But when we'd talk about Billy, you'd see a tear." Here, Anne wipes one from her right eye and begins to weep softly. "She doesn't explode," she manages to add. "Maybe she does in her own time, but you don't see it. I would be very emotional. I knew she'd be keeping things to herself, but the only way she could cope, she said, one of the ways, was to keep it inside. If she blurted it out, she'd fall apart."

Anne sees the Trust as another kind of glue. "It's probably kept her sane," she says. "It's a calling.

"But even before Billy, she went to Bosnia with food. It wasn't just Billy that made her do it, she just went. They went door to door in Bosnia with bags of food. I remember her coming home. 'God,' she said, 'it was like a bomb dropped, everybody has lost everything.'

"It's a funny old world. Why's it's always Africa that gets that. You just wonder why they get all this shit thrown at them. Floods, et cetera. We might have it rough here in Ireland right now but they're not online wondering what coat they're gonna buy. There is no comparison. They need a hospital, there is no hospital there. Here in Tralee people are lying on hospital trolleys, but at the Cape they don't have a trolley to lie on."

Before the clinic, Anne had heard of Malawi, "but I wouldn't have taken any notice. When we were small we had books for Lenten (donations to Africa). I had a cousin who was a priest in Nigeria. I would have heard bits and pieces of it about him. But, for an ordinary person to take off and do what she did, I don't know. I remember thinking, 'She'll do it and she'll set her mind to it.' I was amazed."

Though a staunch supporter, Anne initially was surprised by the local response.

"I was amazed so many local people wanted to help. So many volunteers, it was no trouble to find them," she says. And that fact, Anne adds, is all the more amazing "when you realize there are so many Mags out there. So many charities needing helping hands." The deciding factor in why someone might give their euros to her friend? "Mags is special and they know that," she says quickly and simply.

Anne's sister Martina died of bone cancer one year before Billy's death. She was thirty-seven.

"Mags was a great support," she says. "Now, she wouldn't have been the big weepy weepy — you don't need that when you're weeping yourself. She was there, strong. She knew Martina."

She follows that with a story very fresh in her heart: when Anne's father died the previous May, Mags happened to be in Ireland and drove five and a half hours north to County Cavan to pay her respects, then turned around and drove back to Dingle. "I certainly didn't expect her to be there," Anne says. "My father was an old man. In his ninety-first year. Her time back (in Ireland) is fleeting. But there's no point in telling her 'Don't come.' My sisters had heard me talking about her, and they met her for the first time after the funeral. They were like, 'This woman, is she for real?'"

Because Mags is that real, Anne, who despises the act of fundraising, has been raising contributions for her participation in the upcoming Dingle half marathon to benefit the Trust. "I hate asking for money," she laughs. "I said, 'This year I'll do it for Billy. Even if I get only a few euro.' A friend collected at work and got 170. Mags is so delighted with anything."

Especially with times so tough in Ireland, and not looking to improve very soon.

"It's harder here but the Irish are great for giving," says Anne, who adds that 12 million euro recently were collected in Ireland for aid in Somalia. "Isn't it amazing? That people can do that at a time like this? Some say we should keep our money at home, but no matter how bad we have it here, it isn't anywhere as bad as it is in Africa. Our experience is so way above what they have there, we can't imagine."

When Mags first returned from Africa, Anne took in all the stories. "She'd say, 'So many people are dead.' Then, twenty died this next time she went. There was nobody there to give a feck whether they lived or died. As (the trips) went on, less people were dying. It was great to see progress."

Anne would like to make the trip to Cape Maclear herself, if only to see where Mags spends so much of her time. Those spans keep them out of direct touch, but it's a friendship that easily picks up where it leaves off. When Mags is back, the two go out for Chinese. "I tell her, 'I can see you're busy,'" Anne says, "but we try to get one meal when she comes." She looks for Mags's car at the house when she passes, even if she knows her friend is on another continent. They e-mail "now and again," with Mags always warning her not to expect a reply for a while, and Anne understanding the challenges of Mags's schedule and Internet access. "I ring her the odd time," Anne says. "It's not that we'd be in touch all the time. But I'd do my best for her."

Anne last saw Billy at Benners Hotel on St. Stephen's Day, the day after Christmas of 1998. He was celebrating the holiday on which "wren boys" clad traditionally in straw — or sometimes more modern dress (including actual dresses) — parade. She can't remember the exact outfit Billy had donned but is pretty certain it was "a dress or a skirt or some women's clothes. I still have visions of him coming to talk when he was passing by. We had a bit of a laugh and then he went."

Her expression falls. She was working in Ventry when word about Billy began circulating one day the following February. "He was missing for a day," she recalls. One of the girls I worked with said, 'Billy Riordan is missing.'" Anne never believes a rumor until the person involved confirms it. After hearing the news about Billy, she says, "That I even went to (Mags's) house says something, that I knew it was true. Even before I drove up I knew it was not good news. All the cars at her house. I knew he was gone. She had always had a feeling she'd lose another one. She'd say, 'I always had a feeling one more would die, I just don't know which one.' How awful must that be?"

Anne gets up and sets another peat briquette on the fire.

"It seems so cruel, to take one away when he's just a baby, the other when he's just becoming a man," she says after settling back on the couch. "But who knows? We don't know the answer. I hope that comes one day. Mags is a survivor. I hope her reward is in heaven."

Billy would approve of Mags's work, Anne believes. But she asks, "When she's gone, who will do it? All that takes time." She remembers trying to make several phone calls for the Trust as a favor to Mags. "I was trying to get somebody by phone and I was thinking, 'Mother of God, what a hassle. How does she find the time?' I was feeling guilty.

"I still think there are people who don't fully appreciate the lives she's saved and differences she's made to those lives. You see people on the telly walking with their kids for days, talking about Somalia, well, she knows how Africa is. She has knowledge of the third world. She's always telling stories about all the bureaucracies. How do you put up with that? I don't know how this travel doesn't wreck her head. She doesn't even like flying. But hold a run or a cake sale and collect 100 or 200 euro and she can do so much with that. Give 200 euro to someone here and what would they do with it? She spends so little on herself."

Anne goes to Billy's grave the five or six times a year she visits Milltown Cemetery.

"The stone is lovely," she says. "I don't know it means a lot to them, with no formal religion, but they have the bones. If you don't have that, what do you have?" She looks the listener in the eye, as if an answer might be at the ready. "Mags would-n't be a Catholic dragging all the kids to Mass, but would be a spiritual person. That keeps her going as well, I sometimes think."

When Mags is in Dingle, Anne carefully assesses her health and stamina. Her current opinion is that her friend looks well, as she told Mags herself a few nights prior to this interview. Mags's response: "Yes, after the malaria."

"I said, 'Did you have malaria?'" Anne gasps. "'Yeah,' she says." Then Anne shrugs, "Well, she looks good."

"Mags is a person who makes it certainly not about her. Hers is not an act. There's no messing, no putting on for show. She has no time for that shit. A couple years ago, she rang the radio to say the clinic needed bedclothes and towels. She put an ad on Kerry radio and got a van and the two of us went into Tralee. We went around collecting donations. She knew exactly where we were going. I'd be slow organizing. I'd be (phoning), 'I'm on Grays Lane — where are you?' She's just off and running. They were just responding with donations. No rubbish. People were really good. I was amazed out and out.

"To Mags, there isn't any problem that can't be sorted. She can do most things she needs to do. But — how long can you actually keep doing something like that? I would like to win the lotto, give her a million to hire somebody."

Anne stops, considers the Trust as it would be then, without Mags at the helm.

"But what job would they do? Who'd want to up sticks, leave home, and would they do better? They'd have to have the passion. Mags has the passion. It'll be 'Mags for President' next time. But she'd be feckin' wasted up in that place."

TWELVE

Ethiopia.

Ethiopia is in Africa, the people there are dying because they have no food or water. Snow and rain hasn't fallen for six years there. Plants didn't grow. Other countries are giving the food clothes and money to buy them. Three thousand five hundred thirty pounds were collected on Gay Byrne's show. And this school has collected 400 pounds.

Line by line, former school principal John Russell translates from Irish this essay written by a long-ago student. One who back in the early '80s in his Irish-language school went by Liam O'Riordan, the name at the top of the assignment to write about a country.

"It would be around 1985, I'd say," John guesses. "That's when Ethiopia was, wasn't it? The thing for Live Aid? That must have been '85. I'd forgotten we'd collected 400 pounds. Ireland was the first country to give money to them. That was Billy, he would love to watch television and learn about things like that."

He reads on, tries to figure out a word — "Oh, government. He says the government in Ethiopia is saying the people are not as badly off as they make out. That's because they don't want to give them money." He sets the paper down. "So there's that one. About sort of a version of what his mother is doing."

172

On this morning in September of 2011, a line of children from the thirty-four-pupil school passes outside the window of the classroom in Ballyhea primary school, where John Russell sits in a child-sized chair, one in a circle of eleven around a table. He recalls Billy Riordan as one of the twenty-seven students, ages nine to twelve, he once taught in this very space, the old section of the renovated schoolhouse founded in 1877 and the oldest national school in West Kerry. The days ran from 8:30 to 3:00 p.m., September through May. The curriculum was totally in Irish, hence the need for Russell to translate from the paper titled *An Ethiopia.*

"Everything was in Irish," he says, "as soon as they went outside the gate, or when they went around the corner, it was English. But when they were here, it was Irish. Billy'd had no problem settling in, like. His Irish was quite good."

The courses were what John calls the usual. "'Twas maths, English, Irish, history. History, geography, religion was a big part of it at the time. A bit of drama when we had the time, a bit of art when we had time, but it was hard to make time for all these things. You had to do English and Irish — those were the important ones. The other ones were bonuses."

As if on cue, a flute from the bonus category of music class plays from another room, and the theme from *Popeye the Sailor Man* echoes down the hall decorated with eleven class photos from over the years. Some of the groups of a dozen or so kids include Billy, with Jennifer in others; Emma did not attend here. The tune makes John smile, as do the memories the building holds for him. He's sixty-one. Retired in 2004 after being at the school since 1971. "A fair bit, all right," he notes. His least favorite part of the job was paperwork. "An awful lot of paperwork," he clarifies. "There were just two teachers, but all the paperwork fell to me." The next line is quickly added: "But I liked it — I loved teaching."

His time now is given to gardening, travel, to golf on Sundays. He lives just down the road from the schoolhouse, in a home in the village of Fionach that still holds some of the related papers.

"I burned everything I was finished with," he says, then motions to a small stack topped with the *An Ethiopia* essay. "I put these in an envelope to give to Mags."

He flips through. There's an essay about a dream, another with a title translating to "In Charge of the House." John notes the comments he wrote alongside the work: *"go mall"* — "That's good" — and *"cueesh"* — "That's fair." He translates another piece, done in response to an assignment to write about a gift.

> *One Christmas myself and my mom went into the bike shop looking at bikes. I saw a BSA Javelin and said it was lovely. The man took it out and i sat on it. It was too big for me. The man took another bike out, the same as that one but was a little bit smaller. i sat on it, 'twas the right height. Mom said, "Is that the one you want?" i said, "It is."*

John smiles again, then shakes his head in mild exasperation, as if the piece in his hand were written for an assignment due this morning.

"I don't know how many times I told him in English — a little *i* with dot on it is for the little *i* — I told him about a hundred times about the capitol *I*."

Though John can't remember any actual conversations about travel with the boy he says "got on good with everybody," he saw hints of an interest in the wider world.

"It must have been evident because, looking back now, we did English, Irish, maths, those would be the important ones, but he was never interested in those. He wanted to be learning about different things. There would have been a globe here, a map of the world, as well. You probably could see him there, young, looking at Ethiopia."

Billy Riordan's mother is usually 8,702 miles southwest of that schoolhouse, but she often visits the ones in her African hometown. Frequent topics of discussion in The Gap's office, on her porch, in the ambulance as she drives from one errand to the next appointment, are the health and education of the youngest members of Chembe Village, Cape Maclear. The woman who initially thought she'd honor Billy's memory by building a school, still continues to hold that thought. For now, she tries to help young students via a bilharzia and worming treatment that will keep them well enough to be studying, and through sponsorships for those who cannot afford secondary school or college.

Neither effort is without its challenges.

The Billy Riordan Memorial Clinic has given bilharzia and worming treatments at the primary school every April and November since 2006. Praziquantel tablets are administered at the primary school, given along with rolls and an orange drink — necessary because the medicine must be taken with food. When the ambulance full of four hundred tablets, four hundred pieces of bread, enough orange drink for four hundred, and half a dozen volunteers arrived on the school grounds one morning in the middle of October, 2010, it was greeted by throngs of children running dangerously close to the vehicle, knowing that on this day, aside from anything else that would be happening, they'd get bread and orange drink.

They mobbed the vehicle, barely permitting the volunteers to exit the doors. Hands held forth grimy and ripped copybooks in which rows of alphabet letters and sums had been practiced, and English phrases ("Hello!" "Who are you?") were repeated. Some climbed the ambulance tires to write in the dust on the windows; others tried to peel off the lettering on the side, or to get a look at the goods inside. Four hundred children alone are in the first year at the Cape's primary school, established in 1875 and at which nine teachers attempt to instruct two thousand students, an exercise Mags says amounts to little more than crowd control. Of the entire student body, one in five boys will complete primary school. One in seven girls.

Half an hour after the ambulance arrives, it has to leave. Mags, who'd managed to wriggle through the sea of kids and get to the principal's office to check in, was told there that the government this season will provide the same medication and this season will be paying each teacher 500 kwacha for interruption of the workday. Over the subsequent few days, the clinic will be informed that the fee the government allegedly will be paying has risen to 1,500 per teacher. Finally, the clinic will be invited to administer the drugs, but is told the Trust will have to pay what the government has promised.

Mags is furious about the scam in progress and about the money wasted on supplies. Far too many medications purchased, and way too much bread and drinks, which now will go to the families of staffers as the power has cut out again, rendering the freezer useless and meaning the bread will only get stale if it can't be frozen. In The Gap's dining area, she is shaking her head. "We're a clinic. We can't give the allowance, and *quasi* is expensive."

"Isn't it hilarious?" Elaine asks from a seat nearby. "Since yesterday, more of an allowance." She thinks for a few seconds. "We do two thousand tablets at a time?"

"One thousand nine hundred and something," Mags corrects as she eats a slice of toast. She knows nearly the exact number of tablets prescribed, one per fifteen kilos of weight. They're large and smelly, and the recipients often try to drop or hide them. "As the years go by," Mags says, "they're getting more savvy."

"Little kids are good," Elaine adds. "Tots just swallow the tablets."

Adults are given the tablets only if they present with symptoms: blood in urine, trouble passing urine, fatigue. Mags once had bilharzia for two months; it was gone after two days of treatments, she says.

That story prompts Sheila, sitting nearby, to recall the volunteer who had a worm in her middle: "We'd watch it migrate from one side of her belly to the other."

"If you were to think of all the things you were going to get here," Mags starts, and Sheila talks about taking worming medicine as a child. That gets Mags remembering her brother Frank's childhood ability to bite worms in half on a dare. "It was his party piece," she says. "He's now a dentist."

While a woman tosses a stack of dishes into the lake, Mags dials a government contact.

"Yeah, no, we don't pay at all, we're a charity," she says into the phone, using a voice that's not sharp but is nearing that level. "We can't pay teachers. It's not in our remit. This is done on a regular basis. The health of children at school is put at risk by the teachers who are doing this. If parents have a problem, that is the only issue."

And it's only one of many facing the village children. For the minority that does complete primary school, secondary school awaits only at a cost. To help where it can, the Trust oversees sponsorships for students going on to second-and third-level educational institutions in Malawi. At the University of Malawi, sponsored students have pursued degrees in majors including nursing, health services, agricultural economics and journalism.

A meeting on the latest sponsorship issues is scheduled for this evening on Mags's porch. She's had a headache and is just up from a nap, ready to tackle a problem regarding a sponsored student. Wearing a black tank top, salmon capris and sandals, she carries in a plate of crackers and cheese and takes a seat on a black pillow. Steve and Dave arrive and, maybe ten minutes later, the power goes out.

"Story time," Steve begins as the voices of children at play carry from the beach below.

The main issue is a sixteen-year-old a Trust donor is sponsoring at Lilongwe Secondary School. He's back in the village, and stood on the beach this afternoon with Mags, telling her at length that he was feeling ill, dizzy, doesn't like the school's Muslim bent, claims the meat served there is uncooked.

"He wants to go elsewhere and he's only been there a week," Mags says. "The sponsor paid 25,000 for the term."

"It could either be treated at the health center," Steve says, "or it could be bullshit from him."

"Probably him," says Mags.

"I'm worrying about the students he's teaming up with," Steve says, "I'm being a parent here, am I not?" He laughs.

Dave, sensing something in what's not being said, asks, "Do you want to trust him?"

"It sounds awful to say, but you can't," Mags says. "You have to double-check, triple-check, get receipts to find if the student is double-dipping." She gestures her hand toward the coffee table, where two receipts from the school rest, proof that the sponsor's money had ended up in the right hands, those of the school's administration.

In a country where sponsored students receive checks directly from donors, then are responsible for paying a school, it's possible a student could be paid for by multiple donors, through multiple charitable organizations. Or could be accepting funds without ever setting foot in a classroom. Mags will be tough with anyone found to be mishandling funds. When one student never attended school but kept a donor's money, she told him she wanted the funds returned or she'd pull out of the school the five or six remaining Trust-sponsored students.

"The kids in the village were weeping and wailing," she remembers. "I said, 'You're all part of the school community, you all bear responsibility.' The chief finally paid, but as part of it wanted his nephew's grad school paid for. I said, 'I don't sponsor postgrad.' That's the story."

"We're talking about kids throwing opportunities away. It's like having teenagers myself," Steve says, then smiles widely.

"Why do we pay for these students," Mags states rather than asks. "What does that have to do with the Trust and clinic? It's capacity building and development. You're never going to build if there's no education."

And there won't be, in so many cases, without that outside help, far from a strange concept in a country where up to 40 percent of the national budget is funded by those Western donors.

"If Malawi would realize they don't have natural resources, but they have people, people who are clever, intelligent," Mags starts, then stops. In a few seconds she continues, "It's like Ireland in the '60s. The nuns and priests said, 'We'll educate you.' We want to help. (Local children are) stuck in a cycle. They can't read, can't write."

The need for a better secondary school education is evident even from one visit to the school at the Cape, located near the

Golden Sands Resort and the National Park entrance, monitored today by a uniformed man and woman who sit in the shade. Four baboons rest nearby, along with three of their babies. Mags speaks again the warning to never, ever come between one of those mothers and one of those babies.

The school is three low brick buildings shaded by a few sparse trees, its windows open to the elements. Electricity or plumbing are nonexistent. Yet, if you want to learn, and you've actually gotten through primary school, it's where you want to go next. Students who've performed well in exams and are selected by the government to attend secondary school study between 7:30 a.m. and 1:30 p.m., paying 2,000 kwacha for each of the three annual terms. Those who are not selected attend in the afternoon and are charged 2,300 per term.

Nine teachers comprise the faculty. In the morning, 153 students study. In the afternoon arrive approximately 120 students not selected by the government. Attendance wavers, depending on family obligations including help at harvest time. Mags would like to build a primary school on this site, in the big open area in front of the secondary school buildings. Facilities could be shared between the two schools, she says, and a feeling of community. Right now, the primary and secondary schools are a good mile apart.

"How is your life now?" the principal asks from a classroom doorway.

Mags responds to his greeting by saying she's pleased, including to see furniture at the school. The pieces in the classroom where he stands are shabby, but they are better than nothing, which was the case last time she stopped by. She greets the three instructors there, all males. Each is seated at a different one of the seven student-sized wooden desks, grading papers. They wear pressed shirts, ties, creased trousers, square-toed dress shoes. A poster titled "Mammals of Malawi Grazers" and a calendar from Christian Literature Action in Malawi are the wall decorations. Shelves hold a mishmash of junk, including two battered soccer balls and a case for a manual typewriter.

A pot of food — lunch for the faculty — its lid topped by a cup, sits on the floor in the middle of the room.

The principal, in black pin-striped jacket, blue-and-white shirt untucked from his gray trousers, says he's happy with the books on history, geography and social studies received from an Irish charity with which Mags is connected.

"I will definitely see if I could get another donation in another six months," Mags says. Then she asks about a particular student sponsored via the trust.

"Teacher says he is a very good student," the principal says, "performing well in class."

Mags nods. "Good," she says. "The people paying the fees want to know."

THIRTEEN

The broken bridge stretching in front of her is such a metaphor for Mags's journey in life, not just for this one to the city of Blantyre, that it seems put there by a Hollywood set designer.

It's not much wider than a railroad track, but that's not out of the ordinary here in the middle of the back of nowhere. More than the width, though Mags is more concerned about the planks it's made of. They're buckled in some places, snapped in others. She peers down. The floor of the ravine, fifteen or so feet beneath the bridge, looks that much farther below from her driver's seat in the Land Cruiser perched at the start of the span. As she does with most everything else, she finds another way to keep moving forward.

This time, it's by going back a bit.

She glances around. Behind the vehicle, four bicyclists leave the road and veer into the bush to the left. Mags throws the Land Cruiser in reverse, then shifts to follow them. Up a rise, down a hill and across a makeshift bridge, this one with gaps between the planks, yet appearing safer. Then she's over and past the first and probably the easiest of the roadblocks she'll face on this overnight errand trip to the city of Blantyre.

Mags and/or Steve make this journey every month or two. Today both of them have set out from the Cape with an arm-long shopping and to-do list that includes purchasing pharmaceuticals, dog food, bug bomb and Pantene, and navigating

182

extensive bureaucracy even to get a spare key cut. The reward: an overnight in a relatively modern place, though the lodging most likely won't be five-star.

Rise with Mags for the 7:00 a.m. departure of such a trip, and the expected image of a charity head once again is challenged. She won't be dining in a boardroom, but picking at an egg roll and sipping from a bottle of Coke at a hole-in-the-wall Chinese eatery curiously playing the same rotation of Garth Brooks at top volume. She won't be blindly signing purchase orders for bulk supplies, but walking back and forth between the region's two grocery stores of any size to check toilet paper rolls for price and number of sheets. She won't be lounging in some private jet, but seated at the wheel of her steed, motoring across an ancient and often lunar-looking landscape, down a dirt road, toward the morning's first destination, the home of the area's Chief Nankumba.

To get there, she follows a road that at times has no edges, is bounded only with endless stretches of rust-colored sand and scraggly brush, and in some places is no wider than the sides of her car, crowded by branches. She's not entirely certain she's headed in the right direction and stops occasionally to ask the rare pedestrian a question that is the chief's name: "Nankumba?"

If the pedestrian doesn't simply look confused, he or she will point down the road. Mags will ask "Five kilometers?" The person carrying a jerry can of water will nod. If she says "Seven kilometers" to the next person, that person will nod. There's a nod for any measure of kilometers she throws out there, but the point is that everyone keeps pointing in the same direction. The point is, she keeps moving. The point is, because of Billy Riordan, Mags Riordan is pulling over to a patch of shade beneath a massive baobab tree in this place so very far from home, leaning out the window and speaking Chichewa, asking directions of a woman dressed in a chitenje that reads "Taking Parliament to the People 21st May 2010."

After a few more such stops, forty minutes into her search, one person points to the right, says the chief's is the first house down there, take a right, look on the left. At the home she finds — modest and brick but palatial compared to the surrounding elevated thatch-roof buildings — the chief's wife steps into the front garden and accepts the letter Mags has written regarding the villager who continues to claim that the land on which the clinic sits is his, land Chief Nankumba's late father granted Mags for the clinic's location. She hops into the ambulance, turns right, then right again, onto the main road, driving on over sand, over rust-toned soil, past villages that appear to be occupied only by goats, others where dozens of people queue in the shade or at boreholes.

The handy *MacMillan Malawi Traveler's Map* in the seat back pocket includes a wildlife chart inviting the traveler to mark the creatures spotted on a journey: rock hyrax, vervet monkey, antbear, klipspringer, black rhino, elephant. None is visible. And only one other vehicle is seen in the next few hours of the four-hour trip, a motorbike far ahead that disappears. Appearing eventually are a few signs of modern life, the first one a billboard:*"Merchants: Start enjoying the benefits of accepting Visa"*

In the passenger seat, the left-hand one in this country where cars travel on the left-hand side of the road, Steve fields texts and flashes and actual phone calls. He receives details about a broken pump at the clinic, an issue to be addressed on this trip. He jots additions to the volunteers' shopping list. All the while, Mags drives past roadside vendors standing next to five-foot-tall burlap-wrapped stacks of charcoal. Veers around the kid standing in the middle of the road and holding a live chicken by its feet, then around the man, also in the center, holding sticks spearing travel snacks of dried birds and mice. In one of the first small towns, police stop each car to check for smuggled items. The steed's green cross on the door designates it as an ambulance, buys it a pass. The police would have found inside nothing but three cases marked "Sabax glucose 5 percent" that, upon opening after the last trip to the city, were long-expired and need to be returned. Along the line of cars delayed by police, men walk to car windows bearing handfuls of tomatoes, shiny purple onions, the latest newspapers, hefty carved candlesticks. Children watch from the roadside, standing barefoot on packed dirt infused with bits of blue plastic bags.

There's a stop for cup of Mzuzu-brand coffee in the Chikondi café, where a soap plays from the elevated television. A man and a woman in bed are visited by the ghost of another woman. Much shrieking ensues. But there is more of a show on the road Mags and Steve head back to after their break. Villages increase in size and traffic and commerce. Open-sided stands are stacked with wooden furniture, hung with legs of meat, pyramided by piles of yams. A truck of bananas is parked along a strip that includes The Style Me in Jesus dress shop, which gets Mags recalling a place called the Pack 'n Go Coffin Shop, and Steve pitching in a favorite, the God Will Answer Telephone Bureau, and its slogan, "You've tried the best, but we're different." Mags stops for a crossing of cattle, moves on, then slows to cross a railroad track. Along the road, anthills stand taller than an NBA star. Beyond, mountains sit huge and dark and rough and wild.

After the three more hours of rather uninterrupted natural landscape, Blantyre just happens. Low, indistinct blocky buildings, packed sidewalks, traffic, smog. There's a shabby and circa-1960s feel to what is the business capital of Malawi and its oldest city, founded in 1876 as a mission station for the Established Church of Scotland and named for the Scottish village birthplace of David Livingstone.

Home to 751,600, Blantyre is the second only to Lilongwe (with 817,300) in being the most populous city in the country. Important commerce flows through the veins of the busy streets, which lead to destinations including the Stock Exchange of Malawi (founded 1998) and Chichiri Mall, the largest shopping destination, complete with the country's only cinema complex. The city is the northwest terminus of the Tete Corridor, which flows from Zimbabwe, into Western Mozambique, and then into Malawi, and once was a popular route for those moving between East Africa and South Africa. Political crises in Mozambique and Zimbabwe over the years led to dangers along the route, but today's might amount to none more frightening than being fined a few dollars for a highway law few have heard of or that exists only in the mind of the officer who flags you down. But the city holds its own fair amount of crime, its haves and the have-nots packed so closely. High cement walls topped by concertina and electric wire delineate many businesses and the homes in wealthy neighborhoods. Only with the permission of watchmen do the sliding gates admit cars.

Mags and Steve will journey only within the city, heading back and forth on their various missions along the main drags of Haile Selassie Road, Glyn Jones Road and Hannover Avenue, which today are choked more than usual due to the president being in town.

"All right, Steve, where'll we start?" There's a feeling of excitement, about seeing how much can be accomplished in the day. Ready with his blue ledger of "First Merchant Bank Limited" checks, which he'll carry throughout the day in a blue Velcro envelope printed with "New Medicines for New Times," Steve consults the list of where some of that money will be spent. The paper in his hand holds a rundown of what volunteers are craving from the big city, including Nali garlic sauce, Pantene Pro V Colour Care shampoo (big bottle), tuna in brine, and a phone that must include a flashlight feature. For The Gap and clinic they'll search for dog food, bleach, toilet rolls. That key needs to be cut, Electricity Supply Company of Malawi (ESCOM) visited, along with the bank, post office, the global health organization PSI, and Skyband.

Chichiri Mall, and its anchor store Shoprite, are first. Mags calls the grocery/department store mix Shopshite, "because they don't have what you want." Maybe so, but compared to Chembe Village's shops — often no more than a plank displaying five bottles of Fanta and a couple bags of sugar or laundry powder — Shoprite looks like Costco. The oddly named Game, another grocery/department store hybrid, is the competition at the other end of the mall, and the middle of the span contains a food court with pizzeria, Italian café, hardware store, phone store, ladies' boutique and shoe shop.

The parking lot is filled with shining SUVs, and the one ambulance from faraway Cape Maclear. The shoppers floating from or to the vehicles mirror the relative opulence of this experience. No chitenjes in this place where business-suited women indeed wear shoes, often stilettos, and men don suits and ties. Clouds of perfume and cologne follow them all. In the parking lot, fathers guide young daughters wearing fun teeny-bopper clothes — shorter flouncy skirts, novelty T-shirts new and from the rack rather than multiply pre-owned and from a distribution by a foreign charity.

A father and daughter pass, the child carrying a grocery bag imprinted with the assurance "You always win at Game."

"This is not the traditional family setting so you will see Dad with his daughter at the shops," Steve says. Due to so much of life in traditional Malawian culture truly being "women's work," he says, "You can count the number of times a dad has come with a child to the clinic."

He talks about those who've moved to the city attempting to duplicate the social groups they would have had in a village, but finding such a different experience here in a much more modern world, one where the shopping center's hardware store is stocked with sacks of food for dogs, animals meant to be no more than pets.

For Ulemu, Lisa and Bo, Steve and Mags consider a powdered brand of food that requires mixing with water, but decide against it.

"They're not that keen on it," says Steve.

"What do they like?" Mags asks.

"They like human food more than anything else."

The Zain store is next, for the phone Elaine has requested, a model containing the flashlight she terms a torch. While there, Mags will purchase an air card for her computer, which makes accessing the Internet easier than via a Skyband card. There's a bit of a wait in line for both, but in no time she and Steve have their purchases and are off to Shoprite, where they start their legendary toilet paper comparisons. Standing before towers of Baby Soft, Rite Brand, Nanas and Softex, they study prices and numbers of sheets. Mags produces the calculator on her phone and does the math. Rite Brand and Baby Soft are determined to be the finalists. After a quick check on prices of rubber cleaning gloves, Mags asks, "Right, shall we go to Game?"

On the sidewalk outside Game, Steve receives another phone call about the clinic's well, which right now is delivering only a trickle. A plumber is expected in the village, but exactly when is not known. As he is caught up on the situation at the clinic, Steve is too long on the line for Mags's liking, so she grabs the shopping cart from him and heads toward the entrance. Steve knows where to find her, and soon he does, in front of the Baby Soft nine-packs.

"These are 1,280," Steve says, reading the price. "That's a better value."

Mags reaches for her phone and calls up the calculator again.

They consider Simple Choice, which should live up to its name, but it's one ply. They settle on the Baby Soft, in the eighteen-roll packs. Then decide to get five ten-packs of that for the clinic, three twelve-packs for The Gap.

"First thing, though," Mags says as they walk to the shampoo shelves, "is to get a system set up where we're not spending wads of money on toilet paper."

Steve agrees but is focusing on shampoo now. He can't find the requested type of Pantene, so he calls Elaine to see if the choice could be altered. He reads patiently and clearly from the selection in front of him: "You've got sheer volume, repair and protect, radiant color or sheer volume." Then, after a pause, says, "OK, right, bye-bye."

The phone rings the second after he ends the call. Steve turns away, comes back to report: "The situation now is we have a clinic with no water. I bet the staff will love that."

On that theme, they head to the plumbing company. It's down the road from the mall, across from a private hospital and next to a Mercedes Benz dealership that hints at a city life-style Steve says few Malawians, like the shoeless woman walking up the sidewalk with a branch of bananas on her head, can afford.

The plumbing company owner is white, paunchy and wears his straight hair a dyed shade of brown. In his South African accent he greets Steve and Mags but right off tells them to return the next day. His plumber actually happens to be arriving at the Cape right now, he announces, and will have a full report tomorrow.

The two head back to the car. Mags doesn't give the expected sigh about having had to negotiate the crowded roads in the extreme heat only to be told to return the next day. She just asks, "What's next, Steve?"

"Should we go to Medi-Surg for sample pots? Vet's for flea stuff, ESCOM?"

Mags has a friend to meet at five. "We'll do Medi-Surg now and vet," she decides as she gets into the driver's seat and rolls the window to ventilate the ambulance.

Medi-Surg is located in a cement white house brightened by a front rose garden. Steve heads inside for specimen pots while Mags walks to the nearby vet supply. Flea preventive and wormer is needed for The Gap's cats, flea preventive for the dogs. When the shoppers again meet, as they do each time they return from an errand, one asks "Sorted?" and the other replies "Sorted!"

Then Mags orders, in a West Kerry accent, "Get out the lisht, biy!"

Steve consults his as the ambulance passes The Miracle Shop, a vendor of secondhand clothing from the United Kingdom. When he's done, he looks out the window at sidewalks overflowing with pedestrians and notes the difference he's seen in Malawians over his few years there. Along with high heels, dresses and perfume are their health status, professions, and the additional weight they carry. They've also fully checked into the online universe. Beneath pink Zain-branded umbrellas reading "It's a wonderful world!" and stationed at most street corners, salespeople in folding chairs sell paper tickets for cell phone minutes. To access the Internet, an account with or card from Skyband is needed. In the wonderfully air-conditioned Skyband office at the base of an office building, Mags asks for permission to purchase cards in bulk. She sells so many to volunteers she should be seen as a provider, she tells the representative, and should receive a provider's discount. The clerk tells her to e-mail that request, rather than state it in person. It will be assessed, Mags is assured.

She just nods. Buys the stack she is allowed then walks out to the ambulance and drives along Haile Selasie Road, past a billboard promoting silk as the best fabric, and to a hotel she knows of down a little alley guarded by a guy in a fake green military uniform complete with beret, who instructs her where to park.

Garth Brooks is playing at top volume in the China Da restaurant, located to the right of the sign pointing to a conference center, at the right, or, to the left, to massages and rooms. Mags loves Garth Brooks. Once went to see him at the O2 arena in Dublin. But even she finds the nonstop Garth a little strange. The exposure is minimal, however. She has that friend to visit and orders only a quick Coke and an egg roll. Steve finishes his meal to the accompaniment of Garth and retires early, the novelty of an air-conditioned bedroom awaiting.

In the morning, Mags whacks through half an hour of emails before coming down to breakfast at 7:30 in black T-shirt and beige pants. She halts at the sight of a spread that's memorable in a bad way: untoasted toast, a lump of fried eggs, unfried sausage, yogurt that's frozen and not to be confused with frozen yogurt, and, rather than real coffee, instant Ricoffy and its "fresh percolated taste."

Steve tries to distract her by narrating the steps needed to use the shower in his room: "You ram the faucet into the wall and water comes out and you step under the bit that sprinkles."

Hacking at her yogurt, Mags comments on what looks to

be another hot day, and on her appreciation of Malawi's climate, especially for someone who hails from a largely grayer one. "Isn't it great to go over every day with blue skies, sun?" she asks. "You don't need three layers of clothes."

The first stop on what indeed is another sunny and baking day is the machine shop that recently worked on the clinic's generator. A bill needs to be paid for that work, and Mags chats with a staffer near a poster touting a Massey Ferguson tractor, something that might also be seen back in Ireland. A woman walks in from the parking lot. Apologizes for the dust out there and everywhere. "We're used to thick mud," Mags says. The shop owner, Mike Mathias, is a Brit who knows his mud and who knows the challenges of his adopted country. He asks about the clinic, how long has it been open now?

"Seven years," Mags says.

"Crikey," Mike gasps, "and you're still smiling?"

Mags tells him about the person whose response to the "Seven years" answer was "Are you bitter and twisted yet?" She'd assured that person, and assures Mike, "I'm not. We're going from strength to strength now."

Like so many structures in this city, Airways Travel is protected behind a concertina-and-electric-wire-topped wall and gate. A gatekeeper materializes when a vehicle approaches or beeps. Here, Mags is allowed access and passes through the gate, snaking the ambulance up a winding driveway to a lovely home on a hill where a built-in pool is a front-lawn feature. The view from its edges is of a dipping, green city valley that includes townships, local parlance for housing projects.

In the ground-level office, Mags meets with her longtime travel agent Shamima Tayub, who was born in England to Indian parents and raised in Malawi. Shamima's office is tidy despite bearing all the usual travel agent *tchotchkes* — statues of Mickey Mouse, Beefeaters, Amsterdam windmills, a Taj Mahal. — and many framed examples of the jigsaw puzzles she does for relaxation. As Shamima consults her computer for Mags's file, Mags sets into her lap her own computer, BRMT once spelled out on the cover in salmon-colored stickers, but the *B* and *R* now missing. The two talk dates and times for her next trip to England and on to Ireland. The costs of each leg are discussed. The Trust will cover Mags's flights related to Trust business; she must pay for any other tickets.

Shamima asks for a returning date.

"That's the burning question, isn't it?" says Mags, who is never certain of her schedule and opens her black diary to check a calendar. She glances at tentative plans for the next few months, including her annual trip to Springfield, Massachusetts, for a Thanksgiving Day "Miles for Malawi" run/walk put on by Billy's Malawi Project USA, a group of supporters who learned of the clinic through Mags's annual visit to the Eastern States Exposition and organized as a nonprofit in 2007. For the two years the run has existed, Mags has made the trip in conjunction with speaking gigs at area Rotary Clubs, ladies' luncheons — whatever the locals can arrange for her — along with trips to see individual donors in the States. She's looking at that calendar now. "I was up at 5:00 a.m.," she tells Shamima, "trying to figure that out. January 17, but you'll probably have to change that."

With the itinerary sort of settled, Mags exits, passing a woman walking up the Airways driveway with a plastic shopping basket of live chickens on her head and one dead bird dangling upside down from her hand.

"What's on the lisht?" she asks Steve, who stayed in the ambulance to make phone calls to suppliers.

"Airways is done, ESCOM is done, I don't want to go to

the pharmacy now, it will sit in the car all day. We'll nearly get finished, go home today? Let's press on and see how we go?"

She drives back downtown, into the busy market-lined streets. Beneath the awnings protecting the sidewalk in front of hardware stores and fabric shops, men sit at sewing machines, stitching away, or awaiting your order for a custom piece made there on the sidewalk. In once-empty lots to the other side of the street, secondhand clothing offered for sale hangs from tree branches. Previously worn shoes are lined up neatly for shopper inspection. A stand for phones is next to one for electronics, and that is next to more footwear, which is next to one offering tote bags, the ones hanging highest decorated with the word PARIS. A man walks the line of traffic, offering wooden spoons for sale. There's no pressure when a driver has no interest.

"The people are lovely," Steve says. "A guy came up to me in the parking lot, I said, 'We're an ambulance, we don't pay parking.' He said, 'Oh, I was only coming to greet you.'"

As she's in the neighborhood, Mags decides to swing by Open Arms, a center for orphaned and abandoned children run by Neville Bevis who, along with his late wife Rosemarie, taught her so much about the Malawian culture." They were my closest friends in Malawi at the start," Mags says. "They gave me my African legs, as I call them."

The agency was founded in 1995 by two women who took in twenty-seven abandoned babies born in a country where ten women die in childbirth daily and where one million children have been orphaned due to HIV and AIDS. In 2000, the Bevises, British nationals living in Malawi, took over the effort that currently cares for one hundred twenty infants and children at locations in both Blantyre and Mangochi. Another three hundred are educated and fed in four separate locations.

At the main building, located off a shaded and rather secluded road not far from the center of the city, Neville is thrilled to greet Mags in the tiny reception area brightened by photographs of residents, including a child named Blessings. Neville is funny, friendly, bold, a spirited talker, eager to explain Open Arms to a visitor, and to stress it "is not an orphanage." While children will be adopted out, certainly, he notes, the difference is stated as "We're returning kids to someone. The mother died and the child was abandoned. Others might have family but might stay for two years and then be returned."

Throughout their time at Open Arms, all residents have a semblance of family. Above each baby's crib is a card noting name, date of birth and "My three mothers are," with space for the names of each shift's nurse. Each "mother" might be assigned seven or eight babies. "We just try to give them mothers when they are growing," says Ennifer, the assistant matron, who's worked at the agency for two years. "When you see the little ones, very tiny, and they grow, you just feel you're doing a great job."

In a room of neat wooden cribs, a toy placed in each, Ennifer stands at that of petite two-month-old Hammiton, whose mother died from complications of his cesarean birth, a common reason for mortality in this country. "They have the father," she says, of Hammiton's family, "but very poor. In our culture, the child belongs to the mother."

So Hammiton is, essentially, an orphan.

A pair of month-old twins, who arrived here weighing 3.3 and 2.9 pounds, share a crib as they await their next feeding. Their Open Arms mother awaits the results of their HIV tests.

Issack, in the next crib, was abandoned the previous week in a trench along a market in a Blantyre township. He is still being assessed. His card reads "I was born on: Unknown."

Richard, his neighbor one crib over, was born two weeks ago, in the road, as his mother made her way to the hospital. He is suffering from sepsis. Grace, in the following crib, roughly the same age, HIV positive and already on ARVs, was abandoned in the hedges along a home, brought to the police and then a hospital. "And then brought to us," Ennifer says.

Twins Tiyese and Joyce were born ten months ago, on Christmas Day. They came to Open Arms the next day, upon the death of their mother, another victim of cesarean complications.

Mothers in Malawi often die just after such a birth, or later the same week. Ennifer blames the ineptness of the government hospitals. "Oh no, it's awful, really dirty," she says. "You are waiting for doctor, you can sit there three hours and no one's been taking your information."

She moves to the crib of Esther, whose twin has died and who is dealing with hydrocephalus. At age one, she is hardly sitting up. Next to her, Osbon, ten months, is being treated for severe anemia.

Ennifer walks outside, to a village hut built in the side yard. As is the case with so many of the village huts Open Arms children move on to, it has a dirt floor and no electricity. As a child is about to be adopted, guardians or parents stay with the child in this hut for three days while the adults learn from staff how to care for the child, and the child gets used to the type of structure that will be his or her future home.

Nearby, tots play in a shaded yard. Hear one of their stories and it's hard not to want to scoop up four or five of them, children representing the main reason much of the world has ever heard about the country of Malawi — because of a pop star who was helpless but to do that scooping.

Madonna's adoptions of Malawians David Banda, in 2006,

and Chifundo "Mercy" James, in 2009, put a spotlight on the country. But Mags has little time for Madonna, saying she makes Malawi look like a shopping center for those seeking children, that anyone can come in and get one or two or three kids without having to observe the prospective parents' residency requirement.

In October of 2006, speaking on the radio via the nationally broadcast Ryan Tubridy Show, Mags called Madonna's adoption of thirteen-month-old Banda a fashion accessory.

"We were there long before Madonna," she told him. "Any exposure is good, but I have a huge problem and huge issues with adopting babies out of Malawi. I think it has given Malawi a bad name, people think Malawi is open for the business of adopting babies. I also don't think it, I know it — it sends the wrong message to people in Malawi — that the government makes laws and if someone comes in with enough money, they can break the laws. The law requires eighteen months of residency before adoption. You can leave afterwards, but in order to adopt a child you must prove residency in the country for a minimum of eighteen months. I don't think Madonna was in the country for longer than a few weeks. What is she doing, is she collecting these children, are they like collection items?"

She was less enthused when Madonna's subsequent grand plans to build girls schools in Malawi crumbled in 2012 after allegations that $6 million was misappropriated by administration and staffers at the planned $15 million four-hundred-student Raising Malawi Academy for Girls. Madonna had announced plans for ten schools that would educate one thousand children, half of them girls, but the Malawian Department of Education stood in her way, saying, according to the *Daily Telegraph* of London, "the government was 'fed up' with her."

"Madonna came to Malawi to build a school, an academy like the one Oprah (Winfrey) build in South Africa, but she changed her mind," President Joyce Banda told the paper at the time. "I have a problem with a lot of things around the adoption of the children and the changing of the mind and then coming back to build community schools."

One of the parcels on which Madonna was to have built a school has been designated as the site of a burial ground for Malawian heroes.

That's how it is, Mags says, people just move on. Not unlike she does, saying goodbye to Neville and heading to her insurance company, where she hopes to get the last statement for coverage on the ambulance explained.

"I'm very dissatisfied," she tells the manager she requested when the clerk was unable to answer her questions. "I might have no choice but to swap insurance carriers."

Steve stands to the side, holding the blue ledger of checks. He and Mags stare at the manager as the manager stares at the statement.

After another half an hour, with some satisfaction achieved about the bottom line of the bill, the two race to the ambulance as rain begins to fall. Mags drives past Praise God Shoppings, toward the pump shop first, then to the Ministry of Transport and Public Works for cutting of the spare key. It'll be the second stop in the normally simple process of obtaining a new key; Steve earlier had to pick up a blank key downtown, a transaction that required him to produce identification, and for the clerk to record that identification.

"We're only getting a flipping key cut. It's the faffing," Mags says of the time wasted. And that includes stopping at a roundabout so the motorcade of Malawi's then-president, Bingu wa Mutharika, can pass. A dozen black SUVs, a camper then another four SUVs speed by.

"What's this costing?" Mags fumes as the rain begins to pour. "There's a diesel shortage, there are no drugs in the hospitals, no teachers in the schools and yet they have this. You don't have to be a genius to know something's wrong here."

At the water pump company, the owner leads her and Steve to a shabby boardroom in which a curtain dangles off the end of a rod and a cracked car windshield sits on the floor, not far from an old computer monitor. A dated map of the country hangs on the wall.

"Who has been playing with your pump?" the owner asks of Mags.

In response to his provocative question and harsh tone, Mags gets defensive, mentions the many phone calls made to his office regarding the various problems the device was experiencing. The owner interrupts her, trying to be calming after what was a failed joke. He assures, "It's a very simple situation we found."

A necktied workman enters the room, carrying a variety of fittings. He gives a lesson about electrical surges, about a gate valve that shut slowly, about the dynamic level of the borehole, this one drilled when the clinic opened in 2004.

"What we've got to do is start looking for rain," Mags concludes.

She tells the workman about the thefts from the well. The owner pitches in his own stories, starting with the latest theft he experienced at his home — the sixteenth burglary there in twelve months, and in a neighborhood where a neighbor across the street was murdered three months ago.

"Four men appeared in my bedroom at 1:00 a.m., carrying lead pipes and looking for valuables," he says. "My wife and I told them to take whatever they wanted. The worst was the personal things they took."

Mags is unfazed. "This place is nothing compared to South Africa. They'll murder you in the streets for your sneakers. Now. The pump . . ."

At the Ministry of Transport and Public Works, a worker swings open the gate. Mags parks the ambulance and Steve goes inside. She flips through a magazine picked up at the insurance company. Glances at a picture of McFussy Kawawa, president of the National Bank of Malawi.

Upon Steve's return in another twenty minutes, there's another trip to the office of PSI — Population Services International, a Washington, D.C.-based health promotion agency. "Clean water, malaria, safe sex — the big three here," explains Steve, who exits the ambulance and returns quickly because the people he needs to see are out.

The ambulance passes the distillery of Malawi Gin, empty bottles of which are the standard candleholders during power outages back at the Cape. Other brands important to The Gap have plants here, and the trip takes the ambulance past several, including the Carlsberg brewery, the Chombe tea company, and the bakeries of Universal, origin of so many of the biscuits eaten in the dining area.

The open windows pour a constant blast of hot air into the vehicle's interior, where Steve consults the list and considers what's been paid for and what's yet to be purchased and how much remains in the account that gets chipped away in a reverse of the racism so much of the white Western world knows. Here, whites are the minority, are the ones often charged higher prices. Past a stretch of brilliantly blooming lilac jacarandas, a quick stop is made for salads and sandwiches at a small café and art gallery in a treed area not far from a major roundabout. Again, Mags asks what's next on the lisht.

There's a feel of being a kid out with Ma, doing errands. The repetition of the same roads bores after a while, the traffic slows, the exhaust adds to the smells filling the car — the grainy dog food, the sharp bleach, the fakey floral of the laundry detergent. Mail is one addition that has no odor. Steve carries the Trust's mailbag from the post office on a side road. It contains only three pieces, two of them from Kate and Lauren's college back in Australia. "It's not worth it to mail things, now that there is the Internet," Steve says. As for parcels, he says, "One volunteer was expecting an express delivery package, it cost eighty pounds sterling ($130) to mail, was mailed in August, got here in March. They were lucky it got there at all."

The mailbag is tossed in the back, and the ambulance continues on to Kleen Kem (PVT) Limited, which bears the slogan, "Warriors against grime." And to SANA, a chemical shop that sells an effective bug spray fittingly called Doom.

The official at CONGOMA — the Council for Non Government Organisations in Malawi — is out of the country when Mags and Steve make another call. When Mags stops at the pharmaceutical supplier, the man she needs to see is at the barber's. There's another roadblock because of the president's motorcade still traveling the cities. "No drugs in the hospital, no teachers in the schools, yet this halfwit can go zipping around wasting fuel," Mags snarls as the ambulance idles in a line of traffic.

She swings back to the pharmaceutical supplier and quickly returns with a worker carrying a carton of zinc tablets, another of paracetemol/Panadol, and credit for the expired glucose she returned. She's pleased at the ease of the transaction in a city that's held a learning curve. "When I first used to come here," she says as she turns from the driveway back into traffic, "it was the blind leading the blind. I didn't know where I was, and the people I was with didn't know."

Mags calls the trip so far "reasonably successful, but you have the reasonable frustration." Red tape is strung ankle high every few feet in this country that at a distance might seem simple and old-fashioned but has as many rules and regulations as the most first-world address, she says. As if to illustrate, there's a third stop to try to pick up the key that wasn't ready during the last stop. "A complete hames," Mags huffs.

She wheels down the road, the rugged and beautiful mountains a backdrop, smoke from cars a closer reality. Much of the traffic is the family-sized white vans used as busses, each jammed with twenty people.

At the next stop, the Royal Laboratory, Steve learns that an $800 hemoglobin machine is being offered for free with the purchase of twenty of the test kit packets it uses. Mags idles in the parking lot as he informs her of the deal, and she thinks aloud: "So if it's below a certain level, you need plasma . . . well, if it's free, we might as well get it."

Steve the nurse leaves to make the deal. Mags the guidance counselor finds a parking space and thinks back to the medical connections of her childhood.

"I would have had a certain familiarity with this as I grew up in a medical house. A lot of the exposure would have been — I wouldn't say bandied about — would have been used," she says. "The biggest advantage I did have growing up in a medical household is that it holds a certain mystique for the average punter. Not for me. From the time I was three, I'd go to the hospital on Sundays with my father. Always spent a part and parcel of my life there. Doctors always calling the house. My dad's surgery was just down the street from school. I'd wait at the surgery and we'd all go home together. I'd play with the scales in the waiting room, chat with patients. I knew a bit of the mystique about doctors and nurses and what goes on, but, as far as I'm concerned, it was just a job for my dad. You just didn't think about it. That's what it was. The same thing can be said for those who grow up in deprivation — for them it wasn't normal to have shoes. It's normal to walk to school each day. Living under the same roof, living cheek by jowl. It's just normal."

She stops talking for a second to see if an approaching car needs her to move farther into the parking lot. Then she says, "One drawback of normal would be twenty, thirty years ago here they didn't know how they had it. Now even the most deprived person has access to a TV screen. Now they know it's not normal. I do think their expectations are much higher now."

Along those lines, she says, she once thought about banning pop culture magazines in the dining area. Brought in by new volunteers or those who've been away on holiday, magazines like England's *Hello!* and their gushing features on the opulent lifestyles of royalty, film stars and models, raise her ire. She doesn't want locals to pick them up, scan a pictorial like the recent *Hello!* piece on the sale of the eye-popping $12 million mansion in England that was home to a Cadbury heiress and her husband, whose father was the former chairman of Dutch Royal Shell, and go away thinking everyone in the world comes from that sort of background. "But that would be anarchy," she says, knowing how in a place with limited flow of news and entertainment from the outside, every such copy is treasured and pored over as it rotates through the volunteers.

No copies of such publications make it into the ambulance before Mags points it north for the trip home. Most every inch of the back of the vehicle — and even the space beneath the front seats — is strategically packed with purchases that will carry the clinic and The Gap through the next month or two. The few seat-belt latches that aren't stuck behind purchases swing and ring brightly as the vehicle rolls away from the city, bearing two administrators who are tired but satisfied. Who've solved problems, or at least argued them well and, sometimes, favorably. Who know that pharmacy shelves, kitchen larders, and toilet paper lockers soon will be restocked, that the pump issue is on the way to being solved, and that all the tasks on the list in Steve's pocket have been ticked or strongly attempted. And that a safe bridge awaits on the road back home.

FOURTEEN

Manager Mr. Chapo brings the letter to the dining room at 6:30 a.m.

School officials, the neat blue-inked handwriting informs, do not want the clinic to administer the bilharzia treatment.

It's been three days since the ambulance full of volunteers and tablets and bread and orange Sobo rolled into the schoolyard. Seated in the dining area in blue shorts and white T-shirt, her hair in a rare single braid, Mags passes the letter around the breakfast table, incredulous. "What parent wouldn't want their child treated?" she asks again. She'll make another call to the government, but that will be later. She's got a staff meeting this morning at seven, a meeting with John The Gap at nine, and then will be giving a tour of the clinic to a visitor, Aidan Ellis, a sub-editor from the Dublin-based Murdoch newspaper *The Sun*. It's one of those days when she'll give a slight nod to the length of her usual to-do list, saying of her workload, "It's a cold fist, isn't it?"

The staff meeting was scheduled early to not interfere with the clinic's work. "If it's before work," Mags says, "then there's only half an hour of faffing off."

She's soon on the clinic porch, standing next to Steve, their backs to the new garden, the mural on the wall to their left. Before them are twenty-three employees, most of the clinic's paid staff, chatting quietly, laughing a bit in the moments before Mags calls out a greeting.

"Everything is running well, you're doing a fantastic job," she starts, with grand enthusiasm. "Little by little the staff is getting bigger. Everybody is working well as a team. Working in an area like this, where we are isolated from a lot, that's important."

Some heads nod; most do not.

Steve begins to cover the recent news about the pump, the issue of the water thefts, and the new fact of the locks on the taps.

"Does anyone want all that translated?" Mags asks, and most heads nod.

Working without notes, Mr. Chapo, standing against the mural in dark pants and wrinkled acrylic shirt with a private school-looking crest, begins to speak. Heads turn his way as he talks and talks, and it's one of those moments of using an interpreter when you wonder if Steve said even half that much. Goats run past the garden; one slips beneath the bottom of the fence. Elaine tries to chase it from the enclosure as Mags asks the crowd for questions.

There are none, so she moves on to the teachers' request for disturbance money. She reads the letter received this morning regarding the bilharzia treatment being nixed, then puts it in a nutshell. "The program has not been welcomed," she says. "What this means is your children will not receive the treatment."

Mr. Chapo translates again.

"The teachers were demanding we pay the entire faculty 12,000 kwacha," Mags continues. "That would pay for a lot of drugs here in the whole community. I would just like the people here to know this is what's happening in their primary school."

Mr. Chapo speaks again.

"Why do the teachers want money?" Wilson calls from his place near the door to the reception office.

"They say the government will pay them if the government comes out to give the treatments," Mags says. "The government hasn't been here for five years. It's all about money, Wilson."

"I think it's horrendous," he answers. "The school will hold children ransom for 1,500 kwacha."

There are a few whispers. Justice speaks: "The children do not belong to the school. The community should make the decision."

Mags shakes her head. Shrugs. "It's up to the teachers now," she says. Then, though no one's asked, she says, "Now, fertilizer?"

Staffers are provided a loan at this time of year, important assistance that pays for fertilizer for the employees' fields of maize. The growing season begins in December; the loans are paid back starting in January. Seventeen of the twenty-three people at the meeting are male. They swap comments about fertilizer prices rising. They wonder if Mags will increase the loan.

"You promised this last rainy season," Justice says.

"I don't make any promises I don't keep," Mags returns firmly. As a woman strides past the clinic with a pile of wood on her head, Mags sets her limits. "It's a loan. I can't give what's not there. It's as simple as that."

Big Dorothy suggests getting a larger loan and paying back more each month.

Mags looks around the room. "Could everybody do that?"

Nods again from most.

"Obviously, we want to facilitate stuff as much as we can," Mags says. "If people feel they could do it, and do it without adversity, we can try." She stops here, then says. "We're not a

bank. We could do 2,000 (more). I personally think that would
be a lot of money. Each person can come to (us) and negotiate
an individual loan." The room is buzzing. Mags raises her hand
to ask for order. "The money is taken from wages. After the
tenth of the month you can get an advance on your salary."

Steve tells the group to come to the office at The Gap between 10:00 a.m. to 1:00 p.m. on Saturday, when loans will be
administered. The applause begins.

Eight thousand seven hundred and two miles away, that
applause is echoed by a mother and daughter sitting at the
kitchen table in a modest home with a billion-dollar view of
Stradbally Strand and Brandon Bay on the Dingle Peninsula.
Having done the first survey of Chembe Village residents'
needs, secondary schoolteacher Norah Flynn and daughter
Katie, an aquarist, know well what such a loan will mean.

Norah, forty-five, works down the hill from that home, in
September of 2011 marking her sixteenth year as a teacher of
civic, social and political education at *Mean Scoil Nua An Leith
Triuigh*, the 130-student secondary school in Castlegregory
where Mags once was guidance counselor for students including Katie.

Katie, twenty-five, works on the other side of the peninsula, at Dingle Oceanworld Aquarium, a conservation and
preservation facility that is home to the country's largest collection of sharks. Also coming and going from the house is
brother Paddy, a marine biology student. The family credits
Norah's father, an avid beachcomber, for instilling in the two
grandchildren an interest in the sea.

Katie has worked at Oceanworld for a year and three
months, tending to the fish and thrilling over the dozen gentoo
penguins recently added to the collection. She majored in zool-

ogy at University College Cork, graduating a year ago — "With honors," Norah pushes in proudly, adding that Katie was first in her class and received a medal for earning the highest grades. She's been accepted for the PhD program at the University of Otago in Dunedin, New Zealand, and will leave early the next year. From their nearly overlapping sentences and shared thought threads, the close connection and camaraderie between mother and daughter is clear, as it's clear that their coming separation will be a challenge.

The pair had traveled together before, to Europe and America, had gone on weekends away — "We get on well," Norah says, and Katie smiles her agreement. The Oceanworld collection includes mbuna fish, "rock dwellers" from Lake Malawi. And Katie's college studies included the topic of bilharzia. Working with children, Norah had seen her share of what challenges a family. But they were unprepared for what they'd encounter in the six weeks. Mags's greeting them in Blantyre upon their arrival, however, did help them get their bearings sooner.

"We went to the bank to change money," Katie recalls. "She's straight out saying, 'Don't make eye contact with anybody, walk straight in and out, don't talk to anybody . . .'"

The two giggle, and ponder what would they have done upon arrival if on their own, or how would they have clambered onto the matola they eventually found?

Norah and Katie had heard of Mags before they ever met. "I think people knew what she was doing," Norah says, "but they might have been thinking, 'Why not stay in Dingle — it's kind of daft to be doing this.' It's a lifetime commitment now."

It was their friendship with Mags that allowed the pair to volunteer for the Trust in the first place. Unable to serve the normal four-month minimum due to their work schedules, they were classified as visitors to the Trust, but ones who would work, doing the population survey. The volunteer force at the time was eight or nine others, including two doctors.

Their first glimpse of Chembe Village was in bright sunlight that illuminated a cloud of lake flies over the water. That memory leads them to others about the local practice of catching and eating flies for protein, the introduction to mice kebabs, and of going with Mags to get timber for a new building at The Gap. They remember the carpenters setting a plank in the back of a truck, and when it hung from the back too much, cutting off a piece, then another, then another, until it fit.

"Mags just stood there and said, 'This is Africa. You have to leave them at it.'"

Once they began their work, Norah and Katie received another reminder of where they were.

"We thought, 'It's a village, like here.' Thought we'd just walk around," Norah says.

"But that wasn't always the best thing," Katie notes.

"They'd be saying, 'Mzungu! Mzungu!'"

"The mothers would want their kids to touch us, they'd be holding them, saying, 'Touch the white person.' That was interesting — we're so used to being white and not the minority. The kids would be bawling."

Norah and Katie walked the village every day from the 6th of June to the 19th of July, from the National Park at the western end of the peninsula to the "wealthier" part of the village, home to many fisherman, just before Chembe Eagles Nest, hyped as the only lodge on the Cape with a private (read: no locals bathing, washing dishes or clothes in front of your cottage) beach.

"The first few days it was new to everyone, then the word got out," Katie says. The chance to enter homes added to the information gathered, as did their personal guide and translator. As Norah says, "We had Matthew. Everybody knew him."

Matthew is Matthew Kasangola, now a twenty-eight-year-old resident of Blantyre whose secondary education sponsor once had evaporated and who then was sponsored by Norah's school — one of its efforts to support the Trust.

With the help of Matthew, Katie and Norah asked their subjects general information the Trust needed to better serve the community, collecting age, employment status, education history, marital status, number of children and number of surviving children.

"One would say, 'I had seven children, only three survived," Norah remembers.

"They'd just reel it off," Katie adds.

"Sometimes they didn't know the ages," Norah says. "They'd debate about them with the sister and mother. It was a totally different experience. You go on holiday some place, you have an outside view. To be in a place for six weeks — and going door to door — you get a different perspective."

As they gained knowledge of the culture and community, they gained a new perspective on Mags.

"I think she's just the most amazing person I ever met," Norah says. "She gets hit by another thing and you think, 'God almighty, how is she going to survive?' She's so upbeat all the time. It must kill her to be at the Cape and hear that of fifteen in a family, they've had six or seven children die."

The sizes of some families amazed them, and a constant reminder was Matthew, whose household included a mother and ten siblings.

"We saw grandparents in their forties, then kids," Katie says, and Norah rushes to add, "Those in their twenties were missing. Dead of AIDS."

Katie remembers a young girl who had good English and

took them in to see her mother, a woman unable to lift her head to greet visitors. Rarely did they meet anyone in their fifties. Katie snapped photos with an elderly couple age eighty-eight and seventy-three who joked about visiting Ireland.

As Katie and Norah asked their questions, they'd be asked some in turn: were they really mother and daughter, and where were their men, Norah's status of divorcee being hard to fathom. Some villagers also asked them for money. "They would be angling, if not outright asking," Norah says.

They learned that, for most items, shops charged a local price and a mzungu one.

"I think Mags made a good point," Norah says. "They'll scam you if they can. But to understand it, Mags said, 'What if your children were dying?'"

"Matthew would say, 'I'll go with you,'" Katie says, and Norah adds, "Or you'd spend ages haggling. Though you were very good."

Katie also was good with the village children, letting them try on her sunglasses, teaching them the children's song "Head, Shoulders, Knees and Toes" in Chichewa and later hearing a woman singing the first line as she was collecting water. She produces a list of the words: *mutu* for head, *mapewa* for shoulders, *mabondo* for knees, *mapazi* for toes. "I never got to the rest," she says. She loved collecting the varied first names found at the Cape, including that of a person called Future. "A good name," she says.

Their home now is decorated with souvenirs of Chembe Village: carved spoons, Noah's Ark creatures, and a windsurfer purchased for Paddy. A photo book includes pictures of the hippos that regularly surface at Kasanka, a village neighboring Chembe. The shots are fascinating but don't regularly see the light of day. "I don't show my pictures to a lot of people," Katie says protectively. "I don't want them to yawn. I want them to appreciate them."

The two say they were changed by the experience of traveling to the Cape.

"I remember coming home, I'd be giving out to my friends about what they were complaining about," Katie says, adding that she would have loved a longer stay. For her mother, who was, as she says, "ready to come home" when they did, the time at the Cape gave her firsthand knowledge to share in her classes. Katie calls the lack of concern for the time "the coolest thing" she encountered in the village. "If Matthew says he's turning up at six in the morning, it could be between 6:00 a.m. and ten at night."

Norah was struck by what Mags has called "cheerful hopelessness," and ventures that the villagers are far better off than residents of the developed world. "If they are sick, the families look after them," she says. "There's a better quality of life in that way."

The stories about the mice kebabs and the missing generation were turned into a presentation Katie and Norah gave to the public one night at school. "People were just blown away," says Norah. "We put out a box for donations, got forty to fifty people — a pretty good turnout for something here."

When they'd made their plans to go to the Cape, mother and daughter had organized a fundraising walk to cover the cost of their flights. Since returning, Katie has done a fundraiser every year — a Christmas raffle or a bake sale at Easter, raising 500 to 600 euro each time, and a seven-mile walk on the beach visible from the house, raising 2,000 euro the past year, a 500-euro decrease from the year before, with fifteen walkers rather than the normal thirty. Norah doesn't need to survey her own community to know the cause of the drop in participants and the resulting drop in the funds that help fuel efforts like an increase in loans for fertilizer back in Chembe Village.

"People are just having a hard time," she says. "When things are tough, charity is the first thing to go."

FIFTEEN

That "whole different world" Mags was talking about when she boarded her latest flight to Malawi certainly is how Cape Maclear appears to most who make the trip from a place considered to be the first world.

The majority who visit the continent for the first time arrive with some picture in their mind of what they might see and encounter, and, aside from the expectations of sweeping vistas chock full of incomparable wildlife, much of that picture is not positive. Everyone they'll encounter will be hungry, living in shacks, suffering from unthinkable medical conditions, and if not coming at you with spears extended, then with outstretched hands. Because the prevailing impression is they need your help. Badly.

With the exception of the occasional television documentary focusing on those sweeping vistas chock full of incomparable wildlife, much of the media over the years have painted Africa as pretty much the most awful place on earth.

In his essay "Writing Through the Frame: Expanding the Boundaries of Story for a Meaningful Interpretation and Response to Suffering", U.S.-born and Kenyan-raised writer Brendan Buzzard says early writings about Africa formed "a relationship with the rest of the world as one of need, a myth of vulnerability searching for a benefactor, a continent requiring the services of missionaries to save souls, entrepreneurs to bring commerce, soldiers to quell the violence, and rulers to oversee it all."

He notes how those of us required to read Joseph Conrad's *Heart of Darkness* in high school or college received the image of drums beating through the night, and, writes Conrad, "Whether it meant war, peace, or prayer we could not tell . . . We were wanderers on prehistoric earth, on an earth that wore the aspect of an unknown planet. We could have fancied ourselves the first of men taking possession of an accursed inheritance, to be subdued at the cost of profound anguish and excessive toil."

"And so the myth was born," Buzzard says. "It is a myth no less alive today than when European letters first turned their frames on Africa; a process that began, as the acclaimed Nigerian writer Chinua Achebe explains, with 'portraying Africa as a place that is different from the rest of the world, a place where humanity is really not recognizable.'

"What is recognized, however, is suffering, and it has dominated the stories of a continent. Suffering has formed the central theme of the images that emerge from Africa, a theme appropriated at various times by imperialists, colonialists, abolitionists, story-tellers, and more recently the humanitarian trying to enlist the empathy of viewers into their cause."

Should the subject of suffering be left out of the story of a place in Africa — especially if it indeed is a fact, and if indeed it helps improve a community there?

Assistant Project Manager Elaine Cosgrove relocated from Ireland to Africa because she learned of a great need there, but she's also someone who doesn't like how that great need is portrayed.

"If you were trying to get money from someone, you show people who are down," she says with an unhappy shrug. "We have so much media at home, they need a shock factor in order for you to react. You look at any news, any news, CNN or whatever, there's just complete bombardment with terrible stories, tragedies, you get it live, you can view it live on the Internet . . ." Her voice trails, and she looks around The Gap, the residence of so many — including herself — who at some point saw, read or heard of some need in this part of the world and responded as they could. She acknowledges that the word must be spread. "You're trying to get money for an issue," she says. "You want to show what's happening. So it's a vicious circle."

It's also, according to some critics, "the pornography of Africa," a term for the way the continent — and developing countries — are shown at their worst. In his satirical essay "How to Write about Africa", Kenyan writer Binyavanga Wainaina gives some guidelines for writing that kind of pornography, suggesting the focus be on "dead bodies. Or, better, naked dead bodies. And especially, rotting naked dead bodies. Remember, any work you submit in which people look filthy and miserable will be referred to as the 'real Africa', and you want that on your dust jacket. Do not feel queasy about this; you are trying to help them get aid from the west . . ."

"It's terrible," Elaine says, "that you have to have pictures of starving babies in order to make money."

But, again, what if that is the reality of a part of a place, she muses. Then she shakes her head.

Elaine studied to be a nurse, graduated, then, as she says plainly, "I realized I didn't want to do it. I really enjoyed it but I knew it wouldn't be for me. I just think you'd have medical students coming in, you'd show them how to do stuff . . ." She pauses to wrinkle her nose. "It wouldn't work for me."

The Kildare native, forty-two, was breaking a family tradition she recounts while sitting at the dinner table near a stack of non-pop-culture reading material brought in by Mags a few weeks back — the *Observer*, *The Times of London*, *The Irish Times*. "My mom was a nurse," she says, "my granddad was a doctor, my father did pharmacy, my sister was a nurse . . ."

Elaine actually had applied to study medicine but missed acceptance by one point. Like fellow volunteer Siobhan, she studied at the Mater Misericordiae University Hospital and then nursed in Italy for a year before moving into nurse recruitment, drawing professionals from all over Europe and developing markets in Canada, Africa and the Philippines. The work included being part of the first company to recruit non-English or Irish nurses into the U.K. health system. And it entailed a lot of travel. After a year of traveling purely for pleasure, she returned home to work for another recruitment agency then fell into a job not unlike the one held by George Clooney in the film *Up in the Air*. "I was working with companies laying off four, five hundred people," she says, "telling them they were being made redundant." She found the task enlightening: "For most people, I really think, at the end of it, it probably was a push they needed. I think they would have left a year later. With redundancy, you're pushed into it. Eighty to ninety percent knew it was the right thing for them."

Several more lines were added to the resume — assisting the laid off in their efforts to find new careers, working with banks undergoing change. Eventually, Elaine grew disinterested. "I find I get bored with stuff after a while, I can do it for three years, I can do it well, but it becomes something you can do in your sleep."

With a longtime desire to volunteer, she began looking at possibilities. At nine or ten years of age, she'd visited a priest uncle assigned to a church in Kenya and didn't consider Africa strongly. India was of interest, as was South America, where she'd enjoyed a trip during which she volunteered for a month with a priest in Argentina. "He literally took children that were abandoned and had physical, mental disabilities. He set up a home for these kids; we worked there for a month. It was grand."

But many of the possibilities Elaine researched weren't.

"A lot of the stuff I looked at were 'volly holly' things — you should just go and travel if that's the case. I went for an interview in Ireland for a place in Calcutta, working with street kids, it seemed to be doing good but you weren't actually working, you were just there." She also received an offer to actually run a children's hospital, despite pointing out she had only nursing credentials. "They were like 'When can you start?' It seemed to be not decent. A lot of the (volunteer opportunities) I saw were similar. I saw something different on Mags's site. They were looking for nurses and doctors. It just seemed very professional. Her ethos is, if you're coming out to volunteer, we're not going to press you to raise money. Fundraising can be off-putting, if you're going off somewhere and also trying to cover bills at home. The project seemed kind of professional, to be honest with you, and you would have something to do rather than just be an extra hand. I liked the length of time, as well. That I could do six months."

Elaine wrote Mags and soon received an invitation to meet in Dublin.

The interview in January of 2008 resulted in an offer to come to Cape Maclear as an assistant project manager. Elaine arrived the following October and initially worked in classes Mags had started in the village.

"I had never taught in my life," she says. "I had all the little tots coming in, with really no attention span, but it was good fun doing it. You really needed someone full-time. You'd have ten in one day, fifteen the next, three the day after. You could try to do anything, but it was quite difficult because they were so young. All I had them doing at the end was dancing, painting, a bit of music, English. The older ones started working in the fields and attendance would be down."

The classes ended, and she then began to work with Steve. "Mainly it was just day-to-day stuff and it takes you a while to know how things work," Elaine remembers. "We tidied systems, computerized things, working on the things that made the place tick, left Mags free to do things. I think the place, for her, was just built so quickly, what we're doing is just to catch up. The boring stuff like accounts. 'This is what we paid for paraffin for the last two years, project what it will be next year. If 20 percent more, this is what I need to raise . . .'"

Elaine returned home in May of '09 and a few months later received an e-mail from Mags, asking her to share her impressions of the project with a volunteer who'd been accepted. "Then, a few weeks later, she e-mailed me and said, 'Oh, she's not coming out.' I remember it was summer, but it was freezing cold. I said 'I might come back out myself.' That was probably August of '09. I came back in October."

Elaine recounts this as she marks the first year of her second stint at the Cape. Affable, outgoing, dressed in black tee and matching capris, a cloth handbag sewn by village tailor Bernard slung over her shoulder, her short blonde hair secured by ponytail, she looks up at the battery-operated emergency LED strip light over the dining room's first window. When it's on, power's off. Right now, it's on.

She was home an additional time this past year, in January, when her mother died. "I'm here for another few months," she says. "I said I'd stay to June, but the visa's 'til September . . ." Making it easy to be flexible is the lack of a job back in Ireland and the fact that she's renting her home in the Dublin suburb of Sandymount.

Far from there, she recalls that trip made to Kenya with her mother and aunt back when she was nine or ten, to visit her uncle Liam Doyle, a Kiltegan Father with St. Patrick's Missionary Society of Co. Wicklow.

"Kenya was more developed," she says, "but there was not a huge difference between here and where my uncle was. The kids in school don't have seat, they had logs, chalk and a board. Not an awful lot has changed."

She's come to feel very much at home at the Cape.

"This village is lovely," she says. "It's very laid back. There's not the urgency you have at home. And I think we're kind of doing good stuff here, workwise. I like the idea of having to do stuff with kind of limited resources. It annoys you when the electricity goes — like now — but you think of alternative ways to do things. At home you can get anything done. Here, you still try to have it as professional as you would have at home, but with absolutely seriously limited resources. If something breaks, you figure it out. The job is very varied, could be anything. Could be a broken pump, you might deal with loans, with people and their human resource issues, salaries, anything that happens. I was trying to get something done — fax Sheila's visa — it took four hours. It nearly took me half the day to literally send something very simple. That frustrates you, then something brilliant happens."

She admires Ireland's John O'Shea, a former sports journalist who in 1977 founded GOAL, a Dublin-based organization helping the disadvantaged in more than fifty countries, distributing $984 million in the process, some of that money donations Mags has made over the years to what is one of her favorite causes.

Following the 2004 tsunami that devastated parts of Indonesia, Sri Lanka and Thailand, John O'Shea said, "To help the poor, you've got to love the poor and this is why governments have failed. They talk about the poor, they issue statements about the poor but you don't get the feeling that Mandela had for his people, because he loved his people. We don't have people of that stature, we don't have people of that moral fiber at the top."

Elaine believes they do exist, and believes she lives among at least one of them.

"I was thinking what's the difference between somebody like Mags, who comes out and actually does it, compared to people who come out and work on what she's set up?" she asks, then without a beat answers, "I dunno. I think it might be the injustice of something, to have something happen to you personally. People who build these things, it could be they're inspired by the injustice of something rather than being all lovey-dovey, thinking 'Oh, these poor people.' And then the rest of us get involved."

Mags's motivation was Billy, but she could have ended her memorial when the stone was set into the beach sands of The Gap's grounds that day one year after his death. She could have folded up and done nothing at all but mourn the fact of three dead children over twenty-six years. She's explained her coping as "It's an Irish thing" and/or "I was born like this," and, looking at her country's long history of care for and aid to the poor, the mentally and physically challenged, both in Ireland and abroad, it's clear there indeed might be something in the water.

Rare is the Irish family who hasn't contributed at least one son to the priesthood or daughter to the convent, or child of either gender to the medical profession. And as common is having at least one of those religious offspring head off to serve in what was fuzzily known as "the missions" — a posting frequently in Africa, often through the Society of African Missions, (known as SMA), founded in France in 1856 to serve the people of Africa and of African descent, established in Ireland in 1878 and currently serving in sixteen African countries.

In pre-'80s Ireland, an entire generation schooled largely in the country's Catholic school system grew up contributing pennies each week for the "Little Black Babies" in Africa. This was most commonly done through a classroom plastic figure named Sammy, a kneeling 3-D textbook-pornography-of-Africa black baby who nodded each time a coin dropped into the box on which he knelt. The donor was rewarded with a card depicting a crying child. Some children also brought to school pennies to donate for another effort, each one allowing them to pierce a bead on a pair of rosary beads printed on a card. When the holder pierced all the beads, he or she could select a Christian name for one child in Africa. Many children saw completion of the card as their ticket to adopting an African baby. Vividly illustrating how this practice has remained in the minds of a certain era of Irish is Clare Boylan's 1989 novel *Black Baby*, in which a dying spinster believes that the young black Londoner who comes to her front door once was the African baby for whom she donated money at age twelve to adopt.

Two of the three SMA churches in Ireland are in Cork, not far from Mags's original neighborhood, where a Sammy figure knelt in the classroom of a young Margaret Dillon, who one day would head her own charitable effort.

Writing in the *Irish Independent* in July of 2012, Brendan O'Connor called John O'Shea "another particular type of Irish person, the kind who sets up a charity." His words about O'Shea could be applied to Mags.

"I know some of them," O'Connor wrote. "They can tend to be charismatic and inspiring but difficult, complicated people. Some of them have seen great tragedy in their own lives. Some of them have just seen the same tragedy elsewhere as the rest of us but they see it differently. We are able to compartmentalise it. They are missing that gene. They just see it and they find they have to do something about it. They find it hard and frustrating that the rest of us don't care as much as they do. And sometimes they think they need to hammer home to us at every available opportunity that we are asleep. How can we not feel the same burning need to fix this as they do? They get frustrated at the authorities too. Like John O'Shea, they see a burning building and someone to be rescued. They don't have any patience for political sensitivities and red tape and bureaucracy."

"What does it matter what sort of guy I am?" John O'Shea asked twenty years prior, "the Titanic is going down and I'm the guy who provides the raft. What does it matter whether I was at Mass on Sunday?"

Twenty years later, in a "mutually acceptable arrangement," John O'Shea retired as GOAL's CEO. A statement from the organization's board noted his "unremitting unwillingness to allow conformity with convention to blunt his drive to replace despair with hope."

"It's just phenomenal — what Mags has done," Elaine says, "and to keep it going, as well. And to keep it going and going. We do the books and know where every penny is spent. That money has to be raised somewhere, and she's it. Because myself and Steve do the books, we see what's coming in and going out, when the money is spent so carefully. You look up three different places to get the cheapest thing. Just to keep going and doing it. And to have that burden — I suppose it's a burden, not getting money from government agencies or anything like that. If you knew 'I'm getting fifty thousand a year for sure that's going to come in from Irish aid or something like that,' you'd have peace of mind. Anything that's done here, she's had to raise money for it. And some of that is done through telling it like it is. I just think that kind of constantly telling the story, telling it again and again to people, that's what does it."

Stories not always easy to hear, but, in the case of this one village, the truth. One Mags Riordan believes needs to be told so change might occur.

SIXTEEN

Telling the hard truths about life on the Cape was how Mags connected with one of the clinic's first volunteer doctors, Paul Moroney.

These days he's living down the end of a twisting, turning road that offers few options but to keep moving forward, yet a visitor can get lost enough on a few detours to have to be rescued by a neighboring husband and wife who hop into their car to lead the way to Fungie Cottage. That's Paul Moroney's home, the right-hand unit of the two that comprise a neat white cement building bounded by a fence in oceanfront Been Ban, just before Dingle Town and the village where Mags and Richie long ago shared a tent.

The view from the front garden is a priceless one of Dingle Harbor and Dingle itself, and the road to the end of the peninsula beyond. Paul's door is open on a mild day in August of 2011; tea and cookies await on a low table. Paintings, carvings, keepsakes are displayed on every wall and surface. The air has a slight smell of incense, and the contents of the house, right down to the T-shirt and work pants attire of its occupant — who could be a stand-in for mogul Richard Branson — are comfortably worn.

Paul, fifty-nine, is a general practitioner from Liverpool. His surname, he explains, is a County Clare one. "I'm first generation," he says. "The family is immigrants. They all went to Liverpool. I came back."

What he does in this country is medicine, and he does it on his own schedule, not working full-time since Cape Maclear. "I work when they ask me," he says. "Because I like to do other things." That includes those paintings — so many on his walls he's running out of room — and sailing. He owns an eighty-six-year-old, thirty-two-foot Looe logger gaffer he's sailed to destinations including the Hebrides. Last year he steered *Moose*, the boat named for the pet name of the wife of the man who built her, to Cornwall, where the boat had been built. "I wanted to take her back for her eighty-fifth birthday," he explains.

Sailing was what got him to Kerry. He dropped into Ventry a dozen years ago, met locals including longtime Dingle general practitioner Micheal Fanning. "He wanted me to do some work for him," Paul says. His on-and-off employment began then. "Loads of people end up here who have no interest in stopping. It was one of those things that happens."

He calls Dingle "away yet involved. It has a lot going on." Says that's not always the case: "A lot of west-coast towns are dead in winter. Dingle isn't."

Paul grew up in Liverpool. Like Mags, he had a father who was a surgeon, his orthopedic. And the father's brother was a general surgeon. The second youngest of five children, Paul has an older brother who is a general practitioner. His first trip to Ireland was a family holiday when he was twelve. After that, he thought he might one day like to stay.

Paul studied at Trinity College in Dublin, earning his primary degree in 1979, then going on to two years of six-month stints practicing in areas including obstetrics and casualty. He then spent one year as a general practitioner trainee.

"I like doing it," he says of medicine. "I like stopping it as well. I could never do it full-time. After six months, I'm good for a break."

The invitation to volunteer came about in the early summer

of 2004.

"I went for a cup of coffee at Benners and Mags was at lunch talking to Ted Creedon, a local journalist," Paul remembers. "He came over and asked would I talk to her for a few moments. Mags then told me about Malawi."

He'd never heard of the place. Though he's been to Europe, including Turkey and Greece, mostly on sailing trips, he doesn't consider himself a world traveler. Right there in Benners he told Mags he would volunteer. He follows that fact with a fast, "I don't know why. Another day, it could have been no. I had no idea what I was getting into."

Including the lack of technology and supplies. But that wasn't a problem he found throughout his stay, from November of 2004 to January of 2005.

"I loved having limited resources. I loved that." He smiles big. "It brings us back to what we're about, really. At home we can have too much, too many tests. Not that there weren't times we couldn't have used a few tests . . ."

He drifts in thought to that time earlier in the clinic's life, a full laboratory yet to exist. Mags would see that one eventually was created, but not without the typical amount of trials. Paul laughs and nods. "She's not fazed by anything," he says. "There's constantly something going on there. Someone constantly trying to act the eejit."

He saw that ability of hers, an experience he partially chronicled in a half-filled album of skillfully shot photos showing The Gap under renovation by two Americans; Aufi posing; and kids playing in the water. He fondly recalls Wilson, always with a stethoscope around his neck, and Sofina, ever at the front window.

But for the memories that cast a warm glow on his face, there's the fact that the trip was startling at first — though in a good way, he notes.

"It was a smack in the face, visually. The colors. The lines of people on either side of the road. Just the visual hit me right from the start. I was lucky Mags met me at the airport. I had boxes and boxes of supplies. We stayed a night in Blantyre, at a place with a garden and peacocks."

He remembers cresting the hill into Chembe Village, seeing the houses and the lake, marveling at the lack of impact all the fifteen thousand inhabitants had on the scenery. Of those fifteen thousand, he can't guess the number he treated. He imagines it might have been a hundred a day. He just knows he treated people until there weren't any waiting. That's the way it was in those early days; that's the way it remains.

Business increased once word of the clinic spread, Paul says. Then, as now, the more dire cases were referred to Monkey Bay. But then, he says, as now, "there wasn't much point — they were coming to us in the opposite direction. There were no drugs at the hospital, the nurses were selling them, so patients were turning up to us. We had a limited supply of drugs, and we had to determine how to ration them for a month."

Paul fell into a routine of work, midday break, then going back down to the clinic to finish the day, often paired with an interpreter named Rosie. "We had a great time," he says. "Patients would come in. She'd say, 'Malaria,' I'd say, 'Cold.' Just as a game. The thing is to try, to try talking to the patient."

One of the most common medications given at the time was iron, because of the great numbers of anemia detected. He saw the average coughs and flu, and lots of malaria, including in children. "Parents wouldn't bring them in and in twenty-four to forty-eight hours they would be cerebral," Paul says. "The main problem was to persuade them to bring the febrile kids in, whether or not it was malaria. Doing this would cut down deaths. The chief said that, until the clinic, there would be a line of coffins headed down the road. Simple stuff slowed that line of coffins."

On Paul's last night in the village, a massive storm hit. "Lightning right into the lake next to us and Aufi came charging in, holding a machete, to protect us. I grabbed it and threw it to the side. We sat beneath the roof, the rain coming in."

He says he marvels at Mags's life, in which the rain is coming in — physically or metaphorically — more days than not.

"Most people wouldn't have the degree of energy or focus that she does," Paul says. "Everyone has a choice. To make something positive or negative of it. Mags has that sort of type of personal character to take a positive approach. It's astounding to see what she does.

"I think everybody does change the world to some extent by every decision they make. Some of us are trundling along and it's not as noticeable. But she's done something really big. Most of us would have given up. But she has things to deal with every day."

His time at the Cape showed him what Mags's effort could have turned into, what he calls "so many skeletons of good intentions," referring to abandoned projects, including the former World Vision building next to the clinic. "The clinic is a long-term project, a full-time project. Everything she does is about the clinic. She won (a People of the Year award) a few years ago and her only comment was, 'It'll be good PR for the clinic.'"

There was much Paul liked about the experience of volunteering, including being reminded why he got into medicine. But there was one facet of life at the Cape he didn't care for.

"I found it difficult constantly being asked for money," he says. "If I was talking to someone, eventually it came down to that. It would rather upset a relationship. I found it dehumanizing. I was being perceived as a dollar. That was the only part I didn't like. It was constantly tiring, even, especially in the clinic. No one had any money. It was a thing that tired the spirit."

But he's not certain it wouldn't prevent him from returning, he says. "I've no plans to do anything elsewhere. But I might be in the humor — I might get asked on the right day..."

SEVENTEEN

Five years and dozens of volunteers after Paul Moroney's time at the clinic, Kate Brennan and Brook Hodges stand there, at the brinks of their own careers as physicians.

The twenty-eight-year-old Australian medical student who'll be done with her studies when she's completed her five-week elective at the clinic, and the twenty-nine-year-old doctor who is ready to become part of a practice near her home in England, work the same daily schedule Paul Moroney did in the clinic's earliest days. Where they'll be in another five years, looking back on their time at the Cape, is anybody's guess. But it's a certainty that they'll be able to claim their place in what by then will be an even lengthier chain of volunteers come and gone, and who in the interim kept the clinic operating. And, in the case of doctors, provide essential specialized skills.

Mags talked to Paul Moroney about the clinic. Friends talked to Kate and fellow medical school student and volunteer Lauren Finlay.

"Malawi sort of found us, rather than us finding Malawi," Kate says, recalling a conversation with students from Oxford University who were visiting Flinders University in Adelaide, where Lauren and she were studying.

"It was big for UK students to come here," she says. As for those from Australia? They're the first, she says, a decision made to fulfill an elective, and, Kate adds, "for both Lauren and I, it was coming back to why we chose medicine in the first place. To work with the underprivileged and those that need medicine the most. Social responsibility is big at our school. Africa is a pretty natural choice if you want to help."

Kate is tall and broad shouldered, with a swimmer's physique. Her short blonde hair is pulled into a ponytail and her teal scrubs have been replaced by a spaghetti-strap top and shorts now that she's off work for the day and thinking about a swim. There's so much water so close to home both here and in her city of Darwin, which, at 180,000 inhabitants, she calls "sort of small." She was raised there by a scientist father and a teacher mother but did her undergrad twenty-five hundred miles south, at the University of Sydney, studying nutrition and dietetics. Science isn't a prerequisite for the med school undergraduates. Classmates including opera majors gave what Kate calls "a real mix of life experience."

That's the same thing she received in the two years she took between her undergraduate studies and medical school, a span that included living in Brazil. "In school I was doing nutrition, I was interested in obesity. Then I traveled," she says, "and I realized I cared more about under-nutrition.

"I could have done an elective in a suburban hospital for six weeks. I prefer primary healthcare, small communities rather than big, and the big hospitals with many levels of care. I'd like to focus a bit more on preventative medicine. Community medicine. I'm interested in public health. While this is an amazing experience, it would drive us crazy if we were here longer and didn't do any public health — surveys and studies on malaria, finding out what the community needed. You have to decide where your legacy lies. Lauren and I are heavily involved in the Health and Human Rights Group at university. The right to healthcare is the right to live as long as everyone else. The group works with refugee health, indigenous health, global health, looking at the world as a big place, without borders."

Kate says she admires Mags's accomplishments within the borders of the Cape.

"She's obviously done a tremendous amount for the community. I didn't see this community beforehand but I can't imagine what one would have done with a child with a fever."

However, she notes, the presence of the clinic doesn't mean everything's easy.

"You have to make tougher decisions here," she notes. "At home, you'd stick a tube down (a patient's) throat, transfer them. That doesn't happen here."

Nor does calling in a specialist.

Kate tells the story of a patient seen the day before, who most likely soon would suffer an aortic abdominal aneurysm.

"She was brought in by her grandsons, who obvious cared and were with her. You know that what she has will burst but you don't tell her. You're not telling her something because you don't have an option. I've found that the hardest thing here. I couldn't tell her because there is no vascular surgeon in Malawi."

But there is a soon-to-be doctor who sees her patients as people.

"On the front of her health passport the age just said 'old,'" Kate says quietly. "She couldn't remember her birthday. She was old, but so precious."

Dr. Brook Hodges is used to working with more of a team, and the absence of the ones that constitute a traditional hospital setting has taken some getting used to.

"At home, there are not just two of you doing things," she says, referring to the two physicians — herself and Dr. Nora

Murray-Cavanagh — currently on staff. "At home, you'd pass that patient onto the intensive care people. You're never there by yourself. I think I've always been slightly thinking, 'Everybody knows everything, everybody knows more than I do.' But when you're the only person, you have to know something!"

Brook is newly graduated from medical school and is about to begin a new job, as a partner in a medical practice half a dozen miles from her home in Sheffield, England.

"That's unusual," she notes. "Partnerships are hard to come by now."

The partners had asked her to begin in the summer, but she already had plans to come to the Cape after completing five years of study at the University of Sheffield in Yorkshire, in Northern England. The partner she will replace will delay his retirement until she returns and becomes one of the three-and-a-half doctors in the practice.

"It would be my ideal," she says. "I had worked there before, and I can definitely imagine being there a long time."

Petite, twenty-nine, dark hair falling to her shoulders, in answer to Nora's game of which movie star would portray you, she says "the actress from *Juno*," and she's right.

She fishes for the woman's name — Ellen Page — and then gives a fact about her own, which really is Victoria. "Brook is from 'babbling brook,'" she says. "My dad called me 'Babbling' before I was born."

That dad is a tenant farmer back in Shropshire, where she grew up the eldest of three girls and one boy. Brook's mom is a histologist. Her grandfather was part of the first cohort of male nurses to be trained in the United Kingdom, usually for psychiatric work in those days. But exactly where Brook's medical ambition came from is a mystery. "I really don't know," she says, wincing and looking away. "I went through lots of possible careers. I thought this could make me useful anywhere, a part of the community."

Television definitely figured as an inspiration.

"I knew I wanted to do something like this," Brook says. "I'd watch *Live Aid* and *Comic Relief* on the telly and I'd think, 'I'll do that someday. I'll have something to do with it.'"

She learned of the clinic from a friend who'd heard of it. She applied, then met Mags in England for an interview in the spring and, to her delight, was in.

"I spent a lot of time trying to find a suitable project. I looked at big agencies like MSF (*Médicines Sans Frontières*), VSO, but they want you to go at least a year, two years," Brook says. "Other places were shorter but wanted a lot of money. That's what you mainly get when you do a search (of volunteer opportunities) — places that want money. Voluntourism."

When it comes to tourism of any kind, Brook isn't as well-traveled as most of the volunteers, but did spend two months in Guatemala and another two in Peru as part of her schooling.

"I always get scared about going places," she explains. "It's the unknown, I guess. It's always so long between trips that I think I won't like it. And, this time, I was going away from my boyfriend — and I was quite settled."

But now she's settled in this Gap.

"I like it here," she says. "Life's very easy. I don't have many responsibilities." She rushes to add with a smile, "Obviously, the job is a responsibility, but that's all you have to worry about. The work's brilliant. Some days it's a bit mundane, lots of children with malaria." She recalls a recent patient who was not breathing when brought to The Gap, and adds, "But the other day was fascinating. You feel like you actually saved a life."

Brook says the variety of conditions and issues contrasts greatly with those she's encountered previously. "I see things I wouldn't see at home. Malaria, for starters. Elephantiasis. Just lots more chest infections, much more extreme abdominal masses, big spleens, profound anemia — textbook things, you actually see here. And, obviously, all the HIV."

Plusses have included knowing what she indeed can achieve on a case, and seeing improvement.

"Before I came," she says, "I didn't think so many sick people could get better so quickly. Back home it's different — I would be uncomfortable without investigating. There's fear of litigation over something possibly overlooked and you don't want to miss it. Here there's a 'freedom' to not investigate. There is no litigation. I now know how much something gets better if you just leave it. Sometimes not, of course. Some things you'd love to scan, but not many. This, being here, will make me want to not investigate as much. To leave things."

The experience has her thinking about what she'd like to do with her career, and thinking about wider issues. "Why should this village have better healthcare than anywhere else in Malawi?" she asks. "But you've got to start somewhere. What I hope to do in my career is set up services, rather than just carry on."

On the negative side of her job, Brook does not enjoy working through translators, but has gotten used to it. "I think I miss out on the nuances of consultation," she says. "As a GP, I learned how to communicate, effectively tease out a hidden agenda, identify people's problems. All that gets lost. If they don't consider something worthy of translating, they just won't translate it. The first couple of weeks, I didn't like working here at all. What I could do well at home, I couldn't do at all. Then I got used to it. I found different ways to get information across."

She echoes Kate Brennan when she says, "It's not anyone's fault. It's just kind of frustrating that there's not a culture here of explaining things to the patient. They think you're mad sometimes when you want to explain a problem or diagnosis. The patient is not expected to hear it. You have people who've been to big hospitals, had parts of their anatomy removed, but no idea what for."

Home isn't on her mind too frequently. Helping was a recent visit by her mother, Jane, and sister, Sally. There are fruits and vegetables she'd like to enjoy more frequently, but she adds, "I don't miss anything else — because it's just a completely different place. You don't expect things to be here. It's the same with people — you make new friends. My boyfriend at home (archaeologist Zach, whom she's been seeing for six years) misses me, but the idea is you don't expect these things and people to be here, so you don't look for them, therefore don't miss them."

At her new practice, "in the poor part of Sheffield, where people would have been miners until the '80s," countless cases await her, countless challenges. She's up for them all, but not up for receiving the sainthood some would bestow on those who choose to volunteer.

"It costs a lot to come here, in comparison to what you're not earning. And it takes you away from things at home," she notes. "But I do feel selfish being here. It doesn't feel to me like I'm giving a lot up. I'm doing this because it's really good fun and really satisfying. It's a slightly odd thing to do, but it's the same as anything — if it's a massive sacrifice, it's no fun."

EIGHTEEN

For Mags Riordan, fun is a word she knows, whatever the language.

Humor, levity, an adventurous spirit, all are part of her life and her days. Some days, however, might hold time only for a wry observation made to crack up Steve in the middle of a difficult meeting. Other days, like Halloween, might find her in the dining room, standing in borrowed blue scrubs, stethoscope around her neck, Elaine liberally applying dripping lines of fake blood to the corners of Mags's mouth before she and The Gap occupants head off to parade their getups through several bars.

Sometimes the fun is in her language and lines. "Poppycock, bunkum and navel-gazing" is how she regards time-wasting seminars. Edward is preparing a meal of goat when she sticks her head in the kitchen to say, "Smells like you're cooking a man or something." Of a complainer she warns, "He better not open his beak." And assured by a government official that a matter will be taken care of, she thanks him then, once alone, says, "Yeah, right, and the Pope is my uncle. They lie as fast as a horse can trot."

Driving the road between Lilongwe and the Cape, she passes a group of men surveying a truck at the roadside, one of them wearing nothing. "It's the naked man!" she exclaims of the twenty-something guy, a sort of local celebrity known for walking around in the buff. "He just brightens up the scenery," she says.

A few weeks later, on the road between the village's Big Market and The Gap, the ambulance jounces to a stop at a kid named Stallone.

"Are you studying?" Mags asks.

"Sure, sure. I want to study law."

"I think you'd make a good lawyer," Mags says. "You talk enough."

There's a big smile from Stallone as Mags puts the ambulance in gear again, waves to Little Dorothy walking past. Military calls to her from over a fence. The sun is setting over a lake clear and inviting. She drives by houses chockablock, the lanes between them tidy. One home is the size of a large doghouse, walls of straw, windows partially covered by faded cloth. A figure sits inside. She points him out, knew he'd be there.

Mags says it took five years for her to feel at home in the village. She's in the ambulance again, steering along a brush-edged lane in Monkey Bay, when she recalls the moment. "I was driving, actually, through the bush. Someone said to me, 'You drive like you're home.' I realized I was."

She says that, for her, there's no strain in the village, no stress — despite the fact of why she's here in the first place, despite all she faces every day, and how steep the learning curve has been, both in how to operate a clinic and how to operate a life in a very different culture.

She thinks of her early visits here, when she first was told that all white people look alike, that they all smell of milk. She says it used to take a day to get in and out of Monkey Bay to make one phone call on a landline. Having dropped Steve and Siobhan at the hospital for a meeting regarding their nursing credentials, she's seated on a bench in front of a tiny Monkey Bay general store, watching bike taxis go by, and women walk past with cordwood, cardboard or rugs stacked on their heads.

At this end of the town are lake services (a large ferry that takes four days to journey to the top of the lake), a secondary school, an army barracks, and that much-maligned hospital. Across from the store, a matola stands idle, travelers queuing. She sips a cold Coke — her only choice of what she calls "minerals" — from a bottle (when away from The Gap, she never accepts a glass, as she never knows how well — or if — it was washed) and waits for a visit from a local friend who'd phoned to say he'd meet up with her in ten minutes. "Ten minutes here is half an hour, at least," she says. "I wouldn't give up for an hour. If they say they'll be here at something past four, it could be five, six, seven, eight, nine." Locals' only excuse when they eventually materialize, she says, is: "'It's Malawi time.' They all say, 'God made time, then he made African time.'"

Mags learned all that back when, as she says, "I had the time to sit around and chew the fat with guys." Some of those guys she got to know well. She recalls an early friend, another man named Steve, who had sarcoma and whom she helped by getting him to a good doctor at a hospital, buying his medicines, then, ultimately, paying for his coffin.

When her friend Mike does arrive after about an hour, he's with a man named D, who's wearing a T-shirt that reads "This is the body, this is the face of HIV/AIDS." Small, compact and handsome, Mike is in the middle of guiding a pair of tourists, taking them to a restaurant, showing them where to buy water, as he's just done by bringing him to this convenience store. What's his job? "This is it," he says. There is no work, he says, no assistance for those who are not working. "There is nothing," he says. "This is Africay." And he smiles.

In that same Africay, Mags has made her home, and by dinnertime is back at The Gap, sitting down in the dining room to catch up on the day, one in which the power quit at 7:00 a.m. and won't return until 8:00 p.m.

The screening of "Spongebob Squarepants" films down the beach, courtesy of a Dutch guy who comes to town a few times a year with a projector, will be postponed. Entertainment is never guaranteed for Mags, anyhow — some crisis might arise at the clinic or with the staff, and she and Steve might have to rush out. Depending on what interests are contained in a group of volunteers at any time, choices for excitement might be a poker game, a yoga session, a boat trip to the hippos who converge off Kasanka. But, basically, Mags enjoys going out to a restaurant, stopping at a pub, taking a rare walk on the beach, and she loves living at The Gap. She agrees with Dr. Nora, who told her friends and family, "We're gonna live with a load of Irish and British volunteers, at a holiday resort with wireless Internet. Don't feel so bad for us."

Even so, will she stay here, and for how long?

"I can see myself being involved for the rest of my life," Mags says. "But back and forth always? I don't know. I will always be involved, obviously, maybe I will stay living here through the year. What I do know is the thought of going back full-time in Ireland fills me with horror. I just don't think I could live in a country now where skies are gray six months of the year. I don't want to live in a society that is so consumer driven. I really don't."

It's also difficult to picture her living in a place where her finger wouldn't be on the pulse of the clinic on a daily basis, where, just today, a local man who'd broken his shoulder badly and was transported the three hours to Mangochi Hospital the other day returned to the clinic to report a doctor had refused to see him, telling the patient, "I'm only here to serve the people of Mangochi."

Mags grimaces at that story. She easily chuckles when she's told how that today, when the companion of another patient was asked, "When did your friend hurt himself?" the answer:

"Tomorrow."

In the dining room, the volunteers are talking about a twenty-one-year-old man who'd had his first sexual encounter three weeks ago and came in on this day with a gaping wound two centimeters deep in his groin.

"I'd thought I'd seen it all," Nora says.

Others express sympathy — "Poor guy" — others have none ——"There's enough education," they say, he should know about hygiene. And look at all the washing — of clothing and person — that goes on here at the edge of the lake. "If they put so much effort into their dryin' as their washin'," Nora says, "there wouldn't be so much fungal groins comin' in to see me."

Mags shakes her head. Checks her phone. An observer tries to picture Madonna living with the faculty of one of her schools, having tea with her volunteers, soaking up stories of the day. The major charity executive Mags knows, other than John O'Shea, is fellow Irishwoman Adi Roche, chief executive of the internationally applauded Chernobyl Children's Project International, which assists those affected by the 1986 explosion and fire at Chernobyl Nuclear Power Plant in the Ukraine. "Who have I met — celebrities?" Mags thinks. "If you're talking about rock stars, I've never met anybody. If you're talking politicians, I've met loads of them, but that's no boast."

Then, "Tommy Tiernan!" she exclaims. The hilarious and often controversial comedian from County Donegal has gone to bat for the Trust more than a few times, earning Mags's gratitude and her friendship.

"I think he's great, he's gold," she says. "He's one heck of a nice guy, completely different to what he is on stage. I find him to be extremely nice — more than a gentleman with us."

Tommy Tiernan had been part of two fundraisers since meeting Mags in 2006, when he and she were among the seven recipients of the People of the Year awards nominated by the Irish public and presented annually since 1975 by the Irish social service network Rehab Group. Past recipients have included Nobel Prize-winning poet Seamus Heaney, slain Irish journalist Veronica Guerin and Northern Ireland peace broker John Hume. Mags's award commends her "For the life changing and often life saving impact of a mother's love on many thousands of people in Malawi." Tiernan, who joined Mags in a class of honorees including actor James Nesbitt and the Munster Rugby Club, was selected for the designation of "Ireland's Funniest Living Person."

"I just said, 'Would you help?'" Mags remembers. "And he said, 'Fine. When you have something organized, let me know and if I can fit it in, I will.' And I did, and he did. Who else have I met? I'm sure there've been one or two more. They obviously didn't make a lasting impression."

Mags's straightforwardness extends to the way she lives her life, including keeping far from any diva tendencies. While walking the Miles for Malawi route through a rhododendron-filled wood in Springfield, Massachusetts' Van Horn Park in the chill of Thanksgiving morning 2011, a donor falls into step with Mags and tells her how greatly she is admired, including for how she copes with life in a place that must lack modern conveniences. The Gap indeed has flush toilets and hot showers, but Mags doesn't get into that. Her answer is only "I could pee in a bucket."

She cleans her skin with drugstore-shelf Anne French products, "the cheapest stuff you can get." She does admit to packing a box of hair color into the large hard-shelled lilac suitcase to keep her blonde locks that shade. "I have to say I take the dye with me. One of the girls does it for me. Otherwise, I'd be gray as a badger."

But the donor wants to canonize her. "Look what you gave up back home," she urges. "Your profession, seeing your family."

Mags shrugs, partly from the cold, mostly with her answer, giving her roots as a young wife and mother on the go. "We were always moving around," she says. "We lived once for a period of time in the North of Scotland, then in England, then in New York, then in California. We were always trucking off somewhere. We went down to Mexico for three months. It's kind of tinker blood — maybe not that, but I suppose I'm just adaptable. Really, I'm not trying to blow my own trumpet, I just think I'm very adaptable, Richie was very adaptable. I'm as happy going down there on the floor to sleep as in the fanciest bed in the world — it doesn't bother me. Things that would faze other people, that they'd be upset about, uptight about, I'm saying 'Whaddaya know!' I think it's just personality type."

It's not unlike the answer she gives when she's asked how she could even breathe after the loss of one, then two, then three children. And maybe she has to be like that to keep herself going.

Mags often is asked advice by and on behalf of others going through some form of tragedy. First, she prefers to speak directly to the person in grief, rather than through a friend or family member asking for them. Secondly, she will recommend they attempt therapy. But she will point out she has no personal experience as she engaged in no such therapy after any of the deaths. The only such effort she's been part of has taken place here, thousands of miles away, the act of living and working at the Cape.

"I never thought about it," she says. "And no one ever told

me, 'I feel you should go (to therapy)'. None of these things happened, so I didn't. It's hard to judge yourself, but I don't know what I would have done differently had I gone to therapy. A lot of people, this would change them, but in a bad way. They'd be badly depressed, it would be never ending. They'd be just not a happy person, ending up not able to cope. I obviously possess an ability to cope."

"I have never felt anger," she told the *Irish Independent* in 2004, when a documentary titled *For Love of Billy*, part of the *Would You Believe* television series, aired nationwide. "I think it's unfair that these things happened but there is no way I can change anything. There is an awful lot of suffering around me — people have been through far worse than me."

Mags credits her parents and her upbringing for her attitude, but backs up a bit on her previous comments that managing to live with tragedy is an Irish thing. She's not sure about that on this day she's asked, over tea in the dining room, but does feel that "coming to a foreign country and getting on well with the locals is 'an Irish thing.'" For the proof, she invites the questioner to look around. "There's mostly Irish and English here. There are others, but with the Irish, there's just a difference. I've had wave after wave of wonderful Irish people. Very often, Steve is the only English person here. It's the level of professionalism that impresses me. Difficult surroundings, equipment they're not used to. Wave after wave, not a penny being paid to them. Not a brass ha'penny."

In the place where Mags lives most of the year, including where she just passed Malawi's Mother's Day, the second Sunday of October, by spending a rare weekend away with friends gathered for the annual Lake of Stars music festival in Mangochi, death is addressed differently than in Ireland. Spirits are said to go to dwell in trees three months after a death, the reason why trees in graveyards aren't chopped down. Immediate family do not attend a funeral — they are left to grieve while the villagers head off to the ceremony. Children are buried in the early morning, adults in the afternoon, elderly in the evening. A year after a death, a person's house is burned and everything inside destroyed, so the survivors can move on.

In the place where Mags lives most of the year, she has her own language for that nebulous and personal act of moving on. "I used to feel it was behind me," she says of her grief. "Following me. Over time, I've come to feel it's no longer in back of me, but next to me. It walks alongside me."

It does that each day, including in this place many might feel wouldn't hold the source of much joy for Mags simply for the reason she ever set foot in it.

She says she thinks of Billy "quite often" in Chembe Village, at The Gap, where she'll soon walk to her flat by passing the stone set in his memory. Then she adds, "I'd think of him at home each day anyhow. But he's on duty upstairs."

She almost smiles as she says, "It's weird, it's weird. There are times I think it was all meant to happen. Sometimes I think that someone up there is pulling all the strings, and we're just being pulled along. I'm very thankful to Billy, as well. This is the best place and I've gotten far more out of it than he ever did. I should be sitting home, babysitting my grandchildren. I probably would have been doing something harebrained in my life. But not this."

The electricity has yet to return. Drumming begins from down the beach. The watchmen laugh from their post below the common-area windows. Fishing-boat lanterns make a long constellation of low stars on the Lake of Stars.

"I'd be lying if I said I didn't enjoy this," Mags says. "At the same time, I say, 'Do I have a drop of sense in my head?' On the other hand, when you finally pop your clogs, you would have made some difference.

"All the money in the world can't change the past but you try and make something positive come of it. So then at the end of the day you can face whoever you will face and say, 'Well, I did my best.'"

NINETEEN

You see her approaching and you think, "There's Mags in a dark wig."

Cathy Dillon, though slightly taller than her sister, has the same slim build, wears the same fitted and cool clothes, offers the same easy manner, and at the same time, the same intense eyes.

In the lobby of a Dublin Ballsbridge Hotel undergoing an ongoing renewal that in 2008 included Mohammed Ali cutting the ribbon to open the small grocery store located next to its restaurant, Cathy takes a seat during a break from work. On a late morning in August of 2011, she's come to the hotel from her desk downtown at *The Irish Times* on Tara Street, her employer for the past ten years. Her title is journalist. She once was film critic for *The Irish Press*, a paper founded by Eamon De Valera, who also helped found the Republic of Ireland. Her resume also includes writing music reviews for Ireland's legendary music and culture magazine *Hot Press*. Like Mags, in that house where *The Irish Times* arrived daily and *The Cork Examiner, The Sunday Times, The Irish Observer* and an Irish-language newspaper also were read regularly at one stage, she veered from the perhaps-expected medical career.

Maybe it's due to asking questions for a living that she considers each one sent her way, ponders her answer for a spell before responding, as she does now with the reason for her own career path: "They say the last child often does something creative. Others take particular jobs. I'm definitely the artistic one. *Never* (she stresses the "never") thought of medicine."

Cathy does teach yoga since becoming certified a year ago, after practicing for fifteen years. She thinks that might be her bow toward a healing art. "Well, in a kind of removed way," she says, "it has to do with health."

She's the baby of the family. There are ten years and three siblings between her and Mags. Due to the age gap, she felt like Mags was another mother. "But a different kind of mother," she notes and smiles, as she remembers Mags taking her to ballet class, "doing those sister kinds of things."

She and Mags always got on. "I don't remember ever fighting with Mags," Cathy says. "I was always pretty much on her side. I don't remember that much conflict. Mags is just part of my life. She's always been my big sister.

"There was a big age difference but I do remember quite vividly her teenage years. Friends coming to the house, going out with boyfriends, college friends. I was in awe of them, because they were cool. Had guitars. In '70, '71, she would have been in college. I remember when she got her first Leonard Cohen record. I've been listening to Leonard Cohen since I was eight."

The fact spurs more facts, including the several Cohen concerts she's attended, and her admiration for Bob Dylan, whom she calls "hit and miss," but adds "I don't even care if he plays — he's alive!"

That love of music was something she shared with nephew Billy.

"When Billy was small, I would spend a lot of time in Dingle," she says with a smile. "We were quite close when he was small. I was older . . . he was like my little brother, really."

Cathy calls him charming and gorgeous. Her role was the cool aunt. They talked rock 'n' roll. Billy liked that she wrote about it.

"I remember a phase when he was into The Cure and we would talk about music," she says. "I have a Philip Glass CD of his. He was into all kinds of stuff. Very wide-ranging interest. I would have had that kind of connection with Billy."

As for family traits, Cathy said he was his own person. "I never think of Billy being anyone but Billy, kind of unique, really. He just kind of had his own take on things. Very much a kind of student of the world. Very smart, very self-possessed. . . Bits of Mags and bits of Richie, but really his own person."

She thinks for a few seconds and then corrects the ratios. "A lot of my mother's energy and a lot of Mags's energy," she says. "It's a lot about the energy." That's what she remembers of him, that is what, for her, set him apart.

Luke and Niamh weren't alive long enough for their aunt to establish anything similar with them. "I didn't know them, really," she says, and the sentence hangs in the air for a bit. "The others were only a few months old."

When Cathy looks at her brother Mike's three children, and brother Frank's two, along with Mags's Jennifer and Emma, she stops to thinks how old Mags's other three would be now.

"I remember the day Mags came to the house with Niamh," she says. "I was thinking recently that if Niamh had lived, she'd be thirty-seven now. Now I feel like I miss her. I have a lot of friends that age."

Tears fill Cathy's eyes.

Along with that niece and two nephews, there's a big sister she misses, too.

"We get very little time together now," she says. "Maybe go to dinner, hang out, have a drink. This is her time, you scale things. She is saying she's going to come to Dublin next time."

The two keep in touch via phone. They Skype and want to do more of that. Cathy would like to visit Malawi, see her sister on her turf, a place about which she initially had mixed feelings.

"I did wonder why she wanted to go there, then go there to stay," she says as other travelers move through the doors of the hotel. "I had been wondering about her going. But she was trying to pull something out of something really traumatic. It's a way of dealing with a major bereavement. We're all very different, but, overall, we all need something."

For Mags, Cathy says, the outreach fit her. "Mags was always a bit of a campaigner, even while in school. She was quite active in the student union, for the school in Dunquin, the power plant, always an activist. She always was the kind of person who saw injustice and wanted to change things. Long before Billy. That was always in her."

Cathy remembers Mags's initial idea to build a school in Billy's memory, and she watched as her sister began thinking more and more about offering medical care. Mags's current thoughts about starting a school in the village, Cathy says, are exciting, though funding possibilities right now are not. "But," she notes with economy and truth, "I'd say she's good at making things happen."

Whatever the ultimate project Mags attempts, Cathy sees it as a very healthy way to deal with loss. "I would have been at the bottom of a bottle," she says. And she watched and felt the ripple effect of grief extended through the layers of family.

"The first few years after Billy died, I was very concerned about Mags and the girls, and keeping their own life going was definitely a concern," Cathy says. "I think it was very difficult for them. The mother was completely bereft, the dad was completely bereft. Even I felt I was going through my own thing. It's very sad — I'd had a great loss, too."

Several losses, over all the years. Something she accepts as just how life is. "I'm a bit of a fatalist," she says. "It could be anyone going through this."

A specific faith hasn't helped her through, as Cathy is an agnostic. "I have been since age nine and I'll probably die an agnostic," she says. "I am firmly considering this random, just bad luck. As a journalist, you see many things in life. You just realize something like this is just really, really bad luck."

She pulls a tissue from her bag, and offers another truth.

"Look at all (Mags) has done — what happened since Billy died — in a positive way. It's good, but you'd prefer it didn't happen. Before Billy died, if someone asked me what would be the worst thing you can think of I'd say, 'Something happening to Billy.' And it happened."

TWENTY

That's life for you. You have it all and for one split second the candle blows out and that's it."

Teresa Parke is talking about her own tragedy. One that, like Mags's, greatly influenced her physical and emotional journeys.

Teresa's loss was Ger Parke, the policeman to whom she was married for just two years when he was killed in a 2002 road accident en route to work, his car struck by a Polish laborer's vehicle veering into oncoming traffic.

She endured what she calls "three very tough years" following his death, but says, "I'm good now, and I'm good because I'm living another dream. He was my dream. Now, I've just found the dreams I lost along the way."

The athletic, brown-haired forty-five-year-old Wicklow native tells her story on a day off that will include a mountain bike ride along the roads of the country she first heard mentioned by a Kiltegan priest, a good friend of Ger's who ended up performing their marriage ceremony.

She states another connection to at least the African continent, one directed by her husband. "Before Ger was killed, we were trying to think what to do with some clothes. He said, 'Why don't we give them to a charity going to Africa?' So that could have been the month before he died, might have been a few days, a week, I can't remember. But when he died I was trying to sort through what to do with his clothes, so they went to a charity. His clothes came to Africa."

The donation was fitting as a memorial to a kind man whose widow describes him as loving children and wanting to help people of any age.

"He used to catch people shoplifting, wouldn't just bang them in prison" is the start to Teresa's recounting how Ger caught a wealthy woman shoplifting in a posh shop. "His response was to take her for a cup of coffee, talk to her. She told him she had a well-to-do husband, but her life was boring. Ger knew if he summonsed her, it would ruin her life. He got her to promise she would never do it again."

Ger Parke died at thirty-eight, a policeman of ordinary rank who was repeating his sergeant exams for the second year. "He had high hopes," says Teresa.

Her own long-term ones echo those held by so many other volunteers: a desire to fly off somewhere and help somebody.

"Always, from the day I started nursing, I wanted to do this. It was one of my dreams. To travel, do volunteer work abroad."

A staff development coordinator in the intensive care unit at Dublin's Saint James's Hospital, where she's worked for seventeen years, Teresa has no connection to medical care in a family where she is second eldest of seven kids.

"My mother always wanted to be a nurse, though, but she ended up nursing her parents at home," she says. "So I think she planted the seed, to be a nurse. For me, it's what I wanted to be from a small age."

As for the inspiration to volunteer, Teresa says, "I suppose as kids you go to Mass and listen to the missionary priests telling stories, raising money in the church for their churches in Africa. We also got the missionary magazine sent by the Kiltegan priests — they always raised money through sending out the magazine."

Teresa followed in her mother's footsteps when she nursed her father after his diagnosis with Alzheimer's and the family's subsequent decision to care for him at home, by themselves.

"I had found the dream of traveling and being a volunteer again," Teresa says. "I knew, though, I had to stay with the family and work our way through minding him at home. I had my dream and really wanted to go somewhere, but I knew I had to stay. I had started doing baby steps. I knew I needed little baby steps first, to get a feel for Africa."

Those included a charity camping trek through the African nation of Lesotho in 2007, and a return trip one year later to work for ten days with tradesmen building an orphanage in response to the poverty the group had seen the previous year.

Teresa already was an avid traveler, taking an annual ski or sun holiday, hitting the slopes in Austria and Italy. She'd once lived overseas, working in America for a year in the renal transplant ward at Boston's famed Deaconess Hospital.

When a friend at home told Teresa about a fundraiser for a nurse who was to be volunteering at the Cape, her response was "Tell me." The friend began giving details about the event. Teresa cut her off with: "'No,' I said, 'tell me where she's going to go.' She told me as much as she knew, and the minute she started telling me, I was interested."

Teresa kept tabs on the volunteer, hearing about the ups and downs she experienced. "I knew from the outset I liked what I heard," she says. "I knew this place was for me. That was it, I had decided then. I got in touch with Mags and talked to Mags about it, had all my questions answered."

Her initial stay was in June of 2009, with a commitment of four months. "I loved it," Teresa says. "From a very short period of time, I knew I'd want to stay longer. I started to realize that stability was needed to carry on what others were doing. I felt there was a place for me. I didn't have anything to rush home for so I decided to stay. I extended for another six months, am now extending again for six months more. I'll probably come back for a shorter stint, but I need to figure out what to do from here."

Ties back home are a house she owns and the fact a position at her hospital is being held for her on an unpaid career break.

Her family offers only encouragement.

"They are happy that I am happy," Teresa says. "I think they saw me sad for long enough. When I came home, they saw the light in my eyes.

"I spent a long time in (Dublin's Saint James's Hospital), working in an acute setting. I was very happy at work the first few years, but then it was not the same satisfaction. I needed a change. This has been the ideal change. What will I do next? I'm kind of at a crossroad. Where I'll go next I don't know. I know it won't be back to the ICU. For me, I just feel like we don't want to let people die any more with dignity, so we take in elderly patients — it doesn't matter what age you are any more, we will torture them until they die and we never now allow people to die normally because they're in renal failure or multiorgan failure. We keep flogging them until they die. No decisions are made to let this person die with dignity and it's like when they die, how quickly can you wrap them up, ship them out because the next patient is coming. There's no thought to the new nurse at the end of the bed, the family who have now lost a loved one."

At the clinic, the contrast is no real ICU, minimal resources, minimal emergency drugs, Teresa says. "If somebody is going to die here, we do our best with little resources. If we see it's gone too far to transfer them to Monkey Bay, we make the decision locally and we allow someone to die with dignity, allow someone to die with family members there. We give them time, I suppose. I wouldn't say life decisions are made simpler here — it's a complete contrast. It's a pity we can't marry the extremes and put them together. That would make it, as I would see it, an ideal world."

She praises the spirit of cooperation that she sees as key to making the clinic work each day.

"A team of people probably can achieve anything. It's like, I look at the clinic up there, a group of us coming out here and not having our translator, not having our counselors, not having the personal care attendants (PCAs), not having the people at reception, not enough nurses around — we need care for the patients, even to pack the pills — Sofina, Justice, Elines, the cleaning ladies, Big Dorothy will pack pills in the room with the doctors, say, 'It's fine, no problem.' It's a huge team effort. For everybody who comes here to act responsible and to have flexibility and work within a team is so important to this whole team running well."

Teresa's first glimpse of Mags was on TV, being interviewed on *The Late Late Show* by Gay Byrne, who for thirty-seven years was Ireland's Johnny Carson.

"I admire Mags greatly because I know what she has gone through with sadness in her life," Teresa says as she checks the clock to make sure she'll have enough daylight for her biking. "And because of struggles I have had in my life, to see what she has done with the sadness, turned it all around to make something very positive — where she got the strength to do something like that I can't figure out. If someone said to me 'Ger will die within two years of your marriage,' I'd have said 'I'll never be able to cope, I can't survive without him.' But I found the strength I never thought I had. I'm so much stronger as a person.

"I admire her strength. I would say her exterior comes off as being very tough, but behind all that, she has that softness in her heart. But she has to be like that, to keep the project going, like. I can't figure out where she gets all of it, her drive to keep going, keep going, no matter what. I don't know if I had the same drive, all the different barriers every day, if I could do it. But here she comes, she keeps fighting, fighting, fighting. And there's nothing made easy. For her, it's the fight to keep it going."

TWENTY-ONE

Hers is the third in a row of them on the left-hand side of a very steep paved road off the very top of Main Street in Dingle, just past the closed-down hospital and just across from a fire brigade headquarters, which is deserted on a gray early afternoon in September of 2011. Katherine "Kitty" Dillon opens that blue front door in a heather blue zip-front sweater with flowers embroidered across the front hem. Her pants are dark blue plaid and her socks are gray. She had foot surgery two months ago and is just starting to get around, to garden. It's raining out, and the two big windows that make up most of the back of her unit show a garden now getting watered — bright low flowers, some lettuce, all looking neat, though she claims the plot has been neglected.

The home is bright, easy to heat, she notes, with the stove insert in the sitting-room hearth, and close to town if she doesn't care to drive. It's not a long walk to the church she attends, St. Mary's Catholic, on Green Street. It's also comfortable, including on this day, when Kitty sits on the long white leather couch perpendicular to those garden windows and talks about her daughter, Mags Riordan. In that conversation, she refers to her as Margaret. Kitty sours her face when asked why she doesn't use the name everyone else does.

"Her name is Margaret," she says, in the firm manner of one who chose that name, and no other, for her child. Then she offers tea. A Kit Kat. Both with a genial "There you are,

260

now."

Kitty is eighty-four, as trim and fit as her daughter, thanks in part to regular swims down at the pool in the Skellig Hotel on the harbor. She and husband Victor would have been married fifty years in April of 1998, had he not died of an aortic aneurysm that January. She looks fondly on their life together, but makes something clear: "I always had a life of my own as well outside the children and charity work. Some people are completely depending on their husbands." As for how hard it was to grieve that husband, she stops to think, then shrugs, saying "Anything unpleasant, I don't remember."

Their eight grandchildren include Mags's Billy, whom she compares to her second son, Frank, also a lover of travel, an uncle whom Billy resembled. "Facially and in mannerisms," she says, "and in not worrying."

When asked for her mental images of Billy, Kitty leans back on her couch. Thinks of the child born in Cork, conveniently near her home at the time.

"I'd say he was a couple hours old when I met him," Kitty says, smiling. "It was excellent to have a grandchild."

He was her second, born after Niamh's death. "That he was the second one, there was obviously a certain anxiety that you can imagine, so it was joyful, but it was mixed."

Kitty saw a lot of Billy, even though the family lived in Dingle.

"I was very fond of him and he was quite attached to me. But of course he was up and down a lot because Margaret was up and down a lot.

"He did the garden with me, we did it together. He liked to pull up the plants. I was busy planting, he was pulling. But he loved that, he loved being out, messing in the garden. I think I remember him talking quite a bit about school. He was very keen on school and he used to tell me all about what he did in school. He made me a dibbler, which is a thing for putting in plants. He made me one of those I still have. It was lovely."

When Billy was old enough, the visits were made solo.

"He would come to Cork, he'd stay for a week," she says. "I wouldn't say I knew him very well. I wouldn't have known him as well as I knew the girls. And he had the trauma of the marriage breakup and didn't discuss that. But he was very pleasant, very likeable, very humorous. But what went on in his life, I wouldn't know."

Even so, he was present, traveling to Cork for summer schools including sailing lessons in Oyster Haven. And for a U2 concert.

"Yes, he would have been ten days with me at that stage," Kitty says. "And himself and a couple others went down to U2. When he was younger he'd come down, not to do anything but to hang out, mess around, play tennis with the others. He used to come down, was always more than welcome, never any trouble at all. I had time at that stage. Someone who had nothing else to do at that stage but look after him."

Kitty blinks back tears when picturing Billy.

"He was active. He was very active. Very tall and slim, you know he was physically fit," she says. "He was a very handsome young man, to start with. Full of bright ideas. Very good at expressing himself. Very kind. Very lovable."

She stops to collect herself. But, as is her habit, she doesn't stop for long. Kitty Dillon is always on the move. In thought, in action. She shared with her grandson Billy a deep love of travel, and remains in fine enough shape to regularly explore the world, recently having returned from a trip to Jordan, having seen much of Europe, and having made three visits to Israel. She's yet to get to China or Japan, she notes, but don't count those out. They would have been covered ages ago, but "Air travel came too late," she says. "I had children by that time."

In 2004, she made the lengthy journey to Malawi for the opening of the Billy Riordan Memorial Clinic. Of all the destinations Kitty's visited, she found Malawi different. She says the Middle East, even in remote places, is more modern than what she saw during her three weeks in Cape Maclear.

"If I was younger I'd love to go back, but the conditions there were very primitive when I stayed there," she says in her quiet and measured and honest manner of speaking. "The food was absolutely atrocious. There were rats running across the floor. The showers were cold. I found it very difficult."

She also found little to do. "I used to do a little bit in the clinic, help with sorting medicines, but the rest of the time was boring. I didn't want to swim — I'd been warned about parasites in the lake. If I was younger, I could skim over these things, but I just found it very difficult. I use to take the kids on the beach and try to teach them a few letters, but if you're not going to be there a long time, it's difficult."

Ever the mother, Kitty remarks that the children, despite the poverty in which they lived, appeared clean. Perhaps, she muses, it was because there's no cooking inside the houses, and because there is no need for indoor heating. On both counts, no resulting ashes. And she visited in the dry season, so there was no mud. "They were beautiful," she says, "and very happy."

And the reason for that, she ventures, is "Because, first of all, they've never known it otherwise. They might never know television exists. Life as we know it, they don't know about it. People had computers long before we in Ireland did, and we wanted them when we knew about it."

She saw village women washing clothes in the lake. "There's a trade-off to throwing things in a machine," she says, "and to washing them with the beauty of nature in front of you."

As Kitty talks about revisiting the Cape these days by checking the online site for the *Nyasa Times*, six-year-old black-and-white terrier Buttons jumps on the couch, pays Kitty total attention. She pets him as she continues on to say she had not heard of Malawi before Billy went there. But she didn't find his interest in the African continent odd, feeling the Irish are very curious about lands beyond their own.

"The number one reason," she says, "is the population by and large has a great imagination. They can imagine what people are going through in other places. We have famine in our history, our ancestors starved. That would make starvation very real to us. Also, the Irish nuns and priests were going to Africa for a long time. The African missions were supported in schools."

Those included the one in her Dublin childhood. The foreign mission box in Kitty's classrooms held that figure of a black baby. "You put in a coin, the black baby nodded," she says, and remembers the message: "'Thank you, thank you, thank you.'" She still donates to African causes, just last week sending twenty euros to the SMA Fathers.

"Apart from giving to Malawi," Kitty says, "I do something every month."

Mags's childhood school supported a convent, and the Dillon family was familiar with the plight of the less fortunate. "My husband was a physician in the North Charitable Infirmary, for twenty-five or more years, for nothing," Kitty says. "Six days a week. It was something to work there, they only took the best of the best. He worked 2:30 to 5:30 and took calls at home at night. House calls. Other than that, he worked a paying job in the morning, at Bon Secours Hospital. But I'd imagine he gave more time to North Infirmary. He might be out two times a night."

Once Mags was born, Kitty did not work outside the home, but did manage to fit in a lot of volunteer work. She spent thirty years with Citizens' Information Centre, which offered information on social services, and logged fifteen at Cura, an agency assisting those in crisis pregnancies. She's not sure her children took much notice of her volunteering, but the actions had to have planted something in her Margaret.

". . . The higher the mountain, the more incredibly difficult to climb, the better. It's simply 'Just go on' — all very, very determined. She's always been like that," Kitty says of a daughter who manages to keep moving, stay busy.

She recalls a twelve-year-old Mags returning home of her own accord after only eight weeks at boarding school.

"She left school, got on a train. She was twelve. How she got to the train is a mystery. I didn't like it. We had bought clothes, blankets, and she rang from the station to say she was home from school, one hundred and sixty miles away. There would be no question about going back. That wouldn't even be thought of."

The determination Mags had even at that age mirrors the type she still bears. But at the time, to have a child make such a decision, and stick to it, wasn't seen as an admirable act by Kitty.

In her life, for her worries and concerns, Kitty has found solace of her own at Mass, and attends St. Mary's regularly. "But I don't go for the same reason as most. My religion is with God, not with Rome or the priest. I don't have a problem with God, though he may have one with me."

With the deaths of Niamh, then of Luke, then of Billy, Kitty saw locals incorporating faith into their reasoning why the tragedies occurred.

"People here are deeply religious and would accept it as the work of God," she says as the rain begins to really beat down, and any color in the garden — the green of the lettuce and the red of the flower petals — is ratcheted up. "You can blame everything on God if you're deeply religious. Then, you would be able to accept it. You can't wonder why God would do such things — 'God works in mysterious ways' and we're not supposed to try to figure them out. . . .

"That didn't help me. But then, I'm not as religious as some . . . There's no questioning something for which there is no answer."

TWENTY-TWO

A idan Ellis went to the Cape as part of a trip organized by Irish Aid, which twice a year flies reporters to other countries to see the effects of Irish charities, a public relations effort that helps them justify funds received from the Irish government.

He's a sub editor for *The Irish Sun*, not a staff reporter — therefore not the first person the paper might send off to cover a story, especially not the first who'd be sent to somewhere so far outside the circulation area. But Mags Riordan's story is one he wanted to write after having heard of her from a County Cork co-worker who told him, "This woman is a gas — you have to meet her."

"I thought we should be covering her," Aidan says. "It's rare when a story comes up that might be of that much interest to our readers — a Kerry woman starting a clinic in Africa?"

He makes it clear the trip was not a junket. "(The Irish-based charity) Concern might fly a group (of journalists) to Sudan. I've been on junkets — they can be a good time. But the famine is not a junket. That would be kinda pathetic. On the Irish Aid trips, you write about what they're doing, but I also wanted to write about what I wanted to write about. I wouldn't have been able to go if I hadn't gone along with Irish Aid."

The Irish Aid part of the trip would be "a Plumpy'Nut type of project," he recalls, referring to the peanut-based paste being used to treat malnutrition. "I would do that and do a little bit on this Irish woman. I talked to my editor and said, 'It won't cost you a penny. I'll do it on my own time.' The Plumpy'Nut story would be great but the Mags story would be very cool. The editor bought it straight away. It's a bit fascinating. A woman from Kerry is doing this, and seems quite determined to stay."

Aidan, thirty-two, knows a good story when he sees one. At the time of his visit to the Cape in October of 2010, he'd been at the paper for four years, since its founding. At midday in a late August of the following year, he's wincing from a long shift the night before, working until eleven on a double murder in Turkey; two women from Northern Ireland killed by the boyfriend of a fifteen-year-old daughter of one of the victims. "TURKISH MURDER HORROR: HOME FROM HELL" reads the head of his main story that day, about the daughter returning via Belfast airport. A small story above that directs you to pages eight and nine for more on "MAD DOG CORNERED", Libyan dictator Muammar Gaddafi on his way out. There's also a story on fugitive drug lord George "The Penguin" Mitchell posing as an international gems dealer, and a piece on shamed Bishop John Magee breaking his silence and begging forgiveness for his role in Ireland's Catholic Church sexual abuse scandals. In the tradition started by *The Sun* in 1970 and subsequently copied by tabs in the United Kingdom and internationally, the paper includes a daily photo of a topless woman on page three, today's with a big smile, bigger breasts and tiny bikini bottoms.

The piece Aidan wrote on Mags, which ran on November 22 of 2010, bore the kicker "IRISH SUN JOINS GRIEVING MOTHER MAGS ON MERCY TRIP TO MALAWI" and the main headline of "My son Billy said I'd love this village . . . when he died here I felt I had to see it."

Large amounts of the Trust story bookend a smaller section about the Irish Aid-funded Lilongwe food distribution program Valid Aid. Aidan has given lots of space to Billy's message to his mother, the trip she ultimately made to see this place he called paradise, and what she ended up doing there.

Seated on a high stool in the bright Kylemore Café on Dublin's O'Connell Street, Aidan wears a black T-shirt on a warm day, black classic Ray-Ban sunglasses, silver ring on his right hand. He recalls the journey to Malawi that was far from his first time in Africa. He has relatives in South Africa, and his childhood family trips often were to that part of the world. He's also been to Kenya and Zimbabwe, and knew of Malawi because of his African interest, because of the Lake of Stars Festival (another topic he covered for *The Irish Sun,* in a separate story) and from living in a country where interest in the world extends far beyond the borders — not the case for every nation around the globe, he notes.

"I think we're a lot more interested in world affairs than other cultures (are)," he says and recalls a cousin from South America marveling that on a recent flight on Aer Lingus, the national airline of Ireland, a videotaped campaign sought passengers' donations for famine victims in the Horn of Africa. The cousin said he'd hardly heard of the problem back on his continent and asked incredulously, "Why do you here on this little island collect money for Sudan?"

Aidan's response, then and now, "I don't know, it goes back to before I was born. It goes back to the black babies and the church. We're a lot more curious about the world. Between traveling, and reading about what happens in other countries, people (in Ireland) seem quite happy to raise money."

The trip lasted ten days, including two given to flying. Three days went to covering stories connected to Irish Aid, and in the rest he concentrated on the Trust and the festival.

The Irish Aid portion of his trip was very structured and

organized, he says, topics he might cover and preferred destinations discussed in advance.

"Then I get to Cape Maclear and meet Mags and she says, 'Get in the van, let's go.' It's that real, full-on, very enjoyable — that's her style — 'Jump in, I have things to do.'"

He went along with her. To the clinic. To the meeting on the chief's sister's porch. To the schools. To The Gap. Though he felt welcome, he also felt Mags initially was sussing him out, perhaps because of the tabloid nature of the Rupert Murdoch-owned paper.

"It's not something we normally cover," Aidan admits. And he repeats that it's a story that deserves covering. "She's made this her mission — for good or bad, she's doing this. I've met a lot of aid workers. They work, but in ten years what they've done is no good. She mapped it right. Said, 'Here's a village, here are people who are sick. It's not this pie-in-the-sky thinking. It's, 'Here's a hospital, here's a clinic.'"

He was surprised by the frequent power cuts — "I didn't think that happened any more" — and a level of poverty he'd not seen before. "To land in the capital and there's nothing," he starts. "The buildings are spread out — they have planned what the city will be, but I doubt if they'll actually get it."

The schools also stuck in his mind, as he wrote:

"Back in Cape Maclear, Mags is also looking to expand her operation. With the medical centre up and running, she's started looking at raising funds to build a second school in the village.

"And with just one teacher looking after a staggering 420 first class children in the existing school you can see why.

"She says: We're looking to build a school at the other end of the village. Ideally, we would have some Malawian teachers working hand in hand with Irish volunteer teachers.

"I see a lot of similarities between here and Ireland. Ireland was in the doldrums until free education started under Donogh O'Malley in the Sixties.

"Everyone thought he was mad. Here, they brought in free education but didn't put any more resources into the schools.

"Primary education is not about just putting kids in a class-room — you also have to provide teachers and books. The schools here have nothing."

As always, it's funding that will be the biggest problem — but Mags is determined, despite the difficulties Aidan included in his piece, and what the Trust once received. As Mags told him, "Bizarrely enough, Anglo Irish Bank gave us 75,000 (euro) during the boom — 25,000 a year for three years.

"It was the biggest single donation this place every got but that's hardly going to happen again any time soon."

The story ends with the Trust's website, in case any reader would like to donate. This type of information tag often runs after *Sun* stories but, says Aidan, "With this one, I was thinking someone from Kerry might say 'She's from here' and write a check."

Someone might have been changed by reading his piece. Was the writer changed by making the trip to research it?

"Leaving, I was sick as a dog," Aidan says, referring to overindulging in the local brew at the Lake of Stars. "Chibuku Shake Shake not a good idea."

Then he gets serious: "In Ireland, we're all doom and gloom, we're all losing our jobs, but there, the kids are running around naked and they're so happy. Here, it's 'I'm from a poor village in Ireland, but I'm sitting here watching Skype.' Since Malawi, I've been thinking why people who have nothing can be so happy. For people to be so poor and be so happy with the world . . ."

Aidan shrugs as the stirred-up memories settle. They've remained with him, as have images of the woman who seeks to

271

serve those in the village he visited.

"She's quite daft — really daft enough to do it. And I don't say that in a bad way. She's serious about this. I think it's a Kerry thing. They're a little different down there." He smiles. "She just has that kind of determination. Takes chances. I don't know many people — or any people, really — who'd do what she does."

TWENTY-THREE

S it with Antonio Fazio to talk about Billy Riordan, and you'll quickly be told the story of another boy who died: the boy who grew into the man telling you the story.

"I was born dead," is how he starts in a swaying Sicilian accent. He states the fact without looking into your eyes for any effect, his concentration instead on the pouch of tobacco he's opening as he prepares to roll a cigarette.

"The doctor said to my mother, 'He's a nice boy, but, unfortunately, he's dead.' They wrapped me in a towel. Thank God, before they buried me they saw my heart was beating. Sometimes I really think I had a dream in that time — that the dream between my dying and them finding I was alive, this is what's happening now. Sometimes I think this is the dream."

If so, for the past nineteen years, Antonio Fazio's dream has been taking place in Ireland, his most recent stop in a life of wandering that began when he left Sicily at fourteen. He found the landscape of stone familiar to that of his island of origin, where he'd once helped his father build a stone hut of rocks, poles and reeds. In Ireland he also found himself fascinated with Celtic art, and since moving to Dingle in 1991 has been carving both three-dimensional work and relief pieces from the sandstone of the peninsula where he's settled.

He tells the story of his birth and death and rebirth while seated outside his carving studio, Art in Stone, a former blacksmith's forge on the R559 road, halfway between Dingle and the next village of any size, Ventry. He's maybe five foot eight inches, with a scruffy dark beard that matches his hair. His red-and-white running jacket and green trousers are loose-fitting but hint at a body made fit by the weight of his chosen medium. In the workspace to Antonio's left, in the gallery room to his right, in the courtyard of the adjacent home and lining the wall along the road are stunning standing stones covered in Celtic knots. A sleeping baby lies in an oval egg. The word *fáilte*, Irish for welcome, is accented with intricate knots.

His mastery, detailed in photos that fill a seventy-one-page book he self-published in 2007 and in which he generously offers readers to "Please feel free to copy any of these designs for personal use," gives no hints of a childhood that didn't afford Antonio such basics as drawing paper or pens, or any formal training. A fundamental lack of self-confidence remains an open wound.

"In Sicily," Antonio says, "If you didn't study, your work isn't considered serious. Your art is not from a college of art."

But the work created at his studio, Art in Stone, still is fine enough to have found enthusiastic customers from all corners of the world, who display their purchases in all those corners of the world. Including in a sandy courtyard in a tiny village at the end of a peninsula in the African country of Malawi.

"I know both Richie and Mags, and Billy," Antonio says. There's a small space after that information, a pause not given to anything but silence before he looks the listener in the eyes as he says, "I was the last person from here ever to see Billy."

In February of 1999, Fazio was in Harare, Zimbabwe, attending a carving festival, the one and only reason he was on his one and only trip to Africa.

"I was with two friends. They were way ahead of me," he begins. "I heard my name. They were headed away from me, not calling me. I heard my name again. Turned around. It's Billy Riordan. I say 'What are you doing here?' He said 'I'm going to Malawi.'"

Antonio and Billy stood in the street and caught up.

"He looked great, tan, happy," Antonio says. "He talked about how he loved Malawi. I said 'I'm going back (home) tomorrow. I'll tell everyone I saw you.'" There's another pause. "I came back, somebody told me that Billy Riordan was missing."

The first stone Antonio carved for the family was the one that stands at the grave in Milltown with its carving of a bird flying into a sun beaming with many rays.

In that cemetery on this warm afternoon in August of 2011, the edges of the lettering glow softly with an accent of gold paint, a request made by Mags to Antonio the last time she saw him. To the left of the lantern that is among the items deposited at its base is the now-dried bridal bouquet brought there by Jennifer after her wedding sixteen months before.

The second stone Antonio carved for a Riordan family member was the one Mags took to Malawi in 2000, delivering it to the Cape two days after the first anniversary of Billy's death. Antonio isn't certain what kind of stone that is, but thinks it might have been basalt. It's got the same ragged-edged top as the one in Milltown, but on this one, Antonio carved the last communication from Billy to his mother: "This is Paradise."

As he has carved that last image into his mind.

"He was so happy when I saw him," says the man who, in the dream that is his life, recorded Billy Riordan's name in stone.

TWENTY-FOUR

On the day after concluding a two-week honeymoon in Norway, Dr. Peadar O'Fionnain and Dr. Maire Curtin are back at their home in Ireland's County Waterford. But not for long. In two weeks they'll be taking one more trip to celebrate their marriage. Next stop: Chembe Village.

It'll be a happy homecoming of sorts for Maire, who served at the clinic for four and a half months in 2010 and 2011. For Peadar, it'll also be a return, but one with bittersweet memories. After a lengthy fundraising campaign, his long-awaited six-month stint at the Cape in October of 2010 was only in its first week when he returned home to Dingle to be with his critically ill father.

General practitioner Micheal Fanning died two months later, on Christmas Eve, after fifty-six years of life that overflowed with accomplishments. He'd run a clinic in Dingle since 1982. He'd written ten books of poetry. He'd helped start the local credit union. In 1994, he founded and became director of *Féile na Bealtaine*, a nationally renowned annual arts and politics festival that takes over Dingle for one week each May. He'd also been the one who once offered Paul Maroney the work that got him rooted in Dingle. Though modern enough to set up one of the country's first primary care teams in 1998, Micheal had been old-school enough to make house calls. During his funeral Mass, the lamp that illuminated his way to remote homes, and the doctor's bag he carried there, were offered as gifts. Farther afield, he was a director of the Irish branch of International Physicians for the Prevention of Nuclear War. And, much farther, he volunteered abroad, first with Concern in Ethiopia from 1984 to 1985, in a Romanian orphanage in 1994, and in Lesotho in 2008.

"He just decided he had to go," Peadar says of that first trip taken by his father, who on that journey left behind his son, and his wife, Noirin, who was pregnant at the time. "So we had to grow up with a strong example of this. I suppose all Irish people would have strong connections to Africa anyway — everyone has an aunt who was a nun or an uncle who was a priest, everybody knows someone who's been there, and there's a connection that leads to fundraising and volunteering and consciousness. But we had it extra in that Dad had been there."

Peadar Fanning would be inspired to travel from his childhood home in Dingle, first to med school at University College Dublin, graduating in 2005 and spending the next year in the Middle East and the one after that in Belgium. He'd been working as a GP in Ireland before leaving for Malawi in 2010.

During an interview done via Skype in early August of 2012, he sits at the table in a kitchen white enough to be mistaken for that of a doctor's office. His light brown hair is spikey, his glasses rectangular, his green T-shirt bears an image of Snoopy. He can't recall where he acquired the shirt, but notes in what is an introduction to his cheekiness, "Most of my clothes are stolen."

He's thirty-two and talks about knowing of Mags since childhood, but was between the ages of Billy, Emma and Jennifer, so didn't directly know the family then. Half a dozen or so years ago, Micheal Fanning had asked Mags to speak at a political symposium that was part of a festival, about development in the third world, and Peadar had paid attention. Also, Micheal had trained general practitioners, some of whom traveled to the clinic to serve four of their assigned twelve months with him, so that provided further information.

In an effort to raise funds for the clinic before he left, Peadar sought pledges for three fundraising efforts done over four months. The first, in June of 2010, consisted of three parts: a cycling trip over Conor Pass (Ireland's highest); a climb/jog over the country's second-highest mountain, Mount Brandon; and a thirteen-kilometer road run and kayak across Dingle Harbor. The second, that July, was a 168-kilometer cycling trip around the Ring of Kerry, done on a thirty-year-old single-speed women's bicycle he found in Maire's mother's shed and painted what he calls a lurid red. The third fundraiser, that September, was the twenty-one-kilometer Dingle Half Marathon.

"People are very generous," he says. "We just wrote a few letters and put a few notices in the newspapers. Maire ran a quiz in a pub. People are looking for ways to help, people like to be asked. If they're given a bona fide thing to support, they like to be included."

Peadar raised 10,000 euro — 3,000 to 4,000 more than he'd anticipated. He'd not set a goal or noted its future use by the clinic. "We didn't feel we should specify," he says. "We felt it would be for mostly day-to-day costs. If you specify it's for something shiny — look, everybody wants to do the shiny stuff. But Mags also says 'I need to pay for electrical cables.' We know she's very tight, like, doesn't spend just to spend. As a volunteer, I paid for milk and lunch, there's no slipping of money anywhere there."

That's just one reason he calls Mags "a real phenomenon."

"You have to be tough in Africa," he points out. "Life is tough there and your money will slide if you're not looking after the nitty gritty — is anyone taking water from you? I think she's steely and at the same time she's very warmhearted, well able to organize, can be super pragmatic. She was very good to me, instantly warm."

When Peader had to return home so soon after arrival, he was impressed further.

"Most people would think of their own problems," he says. "'Now I don't have a doctor volunteer.' But she thought of me. She's really human. She's fun. She's gossipy and yet she doesn't allow the small-town frame of mind to get in the way. She's doing what she wants to do. In Dingle, she's driving around in an old convertible. She's modest in her aspirations. Doesn't want to become famous, just looks after her cabbage patch."

Which is part of why he wants to return. Another big part is going through with the plan he'd had for his trip in 2010.

"My parents were very supportive overall but there was just a bit of anxiety because my father's health wasn't clear. We were happy enough with the decision in the end. They were uncertain about their own future, but were hoping I wouldn't throw it off and wouldn't not go to Africa. When I came back, our attitudes changed — this is the reality. We found he was actually dying and not recovering. I went back to kind of re-place him. That's what I did for the next year."

The Clinic *Cois Abhann* — Irish for "beside the river" — closed in June of 2011, when Peadar was unable to receive a contract from the Health Service Executive (the equivalent of the National Health Service) to provide medical care services, which he told *The Kerryman* newspaper at the time is "the core business of general practice everywhere in Ireland, apart from the richer parts of Dublin."

He and the remaining three other staffers, including his

mother, a practice nurse who helped run the clinic, would become unemployed.

"I'm going to take a few weeks off and then do some work around Ireland for the next year and think about the future," he told the paper. The story closed with the line, "I may go back to the Billy Riordan Memorial Clinic in Malawi at some stage."

In the next year, Peadar worked for other doctors. He served as chief functionary of the *Féile na Bealtaine*. He joined Maire in planning his wedding. And then they started planning a new clinic for Dingle. Upon their return from Malawi, he and Maire, thirty-one, will work toward opening it.

"We did have to prioritize Malawi," Peadar says. "It's high on both of our agendas. It would make a lot more sense to set up a clinic in Dingle now. It's possible that in six months' time a new law will allow people to set up clinics anywhere — it's possible someone could do it in the meantime. But we want to get a chance to work in Malawi together. It's a really nice way to start our life together."

Peadar met Maire at another festival, the Electric Picnic, held every summer since 2004 on the six hundred-acre Stradbally Hall estate in County Laois, just under an hour's drive from Dublin and called by *Billboard* "a magnificent rock 'n' roll circus, a textbook example of everything a festival should be."

"We spent a few hours together, were pretty much hooked on each other, before we realized we were doctors," Peadar says, then adds a clear untruth: "We were both mutually disgusted."

Maire, who's been bustling about in the background, takes a seat at the computer screen. Peadar pushes back her short dark hair, which falls to the collar of her purple sweater. There's plenty of time to talk, she says, as if returning from one country and blasting off to another were an everyday occurrence. The home she's leaving is her longtime one — she hails from Dungarvan in County Waterford. She has an uncle who's a doctor in England, but can't recall her inspiration for her career. "I know that seems silly," she says. "I wanted to be a scientist but obviously chose medicine. I don't even like the science aspect. I just like the people."

She studied science — and all the rest involved with a medical degree — at University College Cork, training in pediatrics, then to be a general practitioner.

Maire first heard of Mags, whom she labels "brilliant and an inspiration," in 2008, through students who'd volunteered at the clinic.

"There's something after medical school called the Waterford training scheme, it's very good for Mags's clinic," she says. "They send an almost steady supply of GP trainees. Sixty percent of the time, doctors from the Waterford scheme are training to be GPs."

"We know a lot of the doctors from the Waterford scheme," Peadar offers. "There's a new one of them every few months coming home (from Cape Maclear). They've been very good working without a diagnosis, using basic clinical skills."

The couple was to have gone to Malawi together back in 2010, but Peadar went a month earlier and was planning on staying six months; Maire would go for four months as part of her general practitioner training scheme.

Maire loves travel, and had been to Malawi for four weeks in 2002, working at St. Gabriel's Hospital in Namitete, a village near where the western border of Malawi meets both Zambia and Mozambique. "I was only helping out, only doing what I could as I was only a medical student, but it had a huge impact on me," she says. She'd also spent three years in pediatrics at a huge hospital in Australia, including three months of bush work there, but calls that "nothing like Africa."

"It was just real," she says of that introduction. "Very real. You do something, you see an end result. Medicine is more complicated here, there you have the cold face of things, no administration."

She returned to Malawi just as Peadar unexpectedly left that early October of 2010. She stayed four and a half months, living at The Gap.

"I would have stayed longer, if he was there," she notes. "I suppose that's why we're going back. I only finished my training last month. The first free time we had was the wedding two weeks ago."

Maire was impressed most by the way the clinic was organized. "It does the best it can with the least amount of resources. I hope that continues. The one thing I worry about is that it continues. You need someone, or a corporation, that keeps things going. When I left, at that time, I was the most senior doctor there. I was thinking, 'How did that happen?' But it was OK. It sat OK with me. I suppose I worry about the future. It's such a local project. You can't change the whole of Malawi. You'd love if Malawi would change themselves. But that's the far distant future."

On this trip, the two want to bring in the element of health education on a community level. And they're hoping to start a new clinic in the next village over from Cape Maclear. Discussions are now taking place with village chiefs and elders in Kasanka village, a community with a population of twelve thousand that has no access to medical services. As for access to the village, the road is so rough it's best done by dugout canoe, and villagers often are seen making the paddle.

"People come (to the clinic) by boat in very bad condition, usually come a week too late," Peadar says. "We're hoping to get over there twice a week. Mags is negotiating at the moment to make that happen."

Peadar and Maire also like the fact that they'll be working in a more remote location, one that, unlike Cape Maclear, is "Not a village lifted by the tide of tourism."

And they're eager to get started.

"I'm not sure if we'll get a chance to go back there very soon," Peadar says, "but we'll definitely keep up our relationship with fundraising. I'm on the board now. I think I'd probably like to keep a cultural thing going on as well. You might keep people aware around Dingle through photographs, long-term funding mechanisms. Once you've been there, you understand how it works, you can kind of stand over that. Keep an ongoing stream of trainees going there as well."

"It was lovely to come home and tell people about it, get them interested in the clinic," Maire says. "I've been trying to tell GPs almost at retiring age — this is the life for them."

"It's what's needed — they need an ongoing stream of volunteers," Peadar says. "The real thing to do would be to increase the number of medical students in Malawi. If we could somehow get involved in integrating training with the clinic operation, that would be very much worth trying to do. Being a stand-alone entity, if you pulled out, there'd be nothing in the morning."

TWENTY-FIVE

The annual report for the year 2011 at the Billy Riordan Memorial Clinic takes up no more than two single-spaced pages.

Written by Mags, as has been each of the previous seven annual reports, it right up front reminds the reader of the poor track records of most NGOs, pointing out that "one project in fifty survived more than five years, many other projects in this area have begun and subsequently ceased since we began to see our first patients on August 24th 2004."

By the end of the year 2011, more than 170,000 patients — sixty to one hundred twenty a day — were seen at the clinic, which has grown from that original staff of one doctor, one nurse and five ancillary workers to four doctors, five nurses, three counselors, seven patient care attendants, two lab technicians, four translators and an ancillary staff of fifteen.

Mags wrote of the four-day-a-week HIV/AIDS clinics, attended by more than eight hundred patients each month. Since testing began in March of 2008, the clinic has given results to 6,473 patients. A hoped-for donation from the Springfield, Massachusetts, Rotary Club will create a new and larger HIV/AIDS clinic to solve overcrowding in that area of the building, where numbers mean meetings must be held in the largest room — the wards — and patients temporarily moved to the hallway.

And she wrote of plans for a noted South African ophthalmologist to hold biennial eye clinics at the clinic the following year, with procedures including cataract surgery to be done in a fully equipped temporary operating theater within the clinic. The visits will mark the only time ophthalmic services will be made available to an area of one million people.

The nutrition clinic for children under five, the family planning efforts and a net distribution and malaria education program make the facility stand out even more, she tells readers, as does the hope that those talks in Kasanka will result in permission for staffers to travel there and provide care.

She mentions a bedding collection she hopes to do soon in Ireland. And she mentions money: "Fundraising has become very challenging for the Trust and we are constantly looking for new and innovative ways of raising money for the project."

Then Mags gives an update on the setting of it all, a country where "Life today for everyone ranges from challenging for some to almost impossible for others. Fuel shortages, foreign currency shortages and electricity outages are inconvenient and make trying to do business at a competitive level very difficult while the constant price increases in basic foodstuffs like sugar, cooking oil and flour is resulting in desperation, hunger and despair for others. Inflation is running at an unprecedented height and many teachers and other government employees are becoming the latest additions to the 75% who already live well below the poverty line."

She also mentions the sudden death by cardiac arrest in March of seventy-eight-year-old President Bingu wa Mutharika. Of his replacement Joyce Banda, a woman who told parliament shortly after taking office, "The economy is a mess. I'm running, please come run with me."

"At this point people are optimistic about her term of office," Mags writes in the report, a sanitized version of her opinion at the time of Banda's taking office: "One thing for sure, she cannot be worse than the last guy."

"Despite the problems and difficulties of Malawian life," Mags closes, "the 'Billy Clinic,' as it is known locally, remains a beacon of hope in an otherwise quite dismal landscape. We have managed so far to provide our patients with the medical expertise and medication, which they so desperately require. We are one of the few clinics, which has medication to dispense, and funds to pay our staff. We have been able to maintain our employee numbers and adhere to the highest standards possible in the clinic.

"We desperately hope we can continue to do this."

On this morning whenever this page is encountered, it's a certainty that "this" is continuing.

There is the sound of footsteps through the sand, a group walking not toward but away from the water, turquoise, inviting Lake Malawi at their backs as the doctors and nurses head through The Gap's gate and up and over the hill, toward their day at the Billy Riordan Memorial Clinic.

The work continues there, as it does for Mags wherever she is on this particular day — in her flat, in the dining room, in the office with Steve, in the ambulance, at the airport, in a plane, in her flat in Dingle. As she navigates the next challenge, her laptop, cell phone and notes always are at the ready, as is her more-life-smart-than-Pollyanna-ish attitude: "I never consider failure. Something always turns up."

What she'd love to see emerge is a fairy godmother — or father.

"We have to find somebody in America who would like to be a major sponsor of this clinic," she says, then clarifies, "For 150,000 ($250,000) a year. How many pay that in taxes a year?

They can be from outer Mongolia or wherever. I don't care. But you think of all the people in America who have shedloads of money — if you could connect with them. It's a race against time. Within three or four years, a major donor is needed to enable me to remain independent of government and other charities. I can't remain independent as long as the entire thing depends on me raising money each year. I can't continue to do this when I'm six feet under."

It's an overcast Friday in late August of 2011. Mags stands in the men's department of the Tralee J.C. Penney, rooting through a display of track pants.

Her own outfit is black cardigan, silver-and-pink scarf, pink capris, black slip-ons. The space between the hem of the pants and the top of the shoes reveals a tattoo above her right ankle, five tiny stars in an arc.

The pant leg rises as she leans into the shelves of track bottoms by Umbro, priced at twelve euro. "You're paying for the brand," she says as she eyes the six-euro house-brand styles on the next display. She counts on her fingers the staffers she'll be dressing — "Yotem, Max, Charles, Jonathan, Mr. Holland, Wanda" — then continues her search for more pairs.

Back at the Cape, there recently was a meeting on the idea of uniforms for watchmen, who currently wear whatever's in their wardrobes, a mix of T-shirts and pants or shorts.

"They said, 'We want black trousers and tops,'" Mags says, "and I said, 'Why do you want that?' and they said, 'The staff at Cape Mac Lodge has black trousers and tops,' and I said, 'I don't care what the staff at Cape Mac Lodge has. You dress in all black, you're black, I'm not going to see you when I drive in the gate.'"

She had a point, and the staff knew it, and they laughed. Everyone agreed on navy. Still dark, but not black. At the house-brand track pants display, there aren't enough of the mediums for the folks back in Malawi, and in a multicultural Ireland, a very Irishly red-haired manager, whose very Polishly named nameplate reads Ms. E. Szczepakowska, sends an Asian clerk to the storeroom for more pairs.

Soon bearing an armload of pants, Mags then heads to the children's section, in search of what she calls a comfort blanket, which sounds like what it is, a small blanket you'd hang onto for comfort. There's a selection for three euros each, bearing choice of dog head or lion head. She rings Emma to figure out what to choose for Callum, Mags's newest grandchild. Emma replies that she wants the plainest. The lion is embroidered with HEAR ME ROAR, which makes Mags turn up her nose. She'd get it but for the slogan. She decides on the aqua-and-gray dog, whose embroidery whispers a quiet I ♥ HUGS. She gets three, as Emma requested, for when one is in the wash or lost.

With the comfort blankets and the track pants purchased and bagged, and a stop made at the Permanent TSB bank branch to check an account she hasn't looked at, as she says, "since Adam was a boy," she glances at the screen of the Samsung Smartphone she recently purchased for its ability to allow her to read e-mail on the road. She then climbs the stairs to Dawson's, a second-floor restaurant in a discount store, its menu featuring selections much finer than its location would imply.

Over a slice of lemon meringue pie, she wiggles a foot and shows off the tattoo she says she'd wanted for years.

"People said I shouldn't," she says, "but I was in Sheffield, and I don't know if you know but it's the home of tattoos. One in three people have tattoos there. The family I stayed with in a hotel there, most had them. I wanted five small birds, one for each of my children. I looked at designs, and to make them look nice, and small, it would be difficult." So she went with stars. Walked into a parlor called The Red Monkey, got the sixty pound estimate and got in line.

It was first thing on a Monday, and the shop was extremely busy. "In front of me was a guy in his late sixties, early seventies, paid eighty pounds for I don't know what," she remembers. "Behind me was a man at least seventy-five, loads of tattoos, had an AC/DC CD cover, asked, 'Can you do that on my arm?' I said, 'At least I'm not the oldest.' Clerk said no, he'd had an eighty-two-year-old woman a few weeks earlier going on a world cruise, after her husband died, she got a rose on her shoulder. It was the clerk's feeling the dead husband had put her through a lot."

As for what Mags endured in the parlor, "It hurt a bit but not that bad," she says. "I wouldn't be rushing off to do another straight away. It hurt, but 'not as bad as having a child', the guy said. I said, 'Not that I'd want to do that again.'"

When she revealed the tattoo to her daughters, Mags said, "Emma told her husband, 'It's not safe to let my mother out. You're never sure what she'll do.'"

Emma is one of the stars on the tattoo Mags waited so long to have, mainly because she wanted to be sure she could handle any questions about it. On this trip, she will spend time with both Emma and Jennifer, making the most of the opportunity to do so. Methods for communication between Malawi and Ireland have improved vastly since her first visits, but there's still nothing like face-to-face time.

"When I first was in Malawi, when I'd come home they'd ask me why I wasn't in touch," Mags recalls. "It was not until they came out themselves that they'd see. It would take a whole day to make a phone call. To go to Monkey Bay for the phone.

Things don't work there, or they work differently, to achieve anything. You have to experience it. Otherwise, it's a closed world to anyone else. It's like someone from Cape Maclear coming here and going back — to explain it to them."

She recalls meeting a Monkey Bay friend after his first trip outside Malawi. What stuck in his mind from the experience? A dishwasher.

"To try to explain that to someone in the Cape," she says. "It's not like the average man on the street works in a factory. There is no factory. There's poverty there, but in a completely different context than in first-world countries. But I don't think it's as bad as slums in some European cities. Into that mix you have to put huge levels of discontentment. You don't have that here. Here, you have capitalism. You must have trainers, you must have Game Boy. It's abuse if you don't have the latest thing, you're short of the mark. To me, that's abuse. Particularly in young people. In the village they're not being bombarded by billboards and advertisements."

The pie is polished off. Next, a stop on the first floor of this building for plastic storage boxes she'll give to the cooks and volunteers ever battling to keep perishables fresh and pest free. She looks at tea towels and compares prices — five lousy ones for three euro, three good ones for five. It's like Steve is standing next to her and this is Game; the calculator will be coming out next.

At the cobbler in the mini-mall down the street, she collects a pair of shoes being repaired for Kitty, listens to a few stories from the couple who's owned the business for thirty years, and heads back to the car, and home.

On a busy Monday a few weeks later, Mags is zipping around Dingle, arranging for a winter home for her car, the convertible roof of which is beginning to corrode from weather; getting an update on her rabies inoculation; interviewing a nurse who came down from Mayo and looks like a lock to be accepted; and doing more banking.

She decides on lunch at *Cul Gairdin*, a three-year-old earthy-menued cash-only place of five thick wooden tables in a small room down a hallway off Main Street.

On that Main Street, Mags is stopped in the road by a driver who calls "I just saw you on television!" He's referring to RTÉ's *Nationwide*, where a spot on her was paired with others who "committed themselves to projects for the larger world," starting with a priest who helped with the nation's TidyTowns project.

Narrator Kieran McConville had done a previous story on Mags and was in Lilongwe earlier in the year when he rang to do another. His narration addresses Malawi's poverty, health challenges facing women and children, and how some patients walk up to thirty miles to be treated at the clinic. Those facts are followed by the irony of the area's beauty, and images of lake and beach are shown, including some of Mags walking the beach in her signature capris. Nurse Sheila talks about types of cases she sees, and how "as a child we had nuns from Africa, foreign mission, I wanted to come to Africa but I didn't want to be a nun."

Staffer Iwell Bryasi is prompted, "Talk to me about Mags."

"She's gorgeous," he beams in answer.

There are shots of gorgeous Mags driving through Chembe Village, talking about building a school one day, and lamenting that the plan is endangered by a fifty-percent drop in donations.

In *Cul Gairdin*, asked what she thought of the piece, Mags says "Brilliant. But, as for what I said, well," — here she adds a wince — "I'm never overly impressed by my own performance."

She digs into her dahl and recounts the high and low lights of the past year. The first, a February lightning strike at the original clinic building.

Eight patients were in the ward at the time. Mags credits a fire drill held not long before that night with the smooth and safe removal of all occupants. The resulting damage wasn't repaired until six months later, but in the interim the clinic had run as usual, nevertheless.

Then she talks about having been in England during the summer and feeling horrible. It was malaria. "I knew what I had. I told the doctor," she says, then adds brightly, "I was in an en suite room, got a menu to choose from every day." Her tone changes again to a flat, "But I did feel awful."

And she had kept running as usual, nevertheless.

Because there's always just so much to be done.

Because, as Sofina would remind you, "A good day should always be busy."

As the applicant for personal care attendant would suggest, "Calm down, everything will be all right, don't worry, be strong."

Because, despite strong evidence to the contrary, this indeed can be, as the pink Zain umbrellas on every Blantyre street corner announce, "a wonderful world."

Especially if that world is a place someone once told you was paradise. Which is what you found when you followed his wish and came here.

People grieve in different ways. This is how you've done it. And you're not afraid of it any longer.

Death is a fact of life in this cool garden, you know, and you know this better than most of us.

But you are a straightforward woman of good courage. Trying, as always, to balance. There is no messing, putting on for show. You have no time for that shit.

To help the poor, you've got to love the poor. You've got to be the person who comes out and actually does it, compared to people who come out and work on what someone else has set up. You were inspired by the injustice of something, rather than being all lovey-dovey, thinking 'Oh, these poor people.' And then the rest of us have followed."

"How is your life now?" asks the man in the doorway.

You could tell him it can be a cold fist. But here, in the warm heart of Africa, you've found so much that is not. The people who've reminded you of this have just landed in your lap. You don't know where they come from or why, but they come to you out of nowhere. And it just keeps happening.

It's weird, it's weird. There are times you think it was all meant to happen. Sometimes you think that someone up there is pulling all the strings, and we're just being pulled along. You were pulled along to this place by a son's invitation. And once you got here, you got pulled along to the next thing you were meant to do. And the next, and the next and the next. And all the while, you hang on.

Because it indeed is, you have learned, sometimes the only thing you can do. All the money in the world can't change the past, but you try and make something positive come of it. And at the end of the day, you can face whomever you will face, and say, "Well, I did my best."

To learn more about the Billy Riordan Memorial Trust

please visit: www.billysmalawiproject.org

An Interview with the Author

Who or what inspired you to write this book?

I met Mags Riordan in 2004, when I was helping my friend Fran Ryan sell her knitwear at the Eastern States Exposition. Fran and her Dingle Linens goods are from Dingle, where Mags lives, and for several years at that point Fran had organized a group of vendors to sell their wares at "the Big E," one of the ten largest fairs in the U.S. Our booth was adjacent to the one in the Irish goods area, where Mags was selling jewelry and art from Cape Maclear, the proceeds going to the then-new clinic. People would walk up to her booth, look at the photos of the village and the kids playing outside the clinic, and they'd ask what the display was about. Mags would start to say something like, "I built a clinic in the village where my son died," and many of the people would just walk away. Others would approach, she'd repeat the same stark information.

I wanted to know who this person was, what had happened to her son, and how does someone go about doing something like starting a clinic — how does one single person do something that? Apart from that, how does someone repeat a horrible truth like that, over and over, very often to disinterested ears? I got to know Mags well by asking a lot of questions over the years since, and feel everyone else needs to get to know her well, too. The first time he heard me talk about Mags, my husband, Tommy Shea, who always has the great idea, said, "That's a book." Thanks again, Tommy Shea.

How long did it take you to write the first draft of your manuscript?

I followed Mags on three continents, starting in November of 2009, and I thank her for being willing to do this project in the first place. I wrote as I went along, and finished the last page on December 18, 2012, at the kitchen table of an apartment in Abu Dhabi, where Tommy was working at the time. I'm delighted the story is seeing the light of day, and am hoping that it will do some good for the Billy Riordan Memorial Trust, and might inspire others to see what they can do in this world. It's not corny to say Mags' story is very inspiring. After the losses she's endured, how does this woman get up every day, never mind get up and does what she does for others? It's a story of how you don't have to be a millionaire or a specialist of some sort to start a charitable effort. Along the way I've been shown that by my dear friend since childhood, Mary (Koss) Grimanis, her husband, Mike, and daughters Julia and Lauren, of Wayland, Massachusetts who had no special training when they started The Akaa Project (www.theakaaproject.org). They had only the urging of Lauren, who, in 2007, newly turned seventeen, volunteered at an orphanage in Ghana and returned to tell her family of the great need she'd seen. The project since has created a school in a rural village and has grown to include healthcare and financial projects. The family had no background in anything like this. The four of them just wanted to help, sat down at their kitchen table, and started planning.

Did you read any comparable stories while writing this book?

I have a stack of books acquired for this experience, but those that accompanied me to Malawi included Dambisa Moyo's *Dead Aid: Why Aid is Not Working and Why There is a Better Way for Africa* (provocative and eye-opening), Tracy Kidder's *Mountains Beyond Mountains: The Quest of Dr. Paul Farmer* (I'm a Tracy Kidder fan and wanted to see how he lassoed so many issues and one large personality) and *Three Cups of Tea* by Greg Mortensen, (I read that for many of the same reasons).

Tracy Kidder did a fabulous job wrapping up his man and the experience, in so many different places and facing so many varied challenges. Mortensen and the late David Oliver Relin kept me spellbound, so I was very disappointed to then learn of the inaccuracies in the book that, for me, then put it in the fiction category. Good fiction, but still not a nonfiction book, not the real story of how this one man brought education to so many in Afghanistan and Pakistan.

What else about your book might pique the readers' interest?

Like Mags, the story doesn't sit still. She works in her office and visits family in Ireland, she spends eight months of her year living in a one-room flat in the volunteer complex at the Cape, she attends fundraisers in the states. The story follows her, and to and through some fascinating places, from the lush green of her Kerry backyard to the rugged rock approach to Cape Maclear, in ways so similar to entering Dingle. As Billy Riordan told her, "It's like Dingle. Dingle in the sunshine." The last thing Billy Riordan e-mailed to his mother was the line "This is paradise." He wanted Mags to visit Cape Maclear, to see the stark beauty. She eventually went there, but to set in place a stone in his memory. She has ended up doing so much more. Readers might find all that of interest, and might start pondering what they themselves might do about a need they see in their immediate or larger world.

This Is Paradise

Reading Group and Discussion Question Guide

What are your perceptions of Africa and how were they affected by this story?

What surprised you about life in Cape Maclear?

Which character could you relate to and why? What were some of his or her personality traits?

Which volunteer's story touched you the most? Could you put yourself in his or her shoes? How has the past shaped his or her life?

The clinic began due to a tragedy in one mother's life. Do you have an example of when a horrible experience sparked something positive in your life?

How do you grieve? Do you talk about grief with your close friends or family?

What experience do you have with volunteering? Have you ever started a volunteer program? If so, what difficulties did you run into? What blessings did the effort provide?

Mags has to deal daily with a culture very different than the one in which she's spent so much of her life. What would be the most difficult parts of living in Malawi? Which would you welcome?

How does the author describe the sense of community in Malawi? How does it compare to your sense of community? What are the dynamics illustrated in the story.

What borders have you crossed in your own life, both geographical and psychological?

Why is there such a strong connection between Ireland and Africa?

What would be a greater challenge for you: the actual hospital work or the fundraising? And in this day of so many competing good causes, how would you raise money for an African project?

What charitable efforts do you support, and what story or stories led you to lend that support. In which ways do you choose to give — time, funds, prayer, others?

What is the moral of this story?

What questions do you have about Mags that weren't answered in the book?

Coming Soon!

Suzanne Strempek Shea's New Novel:
Make a Wish But Not for Money

Rosie Pilch's lifelong job as a bank teller is lost in the recession, and her subsequent depression ends only when a friend elopes, moves and leaves Rosie her palm-reading business at Orchard Mall, once a groundbreaking shopping experience touted as "Main Street Recreated," now a sluggish "dead mall" in its last months of existence before the wrecking ball arrives.

Knowing nothing about palm reading, but needing to leave her house, Rosie becomes her friend's alter ego, "Irene, Queen of the Unseen," who knows all and sees all. Rosie expects to know and see nothing except outstretched palms bearing ten-dollar bills, but is more than startled to find she indeed can read palms, and provide information about both the past and future. Her newfound ability attracts a steady line of customers, including the mall's maintenance man, Dennis Edwards, who causes Rosie to reassess her future with her self-centered fiancé. As the mall's few remaining tenants prepare for the end of their businesses, Rosie's abilities figure in a new start for them, the mall and herself.